Praise for *China's Guaranteed Bubble*

Professor Ning Zhu's book *China's Guaranteed Bubble* explains the drivers behind the massive excess capacity in China's traditional industries, the explosive growth of credit and of corporate and local government debt and the efforts (only partly successful) by the state to protect savers and investors–households as well as private and public corporates–as well as households against the consequences of unlucky, unwise and reckless investment decisions.

A culture of pervasive implicit state guarantees has led to state support of stock prices, house prices, and wealth management products. Insolvency, bankruptcy, debt restructuring, bail-ins of unsecured creditors and other laws, rules and procedures to limit moral hazard are applied reluctantly, rarely and late. "You break it, you own it," is not part of the cognitive "acquis."

The book is also a call for action. Unless the Chinese authorities clean up the current leverage and excess capacity mess and end the culture of implicit guarantees that created the boom, bubble and bust (and will ensure their recurrence), China faces the near-certainty of a serious financial crisis and a post-crisis zombified financial system.

Everyone interested in finance and human folly, in China and in global macroeconomic and financial prospects should read this book–but not just before going to sleep.

WILLEM H. BUITER
Global Chief Economist, Citi Group

China cannot "let the market play a maximal role in allocating resources" without market discipline. Professor Zhu Ning's book provides a lively depiction of the prevalent "implicit guarantee" in the Chinese financial sector and economy, and its impact on the Chinese economy, culture of credit, debt crisis, and financial stability. This book is a great read for regulators, financial institutions, investors around the globe.

FRED HU
Chairman, Primavera Group
Formerly, Chairman, Goldman Sachs (Greater China)

Ning Zhu's *China's Guaranteed Bubble* is a fascinating description and analysis of credit systems in contemporary China—a network of private and state-owned businesses, banks, shadow banks, governments in various regions and cities, and households borrowing and lending to one another, sometimes explicitly, sometimes implicitly. Zhu analyzes challenges in constructing and administering a credit system that efficiently allocates resources to socially worthy investments in ways that protect savers.

THOMAS J. SARGENT
Professor of Economics, New York University
Nobel Laureate in Economics, 2011

China's economy faces a huge transition challenge. Rapid growth has in the past been driven by a hybrid model which combines elements of competitive market discipline with a financial system shot through with implicit guarantees and rapidly rising leverage. But as Zhu Ning's book makes crystal clear, that model has reached its limit, and now threatens to produce inefficient resource allocation and increasing instability. The new growth model now required must combine a reformed financial system, hard budget disciplines in which default plays an appropriate role, and a still important but transparent role for the Chinese state. Zhu Ning's book is an excellent empirical and theoretical guide to the complex challenges which this reform programme must overcome.

LORD ADAIR TURNER
Senior Fellow, Institute for New Economic Thinking
Former Chairman, Financial Services Authority, Great Britain

China's Guaranteed Bubble

Ning Zhu

New York   Chicago   San Francisco   Athens   London
Madrid   Mexico City   Milan   New Delhi
Singapore   Sydney   Toronto

ISBN 978-1-259-64458-0
MHID 1-259-64458-8

For my family

Contents

Preface   iv

Foreword by Robert Shiller, Ph.D.   viii

1. The Faultless Default   1

2. Failure is an Option (in China's Shadow Banking Problem)   31

3. Homebuyers Who Cannot Lose   55

4. Petition Against the CSRC   85

5. Alternative Financial Innovations   109

6. Behind the Growth Engine: The Great Slowdown   131

7. An Abundance of Overcapacity   151

8. From Fortune 500 to Truly Internationally Competitive Companies   175

9. The Mother of All Credit: The Government that Never Defaults   199

10. Voodoo Statistics   223

11. Guaranteed to Fail? International Lessons on Implicit Guarantees   245

12. When the Tide Goes Out: How to Reform   269

Index   301

Preface

Preventing the Guaranteed Bubble

The financial or speculative *bubble* has been arguably one of the most studied and yet least understood areas in economics.

China has been arguably the fastest growing and yet least understood economy in the world over the past several decades.

By utilizing a large army of cheap labor, unleashing labor productivity and entrepreneurship, and increasing capital inputs, China has accomplished astonishing economic miracles over the past three decades. Such economic growth has not only drastically improved the standard of living in China, but also jump started Chinese economic, political, and military influence around the globe.

After some fundamental restructuring in the world's economic and financial systems in the wake of the 2008 global financial crisis, and with increasing labor costs, diminishing investment return, worsening environmental conditions, and diminished natural resources, China's economy is currently facing unprecedentedly complicated and challenging situations.

Begun in early 2014, this book intends to examine economic growth in China from the perspective of the government providing implicit guarantees. Government guarantee, which has provided tremendous and highly valuable impetus to Chinese economic growth during the past three decades, is also largely responsible for the challenges China currently faces. By reviewing the potential risks involved in government guarantees in many different forms, the current book proposes potential solutions that will help China's sustainable, high-quality economic growth in the long run.

With slowing economic growth, diminishing corporate earnings, and as small- and medium-sized businesses find it increasingly difficult to access financing, China's government and its corporations and households have witnessed considerable increases in their respective leverage ratios in recent years. China's debt trouble has attracted more and more attention from governments, scholars, corporations, and investors from around the world.

In the short term, debt financing has the clear advantages of lower financing costs and easier financing procedures and has the potential to catapult the growth of enterprises and even countries.

However, the potential for default and bankruptcy and the substantial costs and reputational damage both involve should limit the debt capacity of any enterprise or country. In some sense, the lost decades of Japan's economy, which used to be the largest in the world some twenty years ago, and the bursting of the twin Japanese housing and stock market bubbles, were consequences of over-leveraging by Japanese corporations and households during Japan's booming '70s and '80s.

As in Japan, banks dominate the Chinese financial sector. Even though the Chinese bond market remains relatively underdeveloped compared to that of Japan or even to its own stock market, there has been a lot of development of "bond-like" investment products in China lately. The fast development of trust products, wealth management products (WMPs), and many products sold by the so-called internet finance platforms, all bear close resemblance to fixed income products in countries with more developed financial markets, such as the U.S.

Unlike the fixed income products offered in the West, many of these "bond-like" products in China carry implicit guarantees from their underwriters, the regulators, and, in the end, the Chinese government. Many investors believe that, as long as the financial institutions are concerned with their reputations, as long as the regulators are concerned with career advancement, and as long as the Chinese government is concerned with social stability, they will take care of the risks that investors themselves should bear when investing in such products.

The investors, on the other hand, need only concern themselves with the high returns offered by such products and to chase products with even higher returns. Such a "heads I win, tails you lose" mentality, is largely responsible for aggressive speculation throughout the Chinese investment arena, such as the housing market, the stock market, the shadow banking markets, and the newly developed "internet finance" field, and eventually will cause asset prices to rise far above their fundamental values and lead to a bubble.

What is more worrisome is that, during the recent past, the financing of local government and local government financing vehicles (LGFV) has heavily relied upon land sales and real estate development in the form of trust products and wealth management products (WMP) with implicit guarantees. Many products that originally were of high risk and had unpromising returns turned into "safe" and attractive investments with the help of financial structuring and in the guise of shadow banking products.

As Chinese investors see through to the implicit guarantee behind these products, they come to believe that the government will take responsibility for the risks that they themselves take when making these investments and therefore decide to actively invest in such products regardless of the risk.

If these products should lose their implicit guarantee from the government, or if one day the government cannot afford to provide such support any longer, the Chinese shadow banking sector, the high returns that investors have been enjoying, the cheap cost of capital many SOEs and LGFVs have been relying on, will all be seriously impacted, casting dark clouds over China's economic growth and its economic growth model transition.

Furthermore, the challenges currently facing China's economy, such as the slowing down of economic growth, serious overcapacity in many sectors, escalating debt at SOE and local governments, excessive volatility in many investment fields, may all be explained by the Chinese investor's willingness and audacity in taking excessive risks and speculating over the past few years. In some sense, the difficulties the Chinese economy is facing right now are indeed direct consequences of the bursting of certain previously created bubbles that were caused by implicit guarantees in the past few years.

The government's good will in seeking to grow the economy, highly effective in reaching the goal of high speed economic growth in the short term, nevertheless shifted the risk preference of investors and enterprises along with the social allocation of risk and capital, the tradeoff between return and risk, and the balance between short-term and long-term objectives. Many of the dilemmas in the Chinese financial sector, such as the difficulty SMEs face in obtaining capital, capital shying away from industry and flowing into investment and speculation, and many mini-bubbles that have burst and will eventually burst, are all merely the tip of the iceberg of the "guaranteed bubble" phenomenon prevalent in the whole country, and in some senses the entire world.

On the one hand, it is understandable that the speed of economic growth still matters dearly to further reform in China, to the improvement of Chinese well being, and to the enhancement of China's international status. On the other hand, the dictum "let the market play a decisive role in resource allocation," as mandated by the 3rd Plenum, means that investors have to (learn to) take responsibility for the risks entailed in their own investment decisions and that the government must gradually taper off its implicit guarantees to various enterprises and investments.

Only when investors are allowed (and required) to take responsibility for risks in their own investing, without the influence of various forms of implicit and explicit guarantee from the government, can investors set proper expectations for the rate of economic growth and for investment returns. It is not until that happens that the market can truly play its decisive role in screening and monitoring, and in efficiently allocating resources and capital.

Otherwise, once the expectation of "the guaranteed bubble" is formed and reinforced, investment speculation and mis-allocation of resources and capital will only become worse. In order to truly let the market play a "decisive" role in allocating resources, it becomes imperative for the Chinese government, and governments around the world, to gradually wind down their guarantees.

As the borderline between the state and the market, the tradeoff between risk and return, and the balance between present and future become transparent and clearly defined, the overcapacity, worsening debt, deteriorating SOE performance, SME financing difficulties, and the resulting mounting systematic financial risks, will all gradually get resolved.

Professor Robert J. Shiller, my advisor, friend, and colleague at Yale University, has offered constant encouragement and assistance in the writing of the book. I have also benefited considerably from many discussions with Thomas J. Sargent (New York University), Eswar S. Prasad (Cornell University), William N. Goetzmann (Yale University), Adam Tooze (Columbia University), Harry Xiaoying Wu (Hitotsubashi University), Yiping Huang (Peking University), Sen Wei (Fudan University), Deborah J. Lucas (M.I.T.), Harrison Hong (Princeton), Wei Xiong (Princeton), Adrienne Cheasty (the IMF), David W. Wilcox (The U.S. Federal Reserve Board of Governors), Adam S. Posen (The Petersen Institute), and members of the Global Agenda Councils on the European Debt Crisis, on Fiscal Sustainability, and on Public and Private Investments, at the World Economic Forum.

My visits at the IMF, the Federal Reserve Board of Governors, Yale University, the University of California, Waseda University, and the Chinese University of Hong Kong during the past several years have been valuable in the writing of this book.

My colleagues at Shanghai Advanced Institute of Finance (SAIF), Shanghai Jiaotong University, in particular Min Zhuang, Yu Chun, Xuemei Wang, Guoxing Liu, Siyu Luo, have provided substantial administrative assistance to me during the writing of the book. Cathy Chenjun Fang provided some of the data collection and data analysis for the book.

My editors and sales team at McGraw-Hill Education, Li Yan and Ying Fan in Beijing and Christopher Brown, Courtney Fischer and P. McCurdy in New York, and my editors for the Chinese version of the book at CITIC Publishing, Peng Tao, Ruoqian Xu, and Beiyan Shi, have been considerably helpful in its publication. I would like to thank Patricia Odean for editing the original draft of the book.

Last but certainly not least, I want to thank my family for their constant love, care and support!

Ning Zhu
November 2015, Beijing

Foreword

Ning Zhu has written a perspicacious, as well as fact-filled, account of the state of the Chinese financial markets and the Chinese economy. It is a real-world account, taking account of all the inconvenient facts that some would like to ignore. It is especially clear on the presence of false promises, faulty evaluations, and the long-run consequences of these. It offers such a sensitive account of China's economy that it should be of interest all over the world, as a case study of how financial markets can underpin the world's most spectacularly growing economy while at the same time involving serious financial defects.

People outside of China will find this book much better reading than the typical large international bank's country study or background paper on China, for this book connects the events in China with a broader and deeper perspective. The perspective is from scholarly research, including behavioral finance. At the same time, it pulls no punches; it is a candid account.

China has emerged from the privations of the Cultural Revolution into a period of renewed greatness and innovation. But it is not as if China had been sleeping during the Cultural Revolution. Indeed, during the very same Cultural Revolution we have examples of brilliance. Youyou Tu began research at the time on a cure for malaria, looking at a number of traditional Chinese medicines. She found one that really worked and then identified and extracted the biologically active component from it. She won the Nobel Prize in medicine in 2015. But the volume and intensity of Chinese innovation was not focused financially at that time and not focused on the international marketplace either. It is interesting to see how such a remarkable transformation has happened in China since then despite financial imperfections.

China after the Cultural Revolution discovered some of the power of modern financial institutions. At the same time, the new China has acquired new problems, the characteristic problems that go along with these institutions, especially as they are new and not as yet fully developed. The newly unleashed Chinese creativity has brought with it some of the same problems that were already well known in western economies even centuries ago.

Ning Zhu argues that it has brought with it errors, including the over-construction of real estate and overcapacity in industry, encouraged by overly optimistic sales promotions for investments.

This new book in some sense parallels a book that I have recently written with George Akerlof, *Phishing for Phools: The Economics of Manipulation and Deception* (Princeton, 2015, China CITIC Press 2016). Our book covers mostly the United States, and barely even mentions China. It details many different facets of trickery, bribery and distorted influence that have been used to get ahead in America. We have encountered some anger here in the United States with our book, perhaps at least in part because some took our criticism personally.

People are basically the same in every country. Problems of corruption, manipulation and deception are basic human problems that are never completely solved, but the outcome can become better and better. There is a good side to all people too, and if the environment is right this side can become stronger.

It is significant that in the World Values Survey, the Chinese come across as particularly trusting of each other. The question in that survey, before translation into local languages and asked in many countries, is, "Generally speaking, would you say that most people can be trusted or that you need to be very careful in dealing with people?" A trust index for each country is created, which is positively related to the fraction who answer that people can be trusted and negatively related to the fraction who answer that you need to be very careful. China has scored very high on this index, as recently as Wave 6 2010–2014, higher than the United States and just about any other country.

Studies have shown that if trust is strong and justified it facilitates economic success. But, as Ning Zhu warns, it is fundamental that this trust be honored, and those in positions of power not abuse it. We see today in China a sense that many people trust that the government will prevent any asset prices from falling, will make up for any financial losses, at least in the long run. So as not to find itself in the future where it cannot help but betray this trust, the government should make it clearer now that it will allow markets to fall in the future, will allow speculators to bet against markets to help prevent bubbles, and enforce a social safety net that only protects individuals from privation rather than trying to guarantee high investment returns.

Working against this need to maintain trust in markets and their independence from excessive government interference is the need to maintain confidence in the direction of the economy. A punishing market crash, if allowed to happen without interference, can cause people to curtail their spending and businesses to cancel plans for further hiring and expansion. Sometimes the dilemma that policy makers face has been compared to that of a president confronted with a military commander who is not performing well in his job, but who should perhaps still be kept in charge because the rank and file below him have come to believe in him, and to replace him would harm morale. Wherever such a situation occurs, the dilemma is fundamental, and policy makers will find it difficult to find decisive opinion about the effects of their actions in maintaining confidence. The dilemma is not easily resolved by any economic theory since it operates in a mostly psychological, or rather social psychological, sphere, and works against the indisputable power of free markets in bringing economic efficiency.

Ning Zhu's book puts the Chinese dilemma at this time of overcapacity and slower economic growth into just such a perspective, and supports the view that the time has come for the Chinese government to be tilting toward pulling back on its implicit guarantee for financial assets and letting market forces have more rein in the economy. He shows significant evidence that the markets should be given more freedom to function on their own in China today.

Robert Shiller
New Haven, Connecticut

The Faultless Default

The truth is incontrovertible, malice may attack it, ignorance
may deride it, but in the end, there it is.

—WINSTON CHURCHILL

IN JANUARY 2014, IT HAD BECOME GRADUALLY CLEAR THAT ONE OF
the trust products sold by the China Credit Trust Company faced
the risk of default. The product, which was backed by assets from a
once highly successful mining business, lacked not only the cash flow to
repay its investment dividends but also the necessary assets to cover the
product's principal, which were both due January 31, 2014.

Shanxi Zhenfu Energy Group, the coal company that had taken
out 3 billion Yuan (about $500 million) from the China Credit Trust
Company and through the Industry and Commerce Bank of China
(ICBC), faced a cash shortage in repaying its interest and principal
obligations. Zhenfu Energy originally took out the 3 billion Yuan
financing to expand its production capacity in hope of increasing coal
prices. However, in light of the tapering off of quantitative easing by
the U.S. Federal Reserve and plunging coal prices, it had to shut down
its production, which resulted in its financial distress.[1]

Adding to the drama of the event was the news that Mr. Xing
Libin, owner of another regional energy company that had borrowed
heavily through trust products and faced repayment pressure, had
thrown a wedding for his daughter costing over 100 million Yuan, not
long before the default.

Of particular interest to investors was the fact that the China Credit Trust Company claimed that it only serves as a distribution channel. The real holder and guarantor of the product is the Shanxi Branch of ICBC, China's largest bank and one of the largest banks in the world based on assets and revenue.

On the other hand, ICBC made it clear that it was not responsible and would not take any responsibility in repaying the principal or the interest on the products. The incident has attracted widespread attention, partly because such symbiosis between banks and trust companies, or the formal and shadow banking systems of China, had worked very well in the past, and nobody really knew what would happen if such a collaborative relationship broke.[2]

Surprisingly, unlike default events in the West (which attract considerable notice), the default in this case left Chinese investors and lawyers seemingly composed. This calm response cannot be attributed to Chinese Taoism or Confucianism. Understanding why the creditors and debtors remained calm is key to understanding not only this interesting case, but also many other phenomena in the economy and financial system of China.

Despite the details about the relative responsibilities of each party involved in the trust product prospectus and sales contract, the stance from both sides sets a very interesting precedent for the entire shadow banking industry in China. Shadow banking includes many high-yield-paying trust products and wealth management products that have mushroomed in the past few years. As a matter of fact, China's shadow banking system has shouldered an increasingly large fraction of financing for not only small- and medium-sized enterprises in China, but also investments in many industries with severe overcapacity, much local government debt, and local government financing vehicles.

For example, the China Credit Trust and the ICBC promised their wealthy clients returns ranging from 9.5 to 11.5 percent per year in selling the products related to the Zhenfu coal mine. Such products have become tremendously popular not only because they provide highly attractive returns (sometimes ranging from 12 to 18 percent per year), but also because they are believed by many to be very safe.

Many investors in such products understand that even though there is clear stipulation in the product prospectus that there is no guarantee of the security of the principal, the trust companies and related commercial banks will guarantee the safety of their investment because of both regulatory and reputation concerns.

To make things even more serious, the phenomenon of implicit guarantee has permeated many other aspects of the Chinese economy. Chinese investors in the real estate market and the Chinese A-share stock market also believe that the government values social stability so much that it will not allow real estate prices or A-share prices to fall in order to avoid potential protests and unrest.

Likewise, overcapacity and resulting pressure on producer prices, an economic problem that has started haunting the Chinese economy, largely comes as a consequence of reckless investment poured into industries such as cement, steel and iron, and solar panels. Such investments were made possible not only due to easy financing through products like the one distributed by China Credit and ICBC, but also by investors' belief that the local government would bail out their investment in case things went sour. The Shanxi province's permission for the Zhenfu coal mine to restart production—and an earlier bailout by Jiangxi province of the solar panel producer Jiangxi Saiwei—all add to investors' confidence that the government will come to the rescue.[3]

Perhaps of greater importance is that the central government and regulators alike gradually have come to realize the size and gravity of the implicit guarantees and the impact on the fiscal sustainability of many Chinese local governments. According to a recent round of auditing conducted by the China Audit Authority in late 2013, local governments' liabilities rose by 70 percent over the three years prior to reach the alarming level of 18 trillion RMB (about 40 percent of China's GDP during the same period). Even though the number itself is arguably largely in line with some previous estimates, the pace at which local government debt increases and the diminishing sources of fiscal revenue for local governments lead many to worry about the soundness of Chinese local governments' financial situations.[4]

As a matter of fact, one key source of financing for such an alarmingly high level of local government debt is the same shadow banking products that trust companies and banks sell to their investors. The matter has grown worrisome because some fundamentally unsound investments have been sold to public investors under the disguise of "safe" products. Chinese investors, under the impression of government guarantee, have probably invested far more than they should have in risky products that promised higher returns.

In some sense, many of the trust company products bear similarities with the collateralized debt obligation (CDO) products in the West before the 2007–2008 global financial crisis, and they have grown tremendously in size in the past few years. It is possible that the CEO of Citigroup at the time, Chuck Prince, was right: "When the music stops, in terms of liquidity, things will be complicated. But as long as the music is playing, you've got to get up and dance. We're still dancing."

The homebuyers who cannot lose

In September 2014, several sales and demonstration centers of various real estate development projects were reported to have been vandalized in broad daylight. Without fear of investigation, the perpetrators of some of the vandalizing showed up right in front of the sales centers they had trashed.[5]

They were none other than recent buyers at the very same development projects. These were the homeowners who had bought their apartments just before the developers decided to slash the pre-sale apartment price by 15 to 30 percent.

With the Chinese housing market weakening nationwide in 2014, there have been numerous similar protest and petition events by new home buyers, though not all of them ended up with as much violence. These were definitely not the first situations in which Chinese home buyers have petitioned against developers who lowered prices; nor will they be the last.

A few years earlier when the Chinese housing market softened, similar situations happened to other developers all over the country.[6, 7] In some extreme cases, the demonstrators went as far as taking the sales manager hostage, demanding compensation for financial damages to recent home buyers who suffered financial loss as a result of the reduced prices.

During various protests, the homebuyers-turned-demonstrators felt wronged by the developers who had sold them properties and righteous about protecting their investments. Some claimed that the developers slashed the prices by some 20 or 30 percent before the properties were even completed.

For example, a project in Hangzhou sold for 18,000 Yuan per square meter in early 2014, before the developer slashed its price to about 15,000 Yuan per square meter a few months later, netting a loss of over 15 percent for those who had bought earlier.[8] This caused previous homebuyers losses ranging from hundreds of thousands to over a million Yuan, quite a fortune to average Chinese households.

Many of the homebuyers claimed that the developers had promised them that there would be no further price cuts or promotions after they bought the apartment months, or even weeks, previously. Some protestors felt that what the developers had done was no different from fraud, providing them misleading information to lure them into purchasing an apartment.

Many such buyers felt that they did what they had to: "What would you feel if you bought a TV and the retailer slashed the prices by 10 percent the next day?"

Indeed, during the market corrections in 2008, 2011, and 2014, real estate prices were reined in for several months. To expedite sales, some real estate developers decided to sell new apartments at lower prices than a few months earlier or to provide more generous incentives to attract buyers.

Whereas some new buyers celebrated a better opportunity to purchase property, those who had just bought property saw their investment turning up losses right after the deals were made. Of course, not a single person protested or boycotted the real estate project or real estate developer when they saw the prices of the apartments that they had just bought *increase* by 10 percent within a couple of months, which has been common in China in the past few years. Nor has it ever been reported that homebuyers provided any form of refund to developers after the apartment that they had bought earlier appreciated by more than 100 percent.

Developers, on the other hand, felt victimized in these situations and refused to give in at first.[9] Granted, during weaker market conditions, some developers promised in the sales contract to buy back the apartments that they sold at a 20 to 40 percent premium over their selling price in the subsequent five years.

While such tactics had proved useful in luring in customers in the past, some developers felt that the substantial price appreciation and uncertain outlook of the housing market might dampen their effectiveness in 2014 and therefore no longer offered such promises in the contract. As a result, the developers argued that without any explicit guarantees in the contract, all of the promises that sales delivered were just that—promises, subject to changes in real market conditions.[10]

One could argue that investors from every corner of the world are similar in that they do not fully understand investment and risk, and they are often naïve about the prospects of their investment. The difference in China is how the government and real estate developers handle such situations.

Often, the local governments will step in and play the role of mediators in such disputes. In most cases, the local government will try to appease the property buyers by asking the developers to make up the buyers' losses or to provide additional incentives to make the homebuyers happy. After all, local governments do not want to have a scene involving a large protesting crowd—it is not a healthy sign for social harmony and definitely not instrumental in helping them getting promoted in the future.

Given the close relationship between real estate developers and the guidelines and pressure on local government, real estate developers usually concede to the protesters by making up the price difference or throwing additional amenities to recent homebuyers at a loss, footing the costs and losses themselves. However, such generous moves are not always met with much appreciation. The homebuyers claim that real estate developers had made so much money during the market boom that it is time for the developers to give up some of their gains.

What is more important, though, is that a market-wide expectation had been formed through such protests and concessions. At least in the real estate sector, investors had come to believe that they would not lose money when they bought a piece of new property. Should anything happen, the real estate developer and government would take responsibility for the irresponsible investment that they had made.

Such beliefs, fueled by the implicit guarantees from the Chinese government and real estate developers, may be the main culprit for high housing prices in China and the bubble-like phenomenon in many other areas of the Chinese economy.

A common practice among the Chinese in social gatherings goes like this: when a circle of business friends gathers for a dinner party, they discuss what to buy as an investment in China. Among the circle of friends, everybody agrees that real estate prices are too high and real estate is no longer a good investment. However, they start asking each other questions like, "What is the best investment they have made in the past decade?" "Has anybody ever lost money in real estate investment?" "Do they feel as though they have bought enough properties in the past decade?" After this round of reflective questions, all agree that real estate is not only the best performing investment of the past decade, it's also the safest. Based on such surprising and seemingly perverse reasons, the friends go out and buy themselves more new apartments.

Real estate investment in China has been so stable in the past decades that it is safe to say that everyone who bought a piece of property in China before 2008 has made quite a lot of money, and that those who bought a piece of property in China before 2012 have made some decent money off their investment.

Oddly, it is not that the Chinese real estate market has not experienced any drops or corrections. Quite to the contrary, there have been quite a few drops and dips in the Chinese real estate market since 2000. Most such market corrections resulted from government curb policies aimed at curtailing national housing prices, but there were also a few times when unexpected events occurred, such as the SARS epidemic in 2004, bird flu in 2005, and the global financial crisis in 2008.

What distinguishes China and Chinese investors from the rest of the world's real estate market is Chinese investors' undisturbed confidence in, and unfazed enthusiasm for (and hence expectations of), housing prices.

At first, property buyers were quite concerned when the government announced its intention to stabilize housing prices or to keep housing prices lower. However, after a few rounds of hide-and-seek games, property buyers became more and more confident that the government would not allow housing prices to fall.

The year 2014 may turn out to be the watershed year. After the government relaxed the curb policy that had been in effect for the past three years, many were surprised not to see the usual feverish rebound in housing prices. Instead, weak sales and prices seemed to be lingering. Had the market expectation finally changed?

Petition against the SEC?

Despite the real estate sector's critical importance to the Chinese economy and finance sector, the protests against real estate developers were largely temporary and scattered examples of the implicit guarantee, largely attributable to ever increasing housing prices in China in the past decade.

In contrast, the Chinese stock market, which boasts over 100 million investors from mainland China, conveys another more prevalent and persistent form of implicit guarantee.

Carson Block, of Muddy Waters Research, rose to fame in 2011 by calling Toronto-listed Chinese logging company Sino Forest a "multibillion-dollar Ponzi Scheme" that was "accompanied by substantial theft."[11] After Block's research release, shares of Sino Forest fell by 82 percent, with prominent investor John Paulson selling his entire stake in the company at a $720 million loss.[12]

In the next couple of years, Muddy Waters and a few similar short-seller companies repeated the same practice on scores of Chinese companies, such as Focus Media and NQ Mobile. Several companies witnessed their shares plummet and eventually the de-listing of their shares.

Such short selling of Chinese companies listed on NASDAQ has triggered considerable controversy back in China. Some Chinese commentators claim that the shorting is targeted at China and may indeed be a way for the United States to intimidate Chinese companies and the Chinese economy. Others blame the incident on short selling, arguing that short selling is responsible for almost all financial crises.[13]

Among internet discussion groups, some suggested that Chinese investors and listed companies impacted by short sellers like Muddy Waters should sue the company for damages, and other went as far as to claim that Chinese investors and companies should petition together in front of the U.S. Securities and Exchange Commission (SEC).

These reactions may seem extreme and shocking to investors around the world, but Chinese investors are not to be blamed entirely. After its introduction to the A-shares market in China in 2007, the practice of short selling has remained very limited. Even after its introduction, regulators and investors in China are substantially more concerned about the idea of short selling than investors in most other countries.

Instead, most participants in China have a deep faith that a rise in the market is a good thing, whereas a drop in the market is a bad thing, and that Chinese government, specifically the Chinese Securities Regulatory Commission (CSRC, the Chinese counterpart of the SEC), can and will keep the market rising forever.

To petition against the CSRC Is not Uncommon

Investors' false confidence is in large part reflected in the mission of the market watchdog, the Chinese Securities Regulatory Commission. According to a statement by the Cabinet, the CSRC should "foster the development of Chinese capital markets."[14]

As a result, many Chinese investors believe that the Chinese government, and specifically the CSRC, will not allow the stock market to drop, at least not by too much, because that would cost investors so much that it could endanger the development of Chinese capital markets and the harmony of society. Such implicit guarantees by the Chinese government attracted a record number of investors who had experienced stock market fluctuations to rush into the market during the 2005–2007 market run-ups.

Triggered partly by the 2007–2008 global financial crisis, the Chinese A-shares market subsequently suffered from one of the worst market routs in global stock market history, with the CSI index dropping from a record high of 6,100 to less than 2,000. Many investors wrote petitions to the CSRC and the cabinet demanding that the government take action to boost share prices in order to protect shareholders.[15, 16]

Not surprisingly, most of those who demanded the government protect their investments were those who had bought shares at market peak prices, and many of them still have not managed to recover from their losses, even in the 2010s. What is interesting is that such protests were simply examples of a series of protests that Chinese investors staged against the CSRC whenever a large number of investors suffered investment losses from market downturns.[17, 18]

Investor Protection?

Similar to the situation in the real estate market, no investor seems to have any issue or complaint when share prices go up quickly. Most investors were occupied with the joy of reaping quick profits from the market run-up and failed to consider the risks of such a speedy market ascent.

What is special in China is that the CSRC indeed feels that it is obligated to keep the stock market afloat and always takes action to prevent the market from dropping, even when this contradicts critical next-step reform in the Chinese stock market.[19]

Some people suspect that it has taken the CSRC so long to push forward the introduction of short sales and financial derivatives related to short sales, such as index futures and treasury futures, because the CSRC's intention is to avoid startling the market with more bad news.

Further, the CSRC argues that the very reason that it sets up very strict IPO requirements is to protect investors from buying "bad apples" and suffering considerable financial loss. This train of thought, of course, leads to massive fraud and manipulation in the IPO process, which eventually leads to unwitting investors suffering even more.

As good as the CSRC intentions are, the protection of investors should go only as far as making sure disclosure is fair, timely, and complete and making sure that retail investors are not taken advantage of by more sophisticated institutional investors and listed companies.

Any attempt to further protect retail investors by artificially installing new requirements and price movement caps can only prolong the process of distortion and mispricing of stock prices. Even worse, once investors, especially retail investors, sense that the government and regulators intend to support the market and their investments, they will smartly begin to take on far more risk than they should or otherwise would, even though they know very little about investment.[20] Because of the ban on any form of gambling activities in mainland China, anybody with an appetite for financial risks turns their eyes to the stock market.

Partly as a result of this, the Chinese Survey of Consumer Finance reveals that Chinese households have been making some very disappointing investments under the auspice of the government's protection. Among the 8 percent of households who do choose to participate in the Chinese A-shares market (with about 15 percent of households' financial assets invested in the Chinese A-shares market), only about 20 percent reported investment gains during the past five years, whereas the remaining 80 some percent of households reported investment losses.[21]

This means that these 80 some percent of households would have been better off putting their money into cash or savings accounts.[22] Bank deposits and cash make up more than 75 percent of Chinese households' financial assets, partly reflecting a lack of interest or trust in the Chinese A-shares market.[23]

Because of the protection from the regulators, investors fall into the false impression that investing does not require skill or education. The same survey shows that more than half of stock market investors did not finish college. So, if anything, it seems that the investor protection engineered by Chinese regulators managed to have accomplished one thing: to encourage uneducated risk taking and speculation.[24]

The companies that would never bankrupt

Following the near default of the China Credit Trust Company's product in January 2014, another noteworthy distressful event in early 2014 was the Chaori 11 bond (Security code 112061.SZ).

THE FAULTLESS DEFAULT 13

The Chaori 11 bond failed to come up with its due payment, making it the first bond to default in the history of the People's Republic of China. Shanghai Chaori Solar Technology, the issuer of the bond, had suffered losses in the past three consecutive years. The company's revenues dropped 66.3 percent in the fiscal year of 2013, compared to the previous fiscal year, and its stock faced the risk of being de-listed based on the Shenzhen Stock Exchange's listing rules. With such adversities, investors in the West would expect that the company would soon have to file for bankruptcy protection.

However, few Chinese investors would feel that way. Bankruptcy has never been a familiar topic in Chinese society, and the Chinese have never been open to this notion. As a matter of fact, the concept of bankruptcy is taboo in China. Most officials, businessmen, and even scholars consider bankruptcy disgraceful and try at all costs to avoid it. Reflecting this attitude, the number of bankruptcy cases filed every year in China is very small, sometimes even less than the number of cases filed in much smaller countries such as the Netherlands or Belgium.[25,26]

Thus, Chinese investors have good reasons to be complacent about their risky investments in the stock market or shadow banking products because Chinese companies are indeed unbelievably safe and seem never to have to face the risk of default or bankruptcy.

This is not to say that Chinese companies are not plagued by an over leverage problem. Quite to the contrary; the Chaori incident is simply a reflection of many Chinese companies' debt problems. The Chinese debt problem has become so dire that Mr. Zhou Xiaochuan, the governor of People's Bank of China, acknowledged at the Bo'Ao International Forum of 2014 that the leverage at Chinese corporations is "alarmingly high."

According to statistics from the People's Bank of China, the Chinese nonfinancial corporate leverage ratio was 106 percent in 2012, and increased to 110 percent in 2013. These figures are far higher than 49 percent for Germany, 72 percent for the United States, and 99 percent for Japan. The Chinese leverage ratio is even higher than that of many other Asian countries that arguably share similar traits in developmental stage and social structures.[27,28]

According to data from the Chinese Ministry of Finance,[29] the Chinese state-owned enterprises' (SOE) total assets are 91.1 trillion dollars and total liabilities are 59.3 trillion, with a leverage ratio of 65 percent—higher than that of the private sector.[30]

By gleaning detailed data from Chinese listed companies, it becomes clear that not all sectors of the Chinese economy suffer from the same high corporate leverage ratio. As a matter of fact, heavily industrial sectors such as petroleum, steel, coal and charcoal, and construction equipment experienced particularly sharp increases in leverage. Most of the companies in heavily industrial sectors are SOEs. Statistics based on bank loans and debt issuance reveal that more than 80 percent of Chinese corporate debt is concentrated in SOEs, and this trend continues as this book is being written.

So why would Chinese investors not worry about such seemingly grave debt problems? The answer again traces back to the implicit guarantee by the Chinese government, extending beyond the Chinese financial sector.

Unlike privately owned companies that would worry very much about their deteriorating leverage, the dual roles of SOEs, as both government branches and enterprises, induces SOEs to stick closely to the SASAC's guidelines to become "bigger and (presumably) stronger."[31] SOEs understand just as well as SOE banks, their counterparts in the financial sector, that the SOE's distressed debts, which would be the SOE banks' non-performing loans, are all implicitly guaranteed by the Chinese government. Should something bad occur, all of the liabilities would be taken care of by the Chinese government in the end.

Overcapacity! Overcapacity!

A direct consequence of overleveraged investing and lack of the exit provided by bankruptcy is overcapacity.

Based on official data on production capacity, people are worried about overcapacity across many industries in China. According to the Bureau of Statistics, the capacity utilization rate is 72 percent, 73.7 percent, 71.9 percent, 73.1 percent, and 75 percent (translated into at least 30 percent overcapacity industry-wide) for the steel, concrete, electrolytic aluminum, flat-panel glass, and the ship building industries, considerably lower than the international average.

Even with existing high capacity, many expect that more new investment will generate another round of capacity expansion in the next few years.[32] The overcapacity problem in certain industries has become so dangerous that China has started a national ban on new investments in the coal-chemical, steel, cement, polycrystalline silicon, wind turbine, flat-panel glass, ship building, electrolytic aluminum, and soybean pressing industries.[33]

Such overcapacity, or capacity overhang, can have serious impact on the Chinese economy. First, with such sudden jumps in capacity in so many industries, competition intensifies and corporate earnings drop rapidly. For example, the Chinese solar panel industry reported a reasonable 30 percent gross margin back in 2010. With the massive industry capacity expansion and cut-throat price wars, gross margin in the solar panel industry dropped to 10 percent in 2011 and further down to 1 percent among Chinese solar manufacturers publicly listed overseas.[34]

Nevertheless, accustomed to the great asset appreciation and expanding market potential in China in the past decade, many Chinese companies have tasted the flavor of highly leveraged growth. With increasing size, entrepreneurs find themselves not only benefitting from having more government attention and support, but also from having greater bargaining power with banks when they have financial woes. Local government, entrepreneurs believe, would be anxious to help them take care of their non-performing loans to ensure local economic growth and employment. With such peace of mind in regard to the debt problem, it just becomes natural for some entrepreneurs to forget about financial soundness for a moment and borrow as if there is no tomorrow.

The deterioration in corporate earnings is quickly and clearly re-flected in investment returns and the asset quality of banks that make loans to such industries. For example, the solar panel industry has had five continuous years of expansion at an annual growth rate of over 100 percent,[35] with almost all major Chinese banks having some exposure to the industry. Now that many companies in this industry are starting to lose money, some banks have started worrying about their loans and investment in bonds issued by such companies, as they did in the case of the Chaori solar company, above.

Failed investments would not only deter future investment in this industry and hold the industry back from progress and upgrade, but also hurt bank and investor confidence in the industry, further limit-ing the industry's growth. Hence, even though short-term excessive investment and speedy growth may seem attractive and appropriate, they may actually draw the ceiling for future investment and growth in-advertently.

Of course, there is a closer and more direct tie between SOE debt and the government. Part of the rapid increase in Chinese SOE's leverage is due to local government's GDP growth competition. Be-cause local government officials are being evaluated by the GDP growth in their areas, it is conceivable that growing by borrowing has become the quickest and easiest way for many governments to boost their economic growth speed. As long as a local government can pro-vide enough incentives and implicit guarantees for companies to invest, the companies, mostly SOEs, are more than happy to kill two birds with one stone by expanding their own business and providing a favor to local government officials at the same time.

Such a push towards high speed growth comes not only from the local government, but sometimes from the central government as well. When the Chinese central government faced economic slowdowns in the past couple of decades, it typically engaged in counter-cyclical expansive fiscal and monetary programs to fight economic cycles. State-owned enterprises, including state-owned banks, become the most powerful channels through which the Chinese government can effectively push through its investment-driven development model.

During the 2008 global financial crisis, almost all countries in the world increased governmental leverage to bail out and help private sectors troubled by irresponsible borrowing and unhealthily high leverage. However, China is exceptional in the sense that the Chinese central government's leverage did not increase much in the same period, even in light of the 4 trillion Yuan stimulus package. The secret? It is probably because leverage at the central SOEs (under SASAC's direct leadership) and local government (through local government financing vehicles and local SOEs) had increased substantially, instead.[36]

The SOE conundrum

Lying at the core of the SOE's increasing and concerning debt level and deteriorating overcapacity problem in many Chinese industries is the long-standing soft budget problem that harrows most SOEs, and particularly the SOEs in socialist countries formerly under Soviet Union governance.

On one hand, state-owned enterprises take up some governmental responsibilities, such as providing infrastructure, social welfare, education, and even government debt. On the other, however, SOEs also enjoy many benefits from a close tie with government.

For example, most SOEs, especially those under direct leadership from SASAC, enjoy access to easy and cheap bank loan financing. Put differently, governments at different levels absorb some of SOE's liabilities and financing costs. Of course, when SOEs really get into trouble, it never fails that government will bail them out from their own budget.

A clear example is the local government financing vehicles (LGFV). Because Chinese local governments are forbidden to raise debt directly, they set up LGFVs to raise debt for them. These LGFVs come into existence with explicit guarantees, financial support, and implicit guarantees for repayment from local governments. In a more transparent market, SOEs and LGFVs make up 90 percent of total publicly traded corporate debt in China. Almost all this LGFV debt, and a part of the SOE debt, is directed at helping local governments with their administrative responsibilities.[37]

So the natural next question is how such debt-laden LGFVs and SOEs survive in the marketplace. The answer is government guarantee and support. In exchange for the favors that SOEs do for the government, the government will use its resources to help the SOEs. Of course, many SOEs also owe their success, or at least survival, to different forms of government support, such as entry into monopolistic areas, legal certification in key projects, governmental purchases, taxation refund, and fiscal appropriation.[38]

But a more direct benefit that SOEs enjoy in China today is their access to capital in a seriously financially repressed economy. Chinese government can persuade, or sometimes order, (SOE) banks to make loans to SOEs or SOEs in certain sectors or certain areas. Because of the financial repression in the Chinese economy, access to credit and loans is itself extremely valuable in keeping SOEs surviving and even thriving. Further, because of credit rationing, the real capital in the marketplace is being artificially held down, which means that whoever has access to capital can easily profit from arbitraging between the regulated state banks and the free-will credit market.

Because SOEs can obtain the loans directly from the banks at lower interest rates with greater ease, many SOEs make some handsome and easy returns by lending out the loans that they obtained from banks. Such loans by SOEs to private enterprises and small- and medium-sized enterprises (SME) can sometimes carry a spread return of up to 10 percent per annum, a return that is higher than that from many SOE's main line of business.

Because the SOEs are confident that capital will flow their way, no matter what their operating performance and financial status is, they are willing to keep borrowing and helping the government. Also because of the government's guarantee, banks are willing to make increasingly large loans to SOEs, part of which can be used to cover a previous loan. Such a symbiosis can explain why SOEs can behave in a way very different from what market forces predict.[39]

Of course, the government's guarantee proves to be most valuable when such SOEs run into trouble. On some occasions, the government will turn its implicit guarantee into an explicit one and use its fiscal income to guarantee the security of the loans made by local companies.[40] On other occasions, the government will provide companies with a much needed government order, which will boost the companies' short-term financial performance. On yet other occasions, the government will forego local government taxes or use fiscal subsidies to reward companies that have helped the government in the past.

In short, with the government's guarantee, the SOEs do not have to worry about the availability or the cost of their debt, and banks do not have to worry about the security of their loans. As a matter of fact, SOEs can sometimes help banks inter-mediate their loans and re-lend some of the bank lending to companies that would not have made the cut to borrow directly from the banks.

By sharing the differences in SOE loan rates and the rates to private companies with the banks, the SOEs seem to be doing everyone a favor, with government support. This too-good-to-be-true situation just cannot seem to get any better. With the overall easy monetary policy and inflation, the real interest rate of borrowing is indeed approaching zero, which allows SOEs to engage in another round of investment and asset purchases, which, by itself, pushes up asset prices and generates rewarding amounts of investment returns.

The above government guarantee and soft budget approach may seem to be effective in containing Chinese corporate leverage problems. Also, with the high savings rate among Chinese households, government sectors, and the regulated financial sector, there is still time and room for Chinese SOEs and SOE banks to work together and put off some of the serious debt overhang problem.

The beauty, and at the same time risk, of the government guarantee under a soft budget is the risk sharing and transfer between the private and public sector. Granted there are many successful examples of such public–private partnerships, especially during financial crises, but their success can engender excessive risk taking and greater crises down the road.

The theory of economics and corporate finance proposes that there is a debt ceiling for an economic entity. In the context of China, we simply do not really know where the border between SOEs and government lies, and therefore the debt ceiling is unclear for Chinese SOEs, especially those with inseparably close ties with the government.

This leads us to the trillion dollar question: Will the Chinese government be able to deal with such mounting debt problems when the time comes? (We will discuss this question in Chapter 9.)

The mother of all credit: The government that never defaults

Be it trust products, real estate, the stock market, or state-owned enterprises, all share one thing in common. They have all survived considerable questioning and pessimism and have come out stronger than ever before.

However, the problems of implicit guarantees seem to be just the tip of the iceberg when compared to Chinese government debt. Since the 2009 stimulus package, Chinese local governments have taken on huge amounts of debt to revive economic growth. The problem has become so grave that it has attracted considerable international attention.

Partly in response to such growing concerns domestically and overseas, China's audit authorities conducted a thorough audit of local government debt in late 2013. The auditing put the total amount of Chinese local government debt at about 18 trillion RMB, far more than many had expected.[41]

More alarming than its sheer size, the Chinese local government debt increased by a whopping 70+ percent over just 3 years. Based on such a projection, Chinese local government debt may increase to 50 trillion—the size of the Chinese GDP in 2013—by 2020.[42]

Apart from the very fast growth in the size of local government debt, what has attracted the most international attention is how local governments have diversified their avenues of borrowing over the past few years. Largely because much local government debt is accrued through new venues and under new cover, it has become a lot harder to accurately pin down the total amount, and from that total amount, distinguish what is local governments' direct and explicit liability and what will become a local government's liability in case of adverse events.

As a result, some remain skeptical about the accuracy of the audit estimate and feel that that number is probably the lower bound of Chinese total local government debt.

Further, the real estate curb policy implemented since 2011 has led to a significant drop in growth in land sales revenues, the single most important source of fiscal income to almost all Chinese local governments. Reversing the historical trend in 2012, land sales resulted in 2.69 trillion of revenue to Chinese local governments, 14.6 percent less than the 3.15 trillion CNY in 2011.

With further uncertainties in the direction of the housing market, it remains unclear whether the local governments' fiscal situation will improve going forward. Further, with China's housing prices higher than those of many developing countries in absolute terms (and among the highest in the entire world in terms of house price-to-rent ratio and house price-to-income ratio), it is unlikely that local governments can substantially increase their fiscal income by auctioning off more land at higher prices.

However, many local governments do not seem worried. Because local governments do not have their own separate balance sheets, they are not held fully accountable for their financial behavior. The central government, as a matter of fact, provides implicit credit endorsement and enhancement on behalf of local governments. This can be reflected in a rather perverse and amusing phenomenon in local government debt issuance in 2012.

Four cities (Shanghai, Zhejiang, Guangdong, and Shenzhen) were allowed to issue local government bonds in a pilot program in 2012, and indeed witnessed a rather peculiar development as their bonds traded at a lower yield than that of the Chinese Central Government Treasuries. By common logic, the lower level governments do not have as strong financial status as the central government, especially in China, and hence would entail greater credit risk and higher bond yield to compensate for such risks.

What happened, though, is that the yield on the local governments' debt was lower, instead of higher, which is the international norm, than the yield on Chinese sovereign government debt. The reason is that investors, who are smart enough and familiar with the notion of the implicit guarantee that the central government provides to local government debt, bet that the central government would not allow such bonds to default. As a result, the local governments' debts enjoy credit support from both local and central government. Hence they are believed to be safer than even the sovereign bonds themselves.

The Chinese central government seems to be in a sound fiscal situation at the moment and a reliable support in providing creditworthiness. The balance sheet of the Chinese government is one of the healthiest among all major economies. The total assets of state-owned enterprises were 53.3 trillion CNY (among which 27.9 trillion belongs to the central government and the remaining 25.5 trillion CNY belongs to local governments) and the total foreign reserve was over $3 trillion USD in 2012. Based on such statistics, the Chinese government's assets can easily cover its entire liability.

In addition, the Chinese government's fiscal income has been growing rapidly during the past decade, which persuades most people that economic growth can solve any fiscal problem for the Chinese government, should there be any problem at all. Further, given the high savings rate and high level of home ownership, the private sector is reasonably well financed and can probably cope with costs associated with aging. This should give the Chinese government less to worry about and allow it to focus on dealing with its own debt problems. Finally, the fast growing domestic capital market has the potential of further enhancing the central and local governments' debt capacity in the years to come.

However, with its economic growth slowing down and its economic growth mode shifting, it becomes imperative for the Chinese government to inspect its fiscal sustainability and pose the question, "Is everything about to change?"

In 2012, two noteworthy patterns emerged in the Chinese central government budget report. First, the growth rate of both fiscal income and expenditure was much slower in 2012 than in 2011 (24.8 percent and 21.2 percent) and slower than it had been in most years of the previous decade. Secondly, the growth in fiscal expenditure outstripped that in fiscal income by a wide margin. The trend of fiscal income growing slower and fiscal expenditures growing faster is taking shape.

At the same time, it is worth stressing that the speed of governmental expenditure is very likely to increase substantially in the future. With the Chinese government's commitment to improving social welfare in such sectors as public education, health care, and environmental protection, government spending has to increase accordingly.

The slowdown in fiscal income growth will trigger a series of problems not confined to economics. The growth of fiscal income has outpaced that of GDP growth for many of the past years. Put differently, more wealth has moved into the public sector as opposed to the private sector. The proportion of household income to GDP dropped from about 56 percent in 1985 to about 40 percent in 2010,[43] far lower than the range of 50–65 percent in most developed economies.[44]

As household income growth slows, the inequality in income distribution within the private sector will draw more attention and cause increasing dissatisfaction and disappointment with the current taxation and fiscal system. According to an official report from the Ministry of Human Resources and Social Security of China, the annual income of the top 10 percent of households in China is 65 times higher than that of the bottom 10 percent of households.[45] Similar to the international trend, the income gap between corporate executives and rank and file corporate employees has been rapidly growing, causing increasing dissatisfaction among the younger generation.

Meanwhile, the government has to deal with its own share of the challenges. With reduced resources, it becomes much harder to balance further investments with the provision of social welfare efforts. Certain areas of public expenditures grew fast in 2012, including educational expenditure (28.3 percent to 466.7 billion RMB—4.08 percent of GDP) and affordable housing expenditure (16.4 percent to 444.6 billion RMB), while some other areas, such as medical expenditure and unemployment benefits and training called for similarly fast growth.[46]

For example, medical expenditure grew by only 12 percent, and unemployment training and benefits grew by only 12.9 percent. With fiscal income slowing down, the government is left with the options of slowing down expenditure growth or the fiscal deficit. In addition, the Chinese government requires additional resources to deal with some of the hardcore reform areas, such as social security, education, and health care—areas that the average Chinese household cares the most about.

So far, the central government has started to take the route of expanding the fiscal deficit to make up the shortfalls in the increasing fiscal expenditure. China maintained a modest budget deficit of 800 billion RMB in 2012, about 1.5 percent of China's 2012 GDP, which remains within the 3 percent safety range set by the European Union. In contrast, the fiscal deficit of the United States stands at $1.56 trillion, 10.9 percent of GDP, and some argue that the fiscal deficit problem in Japan may be even worse.[47]

At the same time, according to the China News Agency, the fiscal deficit of 2013 was projected to increase by about 50 percent from its

2012 levels, with a budget of 1.2 trillion RMB. Even with its modest size at the moment, such a growth rate in fiscal deficit would surely raise some eyebrows and concern some investors.

Interdependence

Like the economies of every country in the world, the Chinese economy has become more closely integrated into the world economy. Together with the process of increasing globalization, the connection between different parts of a country's economy has also become ever more closely related.

China's implicit guarantee problem is no exception.

Under the auspices of a government implicit guarantee, investors set aside their aversion to risk and pour huge amounts of wealth into risky investments such as Chinese trust products, real estate, and the stock market, under the impression that the Chinese government will guarantee their investment returns, or that they will not suffer losses.

Such confidence in risky assets leads Chinese households and corporations to take more risks than they fully understand and push forward the development of and exuberance in the banking and shadow banking sectors, the real estate market, and the stock market.

One new high after another has been observed in the Chinese housing market, with the stock market going through roller coaster rides rising from nadir to zenith, before falling back to another market bottom.

The capital that the Chinese financial sector raises is then transferred to enterprises with the strongest need to finance and the highest willingness to pay. In many cases, these include Chinese local governments, real estate developers, and companies in industries with already excessive capacities.

Local governments may need to borrow more or start a new round of infra-structure building for another new city, which is bound to boost local economic growth by another percentage point or two. Real estate developers borrow so that they can buy more land from local governments, which will make them billions in the next round of economic boom and housing price surge. Companies from industries with overcapacities need new capital to sustain their operations and to fend off price wars from competitors who are willing to borrow even more in order to drive other companies out of the competition. Or maybe all these enterprises simply borrow to repay their previous debts.

No matter what their motivations are, the government guarantee provides investors much-needed capital, without which the Chinese economic growth miracle may not have grown as quickly or as impressively.

However, as with all good things in life, there is a limit to how far the Chinese government can extend its implicit guarantee. After years of continuous rise, more and more people feel that the Chinese housing market cannot grow like this forever without facing some considerable corrections.

Interestingly, real estate serves as the poster child of Chinese overcapacity problems. With overcapacity problems ranging from 50 to 100 percent in many major Chinese industries, it is not clear how far this growing-by-borrowing model can keep going.

As shown in the previous section, the speed of Chinese economic growth has had profound impact on the Chinese government's fiscal soundness and creditworthiness, which largely determines the value of the implicit guarantees that the Chinese government provides to all participants in the economy.

With economic growth slowing down, the Chinese central government's fiscal income likewise has shown signs of slowing down. This could not have come at a worse time, given the Chinese government's commitment to substantially revamp social welfare areas such as education, health care, and the pension system.

Local governments, whose primary source of fiscal income comes from land sales, have felt an even greater pinch with the cooling off of the real estate market and the increasing financing costs demanded by investors, who are less confident about the central government's resoluteness and capabilities to bail out lower level government.

Without the ability to sell off new land at ever higher prices, local governments are having a hard time making ends meet, let alone mobilizing resources for further stimulus actions.

Without such guarantees and stimulus from central and local governments, however, it is hard, if not impossible, to imagine how the Chinese economy can keep up with the speed that it has enjoyed in the past decade. Lacking economic growth, a new round of depreciation of government implicit guarantees would start. So too will the contraction cycle start. ...

In some ways, the Chinese government guarantee has been the engine behind the Chinese economic spectacle of the past decades. With economic transition and further reform, this propelling force, if not harnessed well, can turn into the leading risk facing Chinese economic growth, sooner rather than later.

Table of Contents

So that is what this book is about: the exciting but concerning reality of the Chinese economy today and tomorrow. How has the government implicit guarantee managed to stimulate the Chinese economic growth miracle in the past decades? How can implicit guarantees gradually exit and what impact will this have on the sustainability of Chinese economic growth and further economic, political, and social reforms?

Chapter 2 discusses the Chinese shadow banking industry as the tip of the iceberg of the implicit guarantee problem. Chapters 3 and 4 focus on two major investment channels in China, namely real estate and the stock market, and how implicit guarantees by the government distort the return to risk balance in these areas and cause feverish investment in highly risky areas.

Following up on the first three chapters, Chapter 5 details the recent developments in financial innovations and new financing channels in the Chinese economy, and how such innovations manage to circumvent the regulations that a traditional financial system would have to face, and hence can engender unprecedented outcomes and risks.

The book then turns to other issues: the economic growth model in Chapter 6, the overcapacity problem in Chapter 7, and the state-owned enterprise problem in Chapter 8. These three chapters will expose how the major problems in the current Chinese economy can trace their roots back to the implicit guarantee problems that abound in the financial sector, as outlined in the previous four chapters.

Chapter 9 focuses on the mother of all credit, the fiscal soundness and credit worthiness of Chinese sovereign and local governments, and investigates the sustainability of their willingness and ability to provide the much needed implicit guarantees in the future. Specifically, the chapter discusses the option of a gradual exit of the implicit guarantees and how that would impact various sectors of the economy.

Because implicit guarantees are implicit, it is not easy to explicitly grasp how serious the problem is. This "unknown unknown" may very well generate another layer of uncertainties and risks for the Chinese economy going forward. Chapter 10, "Voodoo Statistics," deals with this topic and focuses on the reliability of official statistics and the potential bias such statistics could create in misleading government policy making. If the Chinese government cannot obtain an accurate assessment of the economic reality, it is hard to imagine how expedient reform can take place in the most needed areas.

In addition to helping readers gain more in-depth understanding of the Chinese financial sector, economic growth mode, and prospects, I will discuss in Chapter 11 how the concept of implicit guarantee has become ever more popular in the more developed Western economies, and the consequences implicit guarantees have on the economic, political, and social shifts in these countries, especially after the 2007–2009 global financial crisis.

Recommendations for reforms in several key areas of the economy and financial sector can be found in the final chapter, "How to Reform," which I hope can help diffuse the time bomb set by the increasingly large implicit guarantees provided by the Chinese government.

Notes

1. http://www.njdaily.cn/2013/0311/346222.shtml
2. http://finance.sina.com.cn/trust/20140123/090718056179.shtml
3. http://news.xinhuanet.com/fortune/2014-01/16/c_126012776.htm
4. The Reports on National Government Debt (June 2013), China National Auditing Office, December, 2013
5. http://finance.ifeng.com/a/20140902/13046908_0.shtml
6. http://house.ifeng.com/column/news/yzdzq/index.shtml
7. http://house.ifeng.com/detail/2011_11_11/20582916_0.shtml
8. http://www.zgfpbd.com/?p=5042
9. Some argue, though, that some of the protests were indeed staged by the developers, to put pressure on local governments for support and subsidies. http://www.zgfpbd.com/?p=5042
10. http://www.bloomberg.com/news/2014-07-01/china-developers-offer-buyback-guarantee-in-weakest-home-markets.html
11. http://dealbook.nytimes.com/2011/08/26/canadian-regulators-order-sino-forest-executives-to-resign/?_php=true&_type=blogs&_r=0
12. http://www.bloomberg.com/news/2011-06-21/paulson-dumping-sino-forest-may-deal-clients-720-million-loss.html
13. http://finance.sina.com.cn/focus/ChinesecompanyinAmericastockmarkekt/
14. http://money.163.com/13/0722/19/94DLCCM400254ITV_all.html
15. http://cn.reuters.com/article/chinaNews/idCNChina-1403920080612
16. http://17173.tv.sohu.com/v_102_613/NzgwMTA2OA.html
17. http://finance.ifeng.com/stock/ssgs/20111212/5254377.shtml
18. http://guba.eastmoney.com/404.aspx?code=002070
19. http://finance.sina.com.cn/stock/y/20080918/16295318752.shtml
20. http://news.cnstock.com/news/sns_bwkx/20140½870302.htm
21. China Survey of Consumer Finance, Southwest University of Finance and Economics
22. http://wenku.baidu.com/view/4f620c10a8114431b90dd87c.html
23. http://news.hexun.com/2013-01-10/150023967.html
24. http://finance.sina.com.cn/zl/china/20140325/152418607856.shtml
25. http://www.sciencedirect.com/science/article/pii/S0929119913000062X

26. http://onlinelibrary.wiley.com/doi/10.1111/j.1540-6261.2008.01325.x/pdf

27. http://money.163.com/14/0519/00/9SINTFNU00253B0H.html

28. It is worth pointing out that this estimate is indeed on the conservative side, according to Mr. YAO, Yudong, author of another research on the same topic, Chinese nonfinancial corporate leverage is as high as 140 percent.

29. http://app.finance.china.com.cn/report/detail.php?id=2115866

30. http://finance.sina.com.cn/china/20140519/011719145466.shtml

31. http://news.xinhuanet.com/fortune/2007-07/20/content_6406776.htm

32. http://www.alu.cn/news/483789/

33. Oct, 17, 2013, The State Cabinet, "Guidance on solve the over-capacity problem"

34. http://finance.eastmoney.com/news/1372,20130711305429891.html

35. http://news.xinhuanet.com/energy/2012-10/29/c_123883520.htm

36. The Reports on National Government Debt (June 2013), China National Auditing Office, December, 2013

37. http://baike.baidu.com/link?url=GWEXgxaCdkBzsdDIEI8ltTu06643c5j JDf7ZURS7oKxdiTRjQ5-2tGQ_Np5SfxQ7YFl8d9P1eOHJnDHKq-Lkq

38. China: 2030, 2012, World Bank and China National Development Center.

39. China: 2030, 2012, World Bank and China National Development Center.

40. http://www.chinanews.com/cj/2012/01-04/3580800.shtml

41. The Reports on National Government Debt (June 2013), China National Auditing Office, December, 2013

42. http://finance.sina.com.cn/money/bond/20131230/163617796897.shtml

43. National Bureau of Statistics of China, 2014

44. World Bank Database

45. Institute for Labor and Wages Studies, 2014

46. 2013 National Budgetary Report, 2013, Chinese State Council.

47. http://news.xinhuanet.com/world/2011-03/11/c_121173817.htm

Failure is an Option (in China's Shadow Banking Problem)

The four most dangerous words in investing are,
"This time it's different."

—John Templeton

I N January 2014, IT GRADUALLY BECAME CLEAR THAT ONE OF THE trust products sold by China Credit Trust Company faced the risk of default. The product, which was backed by assets from a once highly successful mining business, not only lacked the cash flow to repay its investment dividends, but also the necessary assets to cover the product's principal, which were both due January 31, 2014.

Shanxi Zhenfu Energy Group, the coal company that had taken out 3 billion Yuan (about $500 million) from the China Credit Trust Company, through ICBC, faced cash shortages in repaying its interest and principal obligations. Zhenfu Energy originally took out the 3 billion Yuan financing to expand its production capacity in hopes of increasing coal prices. However, with the tapering off of the quantitative easing by the U.S. Federal Reserve, and with plunging coal prices, it had to shut down its production, which resulted in its financial distress.

Interestingly, the China Credit Trust Company claims that it only plays the role of a distribution channel for the Shanxi Branch of ICBC, the real holder and guarantor of the product.

In contrast, ICBC, China's largest bank and one of the largest banks in the entire world based on assets and revenues, made it clear in the trust products' prospectus and sales process that it does not bear these responsibilities and will not take any responsibility in repaying the principal or the interest of the products.

The incident has attracted widespread attention, partly because this symbiotic relationship between banks and trust companies, or the formal and shadow banking systems of China, has worked very well in the past few years, until now, and nobody really knows what would happen if this collaborative relationship breaks down.[1]

Despite the details about the relative responsibilities of each party involved in the product, the stance on both sides sets a very interesting precedent for the entire shadow banking industry in China. Shadow banking, including many high-yield-paying trust products and wealth management products(WMPs) that have mushroomed in the past few years (China Credit Trust and ICBC promised their wealthy clients returns ranging from 9.5 to 11.5 percent per year in selling the products related to the Zhenfu coal mine),has shouldered a large fraction of financing for not only small- and medium-sized enterprises in China, but also for investments in many industries with severe overcapacity and many local government debts and local government financing vehicles.

Such products have become tremendously popular, not only because they provide highly attractive returns (sometimes ranging from 12 to 18 percent per year), but also because they are believed by many to be very safe. Many investors in these products understand that, even though there is clear stipulation in the product prospectus that there is no guarantee of the security of the principal, the trust companies and related commercial banks will guarantee the safety of their investment because of both regulatory and reputation concerns.

The default of January 2014 may be the epitome or a preface to many similar defaults that are about to take place. In addition to sluggish housing prices and neutral monetary policy (as opposed to the super-easy monetary policy from 2009–2011), many suspect that there are some fundamental shifts in regulators' attitudes towards such shadow banking products. The regulators' willingness to eventually let some products default and investors lose money may be responsible for this and several other similar default events in 2014.

The new China Banking Regulatory Committee (CBRC) policy (No.107 article by the State Cabinet) instituted in 2013 was intended to rein in shadow banking lending and forbid all state-owned trust companies from using so-called "fund pools" to invest in non-standardized assets, as in the case of the China Credit Trust Company.

Such non-standardized assets make up the majority of the high-return portion of trust companies' assets. If a trust company's fund pool can no longer chase such high-return investments, the trust products' portfolio size would be expected to shrink considerably because the company could no longer offer better returns than other WMPs (especially those directly offered by traditional commercial banks).

Further, the new rules also forbid trust companies from operating fund pools that enable them to fund cash payouts on maturing products with the capital raised from sales of new trust products. By pooling funds from different products, trust companies enjoy the benefits of having the flexibility of salvaging one product with funding raised from other projects temporarily. Until the change in the policy, fund pooling had become a common practice among most trust companies and the bloodlines for some troubled existing products.

By pooling funds from new product sales to repay maturing products' obligations, trust companies and other financial institutions find great leeway and incentive to expand their fund pools. As long as the cash flow generated from new product sales can meet the obligations to repay maturing products, trust companies can keep increasing their fund pool and assets under management (AUM) continuously. In some ways, this mimics a Ponzi scheme, promising unrealistically high returns as long as new funds can be obtained, often through China's interbank money market.

The credit crunch (liquidity squeeze) in June and December 2013 witnessed short-term interbank lending rates skyrocketing to an astonishing high of 25 percent (annualized).[2] Some experts argue that the credit crunch in June 2013 coincided with a period of concentrated maturity of trust products and WMPs, highlighting the reliance of trust products and WMPs on such fund pools and refinancing through the cheaper and shorter-term interbank lending market.

The year 2014 was a year with peak repayment obligations for most trust companies, many of which had become accustomed to financing real estate development projects. When Chinese real estate sales slowed due to stalling housing prices, many observers expected that a clampdown on the practice of fund pools would further endanger real estate developers. As a result, trust companies' ability to cover their cash flow would decrease further and result in more defaults on trust products. If more trust products were to default, it would dampen developer sentiment and their ability to develop their land, because many developers and projects rely heavily on trust products to keep up their cash flow.[3]

The Origin of Shadow Banking: Three Constraints

China has arguably one of the world's largest banking systems.

Unlike many other countries that rely heavily on capital markets, namely the stock market and the bond markets, China's banking system dominates household and corporate financing activities, and, as a result, the national economy. By the end of 2013, the Chinese banking sector, not including shadow banking, boasted over 100 trillion Yuan worth of assets and ranked among the largest banking sectors in the world.

Chinese banks command a total of 148 trillion Yuan in assets,[4] which makes up more than 90 percent of the assets in the Chinese financial system. (Insurance companies, securities companies, trust companies, and mutual fund companies command 8.28, 2, 0.38, and 0.37 trillion worth of assets, respectively.[5])Not surprisingly, the four largest state-owned banks of China, namely the Industrial and Commerce Bank of China (ICBC), China Construction Bank (CCB), Agricultural Bank of China (ABC), and Bank of China (BoC) rank among the largest banks in the entire world.

Given the Chinese banking sector's predominance in the economy, it seems surprising that China appears to need another, parallel, shadow banking system. To make things even more intriguing, Chinese shadow banking has grown at an astonishing speed over the past 5 years, with the traditional banking sector growing at the same time.

According to statistics published by the People's Bank of China (PBoC), the Chinese central bank, nonbank financing made up about 15 percent of bank loans in 2008 (about 2.3 trillion Yuan), and about 15 percent of bank loans in 2013 (about 20 trillion Yuan). According to the Chinese Academy of Social Sciences (CASS), the official number may have been underestimated and the real figure may be as big as 27 trillion Yuan, or about one-fifth the size of the Chinese formal banking sector.[6]

Not only is the size of the shadow banking system greater than that of the shadow banking system in the United States before the 2007–2008 global financial crisis, but the speed of its growth has raised some international concerns. The Chinese shadow banking sector has been growing more than 20 percent per year for some time, causing the ratio of shadow banking to traditional banking to approach the United States' figure during the pre-crisis period (about 1.2 times). Both numbers signal that Chinese shadow banking has grown to become a critically important part of the Chinese financial system.[7]

So why has China's shadow banking grown so fast? There are three primary reasons.

1. Financial repression and thirst for funding (especially after the 2009 stimulus package in China)

In any fast-growing economy, capital becomes a scarce asset that all companies vie for. This demand is even stronger, and unfortunately less well met, in emerging economies like China, where financial development and financing channels are limited and underdeveloped compared to other sectors of the economy and to financial sectors in developed economies.

Under such circumstances, banks hold a strong position in the economy and are motivated to make as many loans as they can afford. However, to keep inflation in check and ensure financial stability, the PBoC and CBRC set targets for credit growth every year, which banks always have incentives to exceed, in order to generate greater revenues and profits.

Things changed drastically with the rolling out of the 2009 stimulus package. In 2009, to prevent economic slowdown, national credit grew at an unprecedented rate, doubling its original target. Credit growth in 2009 was twice as much as that in 2008, and greater than the combination of credit growth in every single year between 1990 and 2000. As expected, such quick credit expansion led directly to inflation and quick asset price appreciation in 2010 and 2011. To counter inflation, the PBoC had no other option but to limit credit growth in 2010 and 2011[8,9].

However, as one old Chinese proverb says, "It is easy to go from frugality to extravagance, but difficult to go from extravagance to frugality." Both borrowers and banks had already become addicted to credit expansion. Investors now seek to borrow and invest in projects that can only be rationalized by expectation of further monetary easing and asset price appreciation. As Hyman Minsky put it, these are "Ponzi borrowers," since "many of (their) investments are not sustainable, if it were not for additional investment and credit to sustain themselves".[10]

Since the amount of (over)investment had grown so large, continuous funding became critical in many instances to sustain existing investments. Banks and companies came to the conclusion that they had to seek credit from other channels and nonbank financial institutions under the stricter rules set by the regulators.

Fortunately, banks and trust companies had started collaborating long before it became critical in 2009. Back in 2006, when the stock market soared, banks had already figured out a way to collaborate with trust companies in order to move credit off banks' balance sheets so they could use the capital to invest in the then burgeoning stock market and generate substantial investment returns within a few days or few weeks. However, it was not until 2009 that banks and trust companies started working so closely with each other with unprecedented scale and volume.

Despite the motivation of banks to make loans in 2009, many companies faced increasing difficulties in obtaining credit. On top of their regular capital need for organic development, many expected asset prices to soar in light of the stimulus package and hence wished to borrow as much as they could to take advantage of the potential rise in asset prices.

When the real estate market started showing a sharp rise in 2009, many banks received guidelines from the regulators to scale back their loans to real estate developers. At the same time, real estate developers themselves remained very bullish about the market and anxiously looked for new ways to raise capital. This unmet financing demand from real estate developers through the regular banking sector prompted banks to move more of their businesses off their balance sheets, which resulted in the surge in Chinese shadow banking.[11]

2. The capital adequacy requirement

In addition to the need from the economy, the fast growth of the trust companies and other forms of collaborations between banks and other types of financial institutions is largely motivated by formal banks' need to circumvent regulatory requirement and obtain "regulatory arbitrage" benefits.[12, 13]

Following the global bank regulatory protocol, Chinese banks faced another constraint when trying to grow: the capital adequacy ratio. The capital adequacy ratio (usually applicable to banks, and now to some other types of financial institutions under the post-crisis Basel III regulatory framework) requires banks to hold a certain proportion of their assets with their own capital.

This requirement was put into effect largely to make sure that banks align their interests with those of their stakeholders (shareholders, bond holders, and other participants in the financial system). Because banks have shown the tendency to take unwarranted risks during financial booms, financial regulators and the rest of the economy would often have to bail banks out during financial busts (the "too big to fail" problem). Given a bank's systematic importance to the entire economy, governments and regulators around the world feel that the rest of the economy is hijacked by the "too big to fail" banks in the aftermath of their excessive risk-taking.

Many attribute this "heads I win, tails you lose" risk-taking mentality by banks and financial institutions to the occurrence of the 2007–2008 global financial crisis and many various financial crises before that. Consequently, global regulators have learned from previous financial crises and require that banks set aside a higher proportion of their assets using their own capital, before another financial crisis takes place. The idea is to prevent banks and bank-like financial institutions from taking risks beyond their capabilities and, should bad things happen, have a credit reserve to offset potential losses for shareholders and bond holders.

With the Chinese stimulus package in 2009 and nerve-wracking fast expansion of its credit, all Chinese banks have every incentive to expand their balance sheets as soon as possible and as much as possible. Given the clear and persistent negative real interest rate (the interest rate was lower than even the nominal inflation rate for many months in 2010, and many people believed that the interest rate was consistently below real inflation during the entire past decade) and strong expectation for asset appreciation, banks find strong incentives in moving transactions off their balance sheets to reduce the required capital that they have to hold.

Given that the Chinese stock market has remained sluggish in the 2010s and that Chinese banks cannot easily raise capital from China's underdeveloped domestic bond market, Chinese banks have to seek ways to hide the tremendous growth in their balance sheets. To meet such a need, shadow banking provides a much needed alternative through which banks can continue to expand their business without having to raise additional capital.

3. The loan-to-savings ratio

On a more technical level, Chinese banks face another major limit set by Chinese banking regulators: the loan-to-deposit ratio. To ensure bank liquidity, Chinese regulators require that banks maintain a loan-to-deposit ratio of 75 percent (subject to adjustment depending on economic conditions). That is, for every dollar a bank collects in deposits, it can only lend out 75 cents.

Thus, to expand its business, a bank would either have to keep expanding its deposit base (which explains the fierce competition for deposits toward quarter- and year-end when the loan-to-deposit ratio is being calculated) or to find an alternative way to make loans not identified as loans by regulators' criteria.

Given the wide savings and loan interest rate spread, banks all have strong incentives to expand their lending, which leads them to reach a point where they would have to expand their deposits before they can make any new loans. Chinese banks quickly find out that the easiest way to get around this loan-to-savings limit is to shift regular lending off their balance sheets through shadow banking (see point one).

According to some research reports by the PBoC and research teams at leading international investment banks, Chinese banks have been working with trust companies, securities companies, and insurance companies to turn their interbank deposits (which do not qualify toward deposits in computing their loan-to-deposit ratio) into ordinary deposits (which *do* qualify as deposits while calculating loan-to-deposit ratios).

What banks do is to use interbank deposits—which come from other banks and financial institutions that trade in the interbank market—to purchase WMPs issued by other financial institutions (i.e., trust companies, securities companies, and insurance companies). Once these nonbank financial institutions receive the funds from banks' purchases of the WMPs, they deposit the funds back into the bank as ordinary deposits. The financial institution boosts its business and earns handsome fees off such transactions, whereby banks manage to increase the size of their deposits relatively quickly and relatively easily.

Trust products

Of all parties involved in the Chinese shadow banking business (small loan companies, securities companies, asset management companies, peer-to-peer financing companies, and other alternative financing channels), trust companies probably started the earliest and have enjoyed the most successes. Trust companies in China are nonbank lenders that raise funds by selling high-yield investments known as wealth management products (WMPs) to investors and then use the proceeds to fund loans to risky borrowers such as property developers, local governments, and others to whom banks are reluctant or unable to lend.[14]

According to the Boston Consulting Group (BCG) in its Global Wealth Report 2014, there were 2,378,000 millionaire households in China in 2013, an increase of 82 percent from 2012. According to the study, the wealthiest Chinese's financial assets grew by a shocking

49 percent to $22 trillion from 2012 to 2013. In particular, the boom in trust products contributed the most to creating more wealth for Chinese households than any other investment channel.[15]

Historically, it took trust companies about five years to catapult their assets by 10 times, from 900 billion Yuan in 2008 to about 9 trillion Yuan in 2013. Even after the CBRC stopped the collaboration between trust companies and banks in July of 2010, trust companies still found huge demand for their services and managed to continue growing their businesses through selling high-return trust products.[16]

Trust companies have become so big and important that some experts blame the concentration of maturing WMPs and the demand for excess cash as partly responsible for the credit crunch in June 2013, when short-term inter-bank lending rates shot to as high as 30 percent per annum.[17]

When the CBRC banned future collaborations between banks and trust companies, it only managed to stop one leaking hole in a sinking boat. Other types of financial institutions, such as securities companies and insurance companies, soon found opportunities in the woes of trust companies and in working with banks. Securities and insurance companies then decided to join the party by offering their share of shadow banking products. Even though the size of trust companies continued to grow, many started noticing that the profit margin of trust companies had come down steadily, primarily because of the competition from securities and insurance companies.[18]

Entrusted loans

Another new addition to the aforementioned formal shadow banking products is entrusted loans. Entrusted loans (loans made directly between companies with banks' intermediation) have become one of the fastest-growing categories of shadow banking in China. Entrusted loans increased from 1.28 trillion Yuan in 2012—a whopping net of

2.55 trillion Yuan ($407 billion)—to 3.83 trillion Yuan in 2013. This put entrusted loans at 29 percent of all new Yuan-denominated bank loans in 2013, as opposed to only 16 percent in 2012.[19]

Several studies in 2012 and 2013 found that probably more than 30 percent of these fast growing loans have been directed to the Chinese real estate sector. If this is the case, entrusted loans indeed provided more capital to the Chinese real estate sector than bank loans and trust products in the five year period ending in 2013. Namely, entrusted loans have become the single most important capital blood-line keeping China's property developers afloat.[20]

Because entrusted loans are essentially private lending, there is greater flexibility by both sides in setting the interest rate and loan contract details. Banks provide intermediary services and collect service fees without committing their own capital in the loans. With the decline in Chinese real estate prices, this type of once high-flying product (often with attractive returns of over 10 percent per year) gradually started showing signs of risks in 2014.

Several listed companies revealed in their quarterly and annual reports in 2014 that, with the softening in the real estate sector, they had started to have trouble collecting the entrusted loans that they made in the previous couple of years. As more listed companies started disclosing their earnings (and losses) from entrusted loans, it became clear that many Chinese listed companies had been involved extensively in the entrusted loan business. These attractive loans that had generated handsome returns for companies during good times were now turning into time bombs that could trigger at any moment.

For example, Zhejiang Longsheng Group Co., Ltd., a chemicals manufacturer in eastern Zhejiang province, reported in its 2013 annual report that it had earned about 20 million Yuan from entrusted loans in 2013, 77 percent lower than its earnings from entrusted loans in 2012. Further, the company reported that some real estate developers that had borrowed hundreds of millions through entrusted loans failed to repay their loans in time and asked for extensions from the company.[21]

Zhejiang Longsheng Group, is not alone in its experience. Many other conglomerate companies like Zhejiang Longsheng Group, which have managed to profit from entrusted loans and transferring funds across different business lines, are now living with the flip side of such cross-subsidization. With many entrusted loans having gone sour, the healthy parts of a conglomerate now end up subsidizing those that are struggling. Without such support, we may witness more default and bankruptcy before the Chinese real estate sector can regain its footing.

Parties involved, forms evolved

According to the investigation and Statistics Bureau of the People's Bank of China, Chinese shadow banking encompasses a very wide range of products and services provided by various financial institutions.

In particular, shadow banking in China includes commercial banks' off balance sheet WMPs, directional asset management products and WMPs offered by securities companies, WMPs offered by mutual fund companies, insurance companies' investment accounts, various non-(weakly-) regulated asset management companies (e.g., industry investment funds, private equity funds, venture capital funds), annuities, small loan companies, nonbank financial leasing companies, specialized factoring companies, financial holdings companies, pawnshops, guarantee companies, third-party payment companies, and unregulated informal lending among companies and individuals.[22][23]

The scale and influence of shadow banking has become apparent when even more components of this rather comprehensive list are considered, such as trade financing, in which merchants use import as collateral to finance and invest for higher returns, and credit guarantees that private companies provide to one another, a phenomenon that we will discuss in Chapter 5 (Alternative Financial Innovations).

Reflecting such complexities, the new regulations on shadow banking now define three different types of shadow banking in China: first, financial intermediaries *without* any financial license and under no financial regulations, such as internet financing companies and independent wealth management companies; second, financial intermediaries *without* financial license and under insufficient regulations, such as guarantee companies and small loan companies; and finally, financial intermediaries *with* financial licenses that are under insufficient regulations, such as money market funds, some asset management companies, and trust companies.[24]

Even though the first two make up the majority of shadow banking institutions in *numbers*, it is the third category, the off-balance-sheet businesses conducted by financial institutions regulated under Chinese financial regulations, that contributes the most to *volume* and *growth* of Chinese shadow banking sector.

Be it trust companies, securities companies, or insurance companies, the shadow banking businesses conducted by these financial institutions have to thank commercial banks for initiating shadow banking practices. With banks' growing need to circumvent regulations and move assets off their balance sheets, trust companies enjoyed phenomenal growth and transformed themselves from once lackluster laggards into the second largest subsector of the Chinese financial system next to banks within a mere five years (from 2009 to 2013).

With trust companies' successes and increasing risks, the regulatory landscape of shadow banking keeps evolving and new parties continue to join as a result of the shifting regulations. With the previous collaboration model between commercial banks and trust companies gradually surfacing and attracting regulatory attention and objection, more and more banks now turn their business to securities companies and insurance companies, which now actively support a new round of bank securities company and bank insurance company collaborations.

For example, Chinese securities companies, under the strict regulation of the Chinese Securities Regulatory Commission (CSRC), historically specialized in investment banking, advisories, and securities dealing businesses, and did not have much to do with the shadow banking business before 2010. However, soon after the CBRC's ban on bank collaboration with asset companies[25], assets managed by the securities companies' asset management arms catapulted almost tenfold, from a merely 282 billion Yuan by the end of 2011 to 1.89 trillion Yuan by the end of 2012, and about 3 trillion Yuan by the end of March 2013.[26]

The PBoC recently highlighted in its 2014 China Financial Stability Report that the directional asset management plans at many securities companies and mutual fund companies are indeed covers for entrusted loans made by commercial banks. According to the report, the outstanding amount of directional asset management plans issued by securities companies increased by a whopping 186 percent to 4.83 trillion in 2013.[27]

Taking a quick glance at a number of banks that have recently filed for IPOs, one would quickly find out from their prospectuses how prevalent and sizeable such directional asset management products have become. For example, by the end of June 2013, the Bank of Chongqing held 3.86 billion Yuan worth of such plans, up from 1.11 billion Yuan merely six months earlier. Harbin Bank, another leading local bank in the North East of China, held 16.3 billion Yuan in such plans by the end of September 2013, more than doubling its holdings in 2012.[28]

So what do securities companies have to do with these banks? According to the PBoC, in its report, such plans allow banks to make off-balance sheet loans. A bank would entrust its funds to a securities company as an investment. The securities companies would then turn to buy a trust product, which is typically backed by a loan to a company, or buy the income stream from a company's accounts receivable. The securities firms then deposit their investments back into their bank accounts, which would appear on the bank's balance sheet as regular deposits. There it is: the banks simply use securities companies as an alternative to engage in loans or investments that they cannot otherwise make. As a result, the banks expand their business and balance sheets, and securities companies happily receive portions of the deal as reward for collaborating with their clients, the commercial banks.

In addition to circumventing the loan-to-deposit ratio, there is another apparent advantage of turning loans into investments. Chinese banks have been blamed for making huge profits from simply making loans and earning loan-deposit rate spread. By turning some of their businesses from loan-related to investment-related businesses, banks would seem to have become less reliant on lending business and more diversified into other business areas, another goal that the Chinese regulators have been pursuing for years.[29]

Alas, unlike the practice of shadow banking in the West, where most of the shadow banking businesses were, strictly speaking, created outside the banking sector or in competition with the banking sector, a large part of the Chinese shadow banking business was indeed initiated, or at the very least supported, by traditional Chinese commercial banks. In the end, it is the banks which needed to create a "bank outside the bank" and to circumvent a series of Chinese regulators' requirements, or their own shadows.

Bypassing the constraints, unleashing the risks

IMF estimates in its 2013 global financial stability report that the size of Chinese WMPs is about 10 trillion Yuan and about 12.5 percent of Chinese household financial assets.[30] Given this relatively low percentage in household assets, and the lack of financial innovation and transaction in shadow banking products, the IMF concludes that the risks of Chinese shadow banking products are still under control, for the time being.

With the slowing down of the Chinese economy and excessive overcapacity looming in many sectors, however, Chinese corporate leverage has been steadily climbing since 2010. In a study by ShenYinWangGuo Securities, the debt-to-asset ratio in their sample of 5,000 companies increased from about 60 percent in 2007 to 95 percent in 2013.[31]

With the tightening in traditional lending made by commercial banks, more companies turn to trust products and wealth management products for alternative channels of financing. As a result of restrictive regulations on banks' lending to certain sectors, industries such as real estate, mining, and steel have become heavily dependent on shadow banking since 2010. The default of ZhenFu in the mining field, as discussed at the beginning of the book, is simply one of many similar cases in which borrowers can no longer service the loans that they took out when the economy was booming and credit was fast expanding.

Another sector that has been relying heavily on shadow banking is real estate. After the 2009 stimulus package, and until 2013, the Chinese real estate sector enjoyed much higher investment returns than the rest of the economy (the real estate sector witnessed its return on equity consistently above 10 percent, which is rare in the Chinese economy nowadays),[32] largely thanks to the super-easy monetary policy and lack of investment channels in China during the rolling out of the 2009 stimulus package.

However, with the cooling off of the real estate sector in 2013, many real estate developers have to turn to shadow banking to raise much needed cash flow. As long as demand remains sluggish in the real estate sector, developers will have trouble repaying their previous borrowings and will borrow to roll over their debt with higher interest rates. If the Chinese housing market were to experience a prolonged period of adjustment, even if housing prices do not drop significantly, the financial costs and dropping collateral value from developers' land reserves may cause many developers to default on their borrowings.

Such risks are not only contained in the private sector. Closely related to the real estate industry in the private sector, Chinese local government financing vehicles(LGFV)—financing platforms set up and implicitly guaranteed by local governments to develop land and build infrastructure—have increased their reliance on shadow banking. With the softening in the housing market, local governments' revenues from land sales will also slow down, undermining local governments' cash flow and ability to provide further guarantees to future infrastructure and real estate projects.

All in all, with the shift in the Chinese economic growth model and a cooling off of its real estate market, it is almost certain that Chinese shadow banking will have to go through its own adjustment, just like the rest of the economy. If anything, because of the lack of regulations and disclosure, shadow banking may turn out to be a trigger for a new financial crisis.

The central bank is clearly concerned with shadow banking and the sharp and steady increase in Chinese leverage. According to Fitch Ratings, China's total nation-wide debt has grown from 128 percent of GDP in 2008 to 216 percent of GDP in 2013—within merely five years. Without government interference, the ratio can climb to 271 percent of GDP by 2017, a number that has preceded the ratio of countries plagued during the past few previous global financial crises.[33]

On one hand, Chinese regulators treat shadow banking as an inevitable result of financial innovation and wish to have shadow banking play an active role in broadening the investment channels for Chinese households, pushing forward further financial reforms and better serving the rest of the economy.

On the other, many come to realize that many of the shadow banking businesses were intended to go beyond the regulatory framework from day one, and it has become increasingly challenging even for regulators to fully understand the scale and impact of Chinese shadow banking.

With collaborations between banks and other types of institutions, particularly trust companies, securities companies, and insurance companies, the border line for regulators has become quite blurred. Because trust companies, securities companies, and insurance companies fall under the purview of three different regulatory authorities in China, and because of the regrettable lack of communication and collaboration across these authorities, gaps in regulatory oversight may even open wider, especially because the Chinese shadow banking system has become so big and complicated.

Based on the experiences of financial crises in other parts of the world, shadow banking's ability to get around regulations and become contagious across many parts of a financial system or an economy is one really intrinsic and worrisome aspect of the practice.

How to reform

Regulators' dilemma

It is worth pointing out that regulators have become aware of and concerned with the ballooning size of Chinese shadow banking. Zhou Xiaochuan, governor of the PBoC, said in 2012 that "shadow banking exists in China, just like it exists in many other countries. … But the nature and the scale of it is nothing compared to that of developed countries, where the problems were exposed during the financial crisis."[34]

Of course, things have developed considerably and rapidly since 2012. The size of the shadow banking sector has catapulted from 2.3 trillion Yuan in 2008 to about 20 trillion Yuan in 2013. In addition to its size, shadow banking has permeated into many new areas of the Chinese financial system (such as securities companies, insurance companies, and asset management companies), reaching to far greater parts of the economy than it had in 2013 (beyond real estate and local government financing). Further, shadow banking itself has morphed, making it harder to identify shadow banking products precisely and hence harder for regulators to monitor and regulate.[35]

Aware of the dynamic nature of Chinese shadow banking businesses, Chinese regulators have taken a consciously conceived plan to gradually de-leverage the Chinese financial system and scale back the Chinese shadow banking sector. This gradual and prudent approach is quite reasonable and understandable.

As long as the Chinese economic growth model does not shift successfully from its investment-dependent path to a slower yet more sustainable consumption-propelled path, China's economic growth, employment, and social stability will remain heavily dependent on investment, which is largely made available by bank lending, given the relatively small size of capital markets (stock market and bond market). With the slowdown in Chinese economic growth speed, a sudden brake on shadow banking could lead to undesired consequences of economic stalling and social unrest.

On the other hand, as discussed earlier, the Chinese shadow banking sector includes many businesses derived from traditional banks' off-balance sheet arms. Therefore, reversing or even slowing down the buildup of debt through shadow banking is bound to hurt the balance sheet of Chinese state-owned banks, some of the largest in the entire world.[36] Therefore, policymakers may lack the resolve to issue rigid requirements to solve the shadow banking problem.

Of course, because many of the shadow banking businesses are established on the basis of collaborations between traditional commercial banks and many other types of financial institutions (such as trust companies, insurance firms, asset management companies, and other alternative financiers, such as pawnbrokers and peer-to-peer lending) any slowdown in shadow banking can mean disaster, not only to traditional banks, but also to the Chinese financial system, infrastructure, and financial investment that rely on shadow banking as their blood lines.

However, the flip side of this gradual approach to the shadow banking system is that any reform in shadow banking regulation is literally a race against time. By not engaging in more drastic reform, Chinese regulators are taking a risky bet that China's debt woes will not turn into a crisis over the next couple of years, when a large number of the shadow banking products with high promised returns will mature.

The paradox in this dilemma is, in the words of Eswar Prasad, ex-IMF China chief, "If problems become apparent in the short term, it reduces the ability to push through reforms that officials think are more important."[37] Without properly setting the expectation, regulators cannot successfully rein in shadow banking. The even bigger

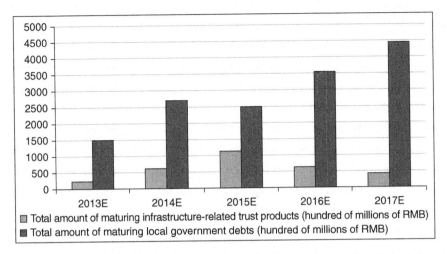

Figure 2.1

problem is that the government and regulators may lack the resolve to shift the expectation for implicit guarantee after all.

Credible threat?

A key to the shadow banking system is, undoubtedly, the implicit guarantees that banks provide to many of the shadow banking products associated with banks—but outside the banks' balance sheet. This is, of course, the beauty of shadow banking, and the first and foremost reason why shadow banking has grown so fast and furiously in China over the past few years.

With the increasing scale and complexities in the Chinese shadow banking sector, regulators have been working hard to expedite reforms to diffuse any potential catastrophic risks to the Chinese traditional financial system and national economy. The introduction of banks' living wills and bankruptcy law, as well as the deposit insurance schemes, reflects the government's determination to eventually break implicit guarantees behind the Chinese shadow banking system.

This could channel credit to commercially viable projects with good risk-adjusted returns, but it seems unlikely that the government will let financial institutions remove implicit guarantees on collective trusts and WMPs completely in the near future, as that may cause severe unintended consequences such as widening in credit spreads, rising bond yields, liquidity crunch, and economic hard landing and social unrest. Therefore, the government is unlikely to conduct severe reforms, but rather it may let the economy gradually grow out of the problem.

Hopefully, reforms in other areas of the economy, such as ending the GDP tournament mentality that is responsible for overcapacity in many sectors of the economy, together with fiscal and taxation reforms that will alleviate the housing boom problem, would also help deflate the size of Chinese shadow banking.

In the end, the key to reform is the ability of the government to communicate its message of phasing out the implicit guarantee that has been supporting shadow banking. The recent establishment of an insurance deposit system is certainly a promising field of reform. Even with the introduction of personal and corporate credit rating systems and the development of a bond market, a lack of a credible default and bankruptcy threat would still distort the return-to-risk tradeoffs facing investors.

Notes

1. http://www.bloomberg.com/news/2014-01-23/china-trust-products-gone-awry-evoke-soros-echoes-of-08-crisis.html
2. http://usa.chinadaily.com.cn/business/2013-06/26/content_16667482.htm
3. http://www.bnppresearch.com/ResearchFiles/29697/China%20 Banks-170114.pdf BNP Paribas Report: Judy Zhang CHINA BANKS: Will the implicit trust product guarantee be gone?
4. http://www.cbrc.gov.cn/chinese/home/docView/987456E5AC9549 BA8FA53EC5F7A66029.html
5. WIND and industry association reports
6. http://news.163.com/14/1101/09/A9V338O700014AEE.html
7. http://www.qqjjsj.com/yjbg/31729.html
8. http://finance.people.com.cn/GB/10681773.html
9. http://money.163.com/12/0214/02/7Q6LA0PP00253B0H.html

10. http://en.wikipedia.org/wiki/Hyman_Minsky#Financial_theory
11. http://ineteconomics.org/%5Btermalias-raw%5D/why-did-chinese-shadow-banking-surge-after-2009
12. http://www.brookings.edu/~/media/research/files/papers/2015/04/01-shadow-banking-china-primer/shadow_banking_china_elliott_kroeber_yu.pdf
13. http://siteresources.worldbank.org/FINANCIALSECTOR/Resources/Session3-LiaoMinShadowBankinginChina.pdf
14. http://www.reuters.com/article/2014/04/14/us-china-regulations-shadowbanking-idUSBREA3D09H20140414
15. http://blogs.wsj.com/chinarealtime/2014/06/10/china-now-has-more-millionaires-than-any-country-but-the-u-s/
16. http://www.nytimes.com/2013/08/07/business/global/growth-slows-in-chinas-trust-sector.html?_r=0
17. http://www.reuters.com/article/2014/04/14/us-china-regulations-shadowbanking-idUSBREA3D09H20140414
18. http://ineteconomics.org/%5Btermalias-raw%5D/why-did-chinese-shadow-banking-surge-after-2009
19. http://blogs.wsj.com/chinarealtime/2014/05/02/a-partial-primer-to-chinas-biggest-shadow-entrusted-loans/
20. http://finance.sina.com.cn/money/bank/bank_hydt/20140516/011919123388.shtml
21. http://blogs.wsj.com/chinarealtime/2014/05/02/a-partial-primer-to-chinas-biggest-shadow-entrusted-loans/
22. http://finance.qq.com/a/20140115/008057.htm
23. Yan, Qingmin, and Li, Jianhua, 2014, A study of Chinese Shadow Banking System, Citic Publisher.
24. http://wallstreetcn.com/node/72008
25. http://bank.hexun.com/2010-08-12/124571244.html
26. http://bank.hexun.com/2013-01-19/150350052.html
27. 2014 China Financial Stability Report
28. http://business.sohu.com/20140505/n399151227.shtml
29. http://blogs.wsj.com/chinarealtime/2014/05/04/securities-companies-take-a-leap-into-shadow-banking/
30. The People's Bank of China, Financial Stability Report, 2014.

31. Lin, Caiyi, Wu, Qihua, How are Chinese Shadow Banking Created, Research Report, ShenYin WanGuo Securities.

32. http://www.sxdaily.com.cn/n/2014/0325/c362-5391340.html

33. http://blogs.wsj.com/moneybeat/2014/01/06/few-specifics-mean-china-banks-could-stay-in-the-shadows/

34. http://finance.people.com.cn/n/2012/1111/c1004-19543760.html

35. http://blogs.wsj.com/moneybeat/2014/01/14/is-chinas-focus-on-reform-clouding-the-picture-on-shadow-banking/

36. As a piece of side evidence, rumors about the State Councils' plan have contributed to a sell-off in China's stock market in early 2014.

37. http://www.brookings.edu/research/testimony/2015/04/22-sustainable-growth-china-prasad

3

Homebuyers Who Cannot Lose

The Fed needs to create a housing bubble to replace
the Nasdaq bubble.

—PAUL KRUGMAN (2002)

I N SEPTEMBER 2014, SEVERAL SALES AND DEMONSTRATION CENTERS
of various real estate development projects were reported to have
been vandalized in broad daylight. Without investigation, the perpetrators in some of the vandalizing showed up themselves right in
front of the now trashed sales center.[1]

They were none others than the recent home buyers at the very
same development projects, who had bought their apartments before
the developers decided to slash the pre-sale apartment price by 15 to
30 percent.

With the Chinese housing market weakening nationwide in 2014,
there have been numerous similar protest and petition events by new
home buyers, though not all of them ended up with as much violence.
These were definitely not the first situations in which Chinese home
buyers have petitioned against developers who lowered prices; nor will
they be the last.

A few years earlier when the Chinese housing market softened, similar situations happened to other developers all over the country.[2,3] In some extreme cases, the demonstrators went as far as taking the sales manager hostage, demanding compensation for financial damages to recent home buyers, who suffered financial losses as a result of the reduced prices.

During various protests, the home buyers turned demonstrators felt wronged by the developers who sold them properties and righteous about protecting their investments. Some claimed that the developers slashed the prices by some 20 or 30 percent before the properties were even completed. For example, a project in Hangzhou sold for 18,000 Yuan per square meter in early 2014, before the developer slashed its price to about 15,000 Yuan per square meter a few months later, netting a loss of over 15 percent to those who had bought earlier.[4] This caused previous home buyers losses ranging from hundreds of thousands, to over a million Yuan, quite a fortune to average Chinese households.

Many of the homebuyers claimed that the developers had promised them that there would be no further price cuts or promotions after they bought the apartment months, or even weeks, before, when they signed their sales contracts. Some protestors felt that what the developers had done was no different from 'fraud,' providing them misleading information to lure them into purchasing an apartment. Many such buyers felt that they did what they had to. "What would you feel if you bought a TV and the retailer slashed the prices by 10 percent the next day"?

Indeed, during the market corrections in 2008, 2011, and 2014, real estate prices were reined in for some months. To expedite sales, some real estate developers decided to sell new apartments at lower prices than a few months previous or to provide more generous incentives to attract buyers. Whereas some new buyers celebrated a better opportunities to purchase property, those who had just bought property saw their investment turning up losses right after the deals were made.

Intriguingly, not a single person protested or boycotted the real estate project or real estate developer when they saw the prices of the apartments that they just bought *increase* by 10 percent within a couple of months, which has been common in China in the past few years. Nor has it ever been reported that home buyers provided any form of 'refund' to developers after the apartment that they had bought earlier appreciated by more than 100 percent.

Developers, on the other hand, felt victimized in these situations and refused to give in at first.[5] Indeed, during weaker market conditions, some developers promised in the sales contract to buy back the apartments that they sold at a 20 to 40 percent premium over their selling prices in the subsequent five years. While such tactics had proved useful in luring in customers in the past, some developers felt that the substantial price appreciation in the past and uncertain outlook of the housing market might dampen their effectiveness in 2014 and therefore no longer offer such promises in the contract. As a result, the developers argued that, without any explicit guarantees in the contract, all of the 'promises' that the sales delivered were just 'promises,' subject to changes in the real market conditions.[6]

One could argue that investors from all over the world are similar in the way that they do not fully understand investment and risks, and they are often naïve about the prospects for their investment. The difference in China is how government and real estate developers handle such situations.

Often, the local governments will step in and play the role of mediators in such disputes. In most cases, the local government would try to appease the property buyers by asking the developers to make up the buyers' losses or to provide additional incentives to make the home buyers happy. After all, local governments do not want to deal with a scene of a large protesting crowd—not a healthy sign for social harmony, and definitely not instrumental in helping them getting promoted in the future.

Given the close ties between real estate developers and local government and local governments' guidelines and pressures, real estate developers usually conceded to the protesters by making up the price differences or throwing additional amenities to recent homebuyers at a loss, footing the costs and losses themselves. However, such generous moves were not always met with much appreciation. The homebuyers claimed that real estate developers had made so much money during the market boom and that it was time for the developers to give up some of their gains.

What is more important, though, is that a market-wide expectation had been formed through such protests and concessions. At least in the real estate sector, investors had come to believe that they would not lose money when they bought a piece of new property. Should anything happen, the real estate developer and government would take responsibility for the irresponsible investment that they had made.

Such beliefs, fueled by the implicit guarantees from the Chinese government and real estate developers, may be a main culprit for high housing prices in China and the bubble-like phenomenon in many other areas of the Chinese economy.

How high are Chinese housing prices?

To people who have never been to China, the question that begs to be answered first probably is, "How high *are* Chinese housing prices?"

There are several ways of assessing housing prices: the speed at which prices increase, the price to income ratio, the price to rental yield, and total land value.

(1) Fast price appreciation

So, how much have housing prices risen in the past decade? This is a very good question, but also unfortunately one without an accurate answer. The official Bureau of Statistics provides one answer, but consensus among the public provides another. Many people contend that the official statistics considerably understate the magnitude of the housing price appreciation to avoid future curbs or a crackdown policy in the real estate sector, at least within their governance. (This will be elaborated on in Chapter 10)

The Chinese National Bureau of Statistics (NBS), which started compiling the Chinese housing index based on 70 large cities in 2004, has by far the longest time series of housing appreciation data. According to the NBS, Chinese national housing prices have risen 77 percent for newly sold apartments and 57 percent for existing apartments in the past decade.[7,8]

Another official data source from the Ministry of Housing and Development (MoHD) covers a smaller sample of cities and reports a bigger increase. According to the MoHD, national housing prices rose by 150 percent from July 2004 to February 2014.[9] Interestingly, this means that one source of official data reports price gains twice as high as the other.

On the surface, the statistics from both sources seem reasonable, or even modest. Housing markets in the U.S. and many developed economies in Europe have reported similar or even bigger price gains in the housing sector before their housing bubble burst in the 2007–2009 global financial crisis.

What sets China apart is that the statistics from both official sources face serious skepticism from the public because they differ drastically from the data compiled by third-party institutions and from residents' first-hand experiences.

Two additional sources come from the private sector. The China Index Institute (CII), affiliated with Sofun.com, one of the largest online real estate listing agencies, started compiling a housing index for 100 representative Chinese cities in June 2010. CII reported that national housing prices rose by 21.7 percent from June 2010 to December 2013 alone, with prices in first tier cities rising at twice this speed.[10]

These numbers, even though already much faster than the two official statistics, seem meager compared to data from another commercial source, Centaline.com, another leading Chinese real estate agent for property sales and rental in major Chinese metropolitan areas. According to Centaline, housing prices in major cities such as Beijing, Shanghai, Guangzhou, and Shenzhen have risen by 374 percent, 346 percent, 505 percent, and 420 percent, from May 2004 to March 2014.[11]

However, as many residents feel (and as will be shown methodologically in Chapter 10)even the data from the China Index Institute and Centaline.com may still seriously underestimate housing price appreciation due to fundamental sampling bias.

(2) Rental Yield

Rental yield, or the ratio of rental income to housing price, is a widely used gauge for housing prices in the world. Because the National Bureau of Statistics and the MoHD do not collect large sample rental information, there is little official data on rental yield in China.

Centaline.com, on the other hand, has been publishing rental yield data in major Chinese cities since 2008 (based on the average rent and average price in each city) using all transactions brokered by Centaline within each city.

According to Centaline, one trend has become very clear since 2008: the rental yield has been decreasing consistently. For example, the rental yields for Beijing, Shanghai, Guangzhou, and Shenzhen were 3.5 percent, 3 percent, 4.5 percent, and 3.9 percent in 2008, and the figures dropped to 1.8 percent, 2.0 percent, 2.5 percent, and 2.2 percent toward the end of 2013.[12]

It is worth pointing out that both housing prices and rents have been increasing during the past five years. What has caused the rental yield to drop by one half is the fact that the speed of increase for housing prices is much faster than that for housing rentals.

For example, Centaline reports that rents increased by 34 percent, 63 percent, 59 percent, and 31 percent from 2009 to the end of 2013 in Beijing, Shanghai, Guangzhou, and Shenzhen, the four major cities of China. At the same time, the price of existing homes in these four cities increased by 69 percent, 107 percent, 167 percent, and 112 percent. The faster appreciation in housing prices directly led to the considerable drop in rent-to-price yield and made investment in real estate less attractive from a fundamental valuation perspective.

The price to rent ratio in Beijing and Shanghai, in particular, has dropped from about a 3–5 percentage range five years ago, to a 1.5–2 percent range in 2013, lower than Chinese banks' deposit rate (about 3.5 percent per year during the same period).[13] This low rent-to-price ratio makes Chinese housing as expensive as Taiwan and Korea, and more expensive than any other major emerging economy.

(3) Housing price-to-income ratio

Another way to evaluate Chinese housing prices is through a commonly used benchmark, the housing price-to-residential-income ratio. This benchmark reflects how affordable the housing is in an area compared to the purchasing power of residents in that area.

According to a recent report by a leading Chinese real estate broker, the average housing-to-income ratio is 10.2 for 35 leading Chinese cities.[14] The situation is indeed a lot worse in the Eastern coastal cities. Beijing, the capital city of China, comes at the top of the list with a housing price-to-income ratio of 19.1. That is, residents in Beijing would have to use their entire disposable income every year for 19 straight years before they could afford a 100-square-meter apartment in Beijing for a family of three. Because housing prices are generally understated in China, some worry that the true situation is even worse.[15]

These numbers are much higher than the international average housing price-to-income ratio of 4.6, based on a survey conducted by the World Bank.[16] The situation is also in stark contrast with the rule of thumb in the United States that one can normally afford a house that costs about three times one's annual salary. Among developed economies, most other developed economies report housing price-to-income ratio of 5–6 times.[17]

(4) Total land value

Another way to look at a national housing market is through the value of total land within a country. At the peak of the Japanese real estate bubble in 1990, the total value of Tokyo land was about 4.1 trillion dollars, about the total land value of the United States during the same year and about 63.3 percent of the contemporary U.S. GDP. Coincidentally, at the peak of Hong Kong's real estate bubble in 1997, the total land value of Hong Kong was about 5.7 trillion dollars, again about 66.3 percent of contemporary U.S. GDP, before the market collapsed and lost almost half of its value in the following decade.

In 2012, the total land value of Beijing was estimated to be about 10 trillion dollars, about 61.6 percent of the U.S. GDP in that year. With considerable price gains from 2012 to 2014, it is highly likely that, proportionally in terms of the U.S. GDP, Beijing's land value is approaching that for Tokyo and Hong Kong, when each market was near the burst of its own real estate bubble.[18]

In sum, all four benchmarks point in the same direction: that Chinese housing prices are very high from the perspectives of total value, historical pricing, affordability, and investment.

The demand side

Demand from households

So if Chinese housing prices are so expensive and unaffordable, how can Chinese households afford to buy apartments, and why have they continued doing that during the past decade?

First, as in many other East Asian economies, households in China have a much higher savings rate than in Western households. This savings buffer supports some of the down payment for buying a first home. If the younger generation cannot save up enough for their down payment, it is almost taken for granted that the older generation will pitch in with their life savings.

Further, the booming housing market has created wealth for many households that use the money from their old apartments as down payments for new apartments, hoping that housing prices will keep rising in the future.

In addition, because buying a house is considered lucrative and necessary for newly married couples, many families forsake other household expenditures, such as education, vacations, and entertainment, to contribute to housing installment. Sometimes, the cost does not come in the form of money. In major metropolitan areas such as Beijing and Shanghai, it is not uncommon for people to spend two hours one way commuting so that they can live in homes they can afford to buy, but which lie far away from city centers.

However, what may really set the Chinese housing market apart from that of any other country in recent history is that the housing boom in the past decade has convinced many that housing is the best investment and has led households to invest in real estate. The Chinese housing market, quite up to people's expectations and hopes, has managed to live up to its attraction and has generated handsome returns to anyone who has been involved in the process.

Expectations and Speculations

One strong argument for the high and rising housing prices is the steely rigorous demand for housing in China. The booming economy, the world's largest population, the relatively low starting point of housing, and the relatively more concentrated geographical distribution of the population are all solid fundamental reasons why Chinese real estate properties should be valuable assets.

However, with the rapid urbanization in the past decade, the glut of existing apartments and apartment developments, and the rapid aging of the Chinese population, it makes one wonder whether demand for housing as a consumer item is really as rigorous as claimed, and whether this trend is going to change in the future.

Even according to the not-so-comprehensive statistics on urbanization, which fail to incorporate the increasing number of migrant workers, China does not lag too far behind the urbanization process of many developed countries (54 percent compared to the 65 percent of most Western countries). Also, as measured by the area per capita, Chinese residents indeed enjoy a similar level of living space to that enjoyed by the citizens of France, the United Kingdom., and Japan. This level is indeed rather high, put in the context of the relatively dense population and low income level, even by East Asian standards.[19]

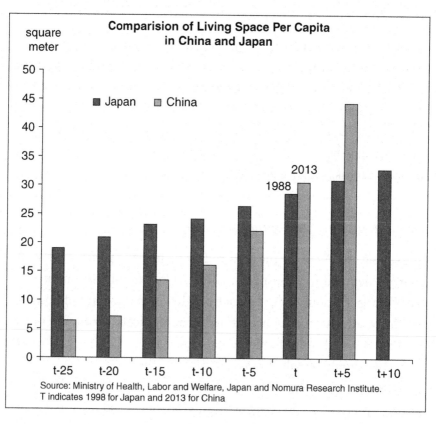

Figure 3.1

Also, it defies the principles of Economics 101 that the demand for a good or service would decrease should the price of the good or service increase. This is indeed how residents of many major metropolises, especially Asian ones, manage their lifestyle. If the housing prices rise, one should expect urban residents to be willing to live in a smaller apartment. Alternatively, if the housing prices rise much faster than housing rentals, one would expect more people to rent instead of buying apartments.

However, because Chinese residents are so convinced that the housing prices will keep rising, most families are not only buying an apartment to live in, but also as a potentially valuable option that could generate millions of Yuan in the future, should housing prices keep going up.

Such expectations may help explain why Chinese housing prices rose to such high levels that even residents from countries with much higher incomes find them out of reach. Partly, it is because Chinese residents consider housing less as a consumer good and more as an investment, and therefore ignore the absurd rent-to-price ratio and buy even more apartments.

This could explain the affordability puzzle in the Chinese housing market. Chinese residents—investors in this context—do not really think about whether they can afford the housing they buy. What they care the most about is whether the property *will* appreciate. As long as housing prices keep going up, borrowing to buy properties can be deemed as leverage for a smart trade, no different from margin trading in the stock market.

This may also explain why even when the rental yield in many Chinese cities is lower than the banks' meager savings rate: residents are still feverish about buying apartments with as much money as they can borrow. The apartment buyers in China have become used to the over 20 percent annual appreciation rate in the past decade and believe that the trend will, and should, continue going forward. After all, it is the strong speculative belief in and demand for housing that has been pushing housing prices higher and rental yield lower.

Steely Demand for Investment?

Whether China's housing prices can continue at such a high level depends on demand for properties. There are two drastically distinct incentives, hence demands, for buying a piece of property. The primary reason is, of course, as a place to live. The secondary reason is to treat an apartment as a kind of security and make money off it.

According to a survey conducted by Southwest University of Finance and Economics (SWUFE) in Chengdu, almost 90 percent of Chinese households own their primary residence, a ratio that is far higher than the 66 percent in the United States and 63 percent in the rest of the world. So it is not clear why the Chinese would want to buy more houses as residences.[20]

What sets China apart seems to be that the secondary demand has become the primary one these days. One simple way to look at this issue is if the primary demand for an apartment is indeed due to the rigorous demand for someone to live in it, then the demand for housing should be fairly stable. After all, there are only so many graduating college kids and newlyweds who need to buy new apartments. If this is the case, one would expect that the past housing curb policy should not have too much impact on the demand and on housing prices.

If instead, a majority of the demand for real estate in China is driven by investment or speculative motivations, then it is conceivable that such speculative demand would drop in light of the curb policy, and with it housing prices. It has become a public secret in China during the past decade that the best investment an average household can make is to buy real estate.

According to the same survey conducted by the SWUFE, Chinese households on average have made 340 percent return on their primary residence.[21] Such expectations generate further demand for housing, which pushes up housing prices and solidifies the expectations with new evidence. Hence, the self-fulfilling prophecy.

Of course, the line between the consumption and speculation purpose of home ownership may not be that clear. A family may consider buying a larger apartment and hoping that the apartment will appreciate in value at the same time. However, if residing in an apartment is really the driver for this purchase transaction, one would expect that there should be at least some people who would rent out their small apartment and rent a bigger apartment to live in. However, few Chinese households do that. It seems that this option of house appreciation is probably just as important in Chinese house purchasing decisions as is living in the house.

Also, one may argue that the several rounds of past curb policies should have already squeezed out a large proportion of the speculative demand. However, like many other interesting phenomena in China, for every policy there are loopholes that one can and will take advantage of.

Fake contracts

Because one would have to pay transaction taxes based on the face value of an apartment transaction agreement, it has become a common practice in China for the buyers, sellers, and real estate agents to work together to bring down the price and total value of the transaction.

By doing so, the buyers can pay less tax and are sometimes willing to share some of the tax savings with the buyers to gain the buyers' collaboration. The real estate agents typically keep their commission as a percentage of the real transaction value, so they have every incentive to facilitate the deal. Once the deal is made, the saved transaction taxes will be split between the buyers and sellers who have collective incentives to cheat the government with a lower value.

The result of such fake contracts is not simply some foregone tax dollars to the tax authority. If fake contracts are very prevalent, it would mean that the official housing prices data would be greatly understated.

In addition, the apparent achievement that the curb policy has managed to make may indeed be due to more aggressive use of contracts with considerably understated prices.

Fake divorces

A rather amusing incident took place in early 2013 when the Chinese government issued a new requirement intended to stabilize housing prices and levy additional taxes and financing costs for second and third properties. This specific curb policy intends to limit the number of properties that a household can buy or hold. To circumvent these regulations and avoid penalties and increasing financing costs, many Chinese families with multiple apartments filed for divorce before the new curb policy took effect so that the wife and husband each could be regarded as a household, thereby increasing the total number of apartments the newly divorced family could have together. Reports came in that before the curb policy could have any meaningful impact on the Chinese housing market, it first generated far reaching impact on the Chinese family structure![22]

False ownership information

To make things even worse, there is no centralized data system which documents property registration and ownership information in China. This means that each household could indeed own multiple properties in various areas of China without even having to face the aforementioned requirement on ownership of multiple properties.

Recently, there were several incidents of corrupt government officials or bank managers who took properties as bribes. They own many properties without selling them off, making one wonder how many similar cases exist and how many apartments in China are vacant because the owners have no desire to live in them or do not dare to bring these apartments into public scrutiny.

For example, Fang Guangyun, who was in charge of urban recon-
struction in Hefei, the capital city of An'Hui province, was charged with
taking bribes of 18 apartments.[23] This is nothing compared to another
official, ZhaoHaibin from the Guangdong Province, who was charged
with owning 192 apartments from various illicit activities.[24]

Such cases are not limited to government officials. Gong Aiai, a
deputy CEO at a small local bank, was found to own over 20 apartments in Beijing, valued at over 1 billion Yuan. Real estate properties
have become major components in illicit activities such as bribery and
embezzlement, and the real owners of most of these properties do not
even surface until the Communist party disciplinary department or law
enforcement is involved.[25]

Renter Protection Act

Of course, there is one key difference between buying and renting—the
control over the apartment and the continuity in consumption.

This is indeed a thorny issue in China. Chinese landlords enjoy
greater power in deciding when they can sell an apartment, and ten-
ants must vacate in compliance with the landlord's decisions. Even
with additional compensation for early termination of the leasing contract, many renters fear that renting would be too much hassle without
proper protection in legal forms.

The problem becomes even worse because of rising housing prices.
So many existing homeowners would like to either cash in their earlier investment or opt for a greater investment in a bigger apartment.
Either way, it would often result in the early termination of rental
contracts and having the ordeal of looking for another place to live.
Put differently, some of the renters were "forced" to buy an expensive
apartment by their landlord.

This is indeed why, in many developed countries, the law limits landlords' power in setting rent or deciding when to terminate
the housing rental agreement. Germany, for example, issued a law in

2013 to forbid landlords to increase rentals by more than 15 percent in three years.[26] Even in Hong Kong, arguably the market with some of the strongest "free market spirit" in the world, renters are very well protected.[27]

However, this falls back into the government's purview. If the Chinese government is really serious about stabilizing the housing market and decreasing the speculative demand for housing, maybe it should consider more renter-friendly policies like those in many developed markets. Tenant-friendly requirements would not only guarantee everyone a safe and sound place to rest at night, but also relieve some speculative demand forced into the market when renters no longer have to worry about being forced out of their rental home.

Guarantees for Housing

It is worth mentioning that some of the loopholes in China's housing market are indeed kept intentionally in case the government needs to fine-tune some of its curb policies on real estate. Over the past decade, the Chinese government has had to face the same dilemma that it has faced again and again: deciding whether or not to curb the real estate sector. In its previous attempts to cool off the housing market in 2005, 2007, and 2012, the Chinese government started with some effective measures at first, but eventually gave in every time under the pressure of economic growth speed and social stability.

By trying to drive down housing prices and then giving up, the Chinese government provided an implicit guarantee that the housing market will not drop. Whenever there is some slight sign of the Chinese housing market losing ground and buyers of apartments realizing they had overpaid, the protests of the buyers have often caused the government to persuade the real estate developers to make sure that the apartment buyers do not face a sudden price drop. Ironically, the real estate developers complained that they have never asked apartment buyers to share the money that they have made from the purchase.

So, the risk sharing is only on the downside for the developers and the government, but not upside for home buyers. This implicit guarantee that property investment always makes money certainly can explain part of the property investment frenzy that has been going on for quite some time in China.

In essence, this guarantee is not too different from the cheap financing backed by Fannie Mae and Freddie Mac under the grand scheme of the "American Dream" of everyone owning a residence. These implicit guarantees offered by the agencies and the U.S. government were directly responsible for America's enthusiasm for real estate investment in the early 2000s and eventually caused the real estate bubble and burst later in that decade.

Real estate developers, with government support and guarantees, also provide their own version of the guarantee to attract real estate buyers. In China, real estate developers, especially in the area of commercial real estate, promise guaranteed rental yield to investors on their development properties. Needless to say, such "too good to be true" rates are much higher than the going market rental yield.

Some investors were indeed attracted by these guaranteed higher returns, only to find out later that the guarantees came with fine print. In many cases, the developers simply defaulted on their original guarantee on higher returns. Lawsuits and disputes occur extensively on this matter, with similar guarantees being offered even now. In many cases, the promised rental yield is between 8 to 10 percent, whereas the going rate for neighboring apartments is only 3 to 5 percent.[28]

The failures of developer guarantees reveal the true problem of all such government and developer guarantees: How credible and sustainable can they be? At times, investment opportunities too good to be true during the bubble's formation did prove not to be true after the bubble's burst.

Belief in the housing market, combined with the government's implicit guarantee that housing price will keep going up (indefinitely), undoubtedly drives the Chinese investors' confidence in the housing market and the housing prices.

Similar situations happened many times in other economies when housing prices reached unprecedentedly high levels (for example, in Japan during the 1980s, in Hong Kong during the 1990s, and in the United States. and the United Kingdom during the 2000s.) Investors in each market managed to convince themselves that real estate prices could only go up, despite very shaky fundamental rental yield.

Unfortunately, the music has to stop and party has to end sometime. What happened in the United States during the 2007–2008 global financial crisis suggests that no assets can escape the very fundamental law of one price in finance and economics. Ironically, the solution to the short-term problem of market correction and economic slowdown can plant seeds of even bigger problems down the road.

Even though some people still blame the curb policy put into effect in 2011 for the disappointing Chinese housing market in 2013 and 2014, others argue that the three-year-old policy at most has marginal impact on recent lackluster housing sales. Instead, some fear that the expectation by investors and speculators has finally started running out of steam and shifting, which could be disastrous for housing sales going forward.

Government Demand for Growth

If anything, speculators seems to have been correct about one thing: that the Chinese government is not serious about driving down Chinese housing prices. To their credit, government officials have communicated this message clearly enough. In Premier Wen Jiabao's "Premier Report" in 2012, he stated several times that the purpose of the curb policy is to "ensure *moderate* growth in the real estate sector."[29] Of course, to Chinese people who are heavily influenced by Confucius's teaching on balancing, there is a lot to muse about exactly what "moderate" means.

In some ways, the Chinese housing market would not have grown to its current stage without the government's encouragement, or at least consent. To see this point, it is easy to note that the few times the government implemented serious curb policies (2005, 2007, and 2012), house prices indeed dropped to different degrees as a result. However, time after time, the Chinese government has decided to change its mind and scrapped its own policy to curb housing prices before any meaningful change could take place in investors' expectation.

The billion, maybe trillion dollar question then is, *why?*

There are of course political and social considerations, given the Chinese government's promise to deliver a better life to everyone in the country. A steady and booming housing market makes almost everyone in the country happy, at least for a little while. This not only improves citizens' satisfaction with the government's policy, but also underscores the government's ability to reach its objectives and deliver its promises.

A key consideration of Chinese government in the past decade is, first and foremost, its *economy*: the speed of Chinese economic growth. Real estate investments make up 26 percent of Chinese social fixed-asset investments. If one were to account for other sectors that are closely related to real estate, such as construction, steel, cement, chemical manufacturing, furniture, household appliances, and leasing services, the real estate and related sectors make at least about 33 percent of Chinese fixed asset investments and about 16 percent of Chinese economic growth.[30]

Based on this data, a slowdown of 10 percent in investment in the real estate sector would drag down Chinese fixed asset investment growth and economic growth by 3.3 and 1.6 percentage points, respectively. This estimate of real estate's impact on Chinese economic growth is probably conservative, given that a slowdown in the real estate market might significantly impact Chinese local governments' fiscal revenue, which comes primarily from land sales, and further slow down local economic growth. Also, slower economic growth and dropping asset prices would hurt Chinese banks' asset quality, which would hinder their willingness to lend and result in further economic slowdown. (These two issues will be discussed further in later chapters.)

Even without such complications, a difference of 1.6 percentage points in the speed of Chinese economic growth could be the deal breaker for the Chinese government's mandate to maintain its economic growth at 8 percent, 7.5 percent, or 7 percent and have profound impact on people's confidence in the Chinese economy.

A closer look at Chinese local governments' fiscal situations provides an even more compelling economic insight on how real estate over the years has become the bloodline for Chinese local government revenues.

In 2013, land sales generated 4.12 trillion Yuan in fiscal income to Chinese local governments. Together with the 1.06 trillion that local governments collected through taxes and fees related to land sales and real estate development, real estate and related activities made up more than 75 percent of Chinese local governments' 2013 budget of 5.2 trillion Yuan.[31]

In other words, land sales eclipsed central government appropriation and any other fiscal income source and became the single most important income source to Chinese local governments. Without growth in the real estate sector, Chinese local governments could barely do any of the development needed to boost local GDP growth. Without GDP growth in local areas, local government officials would have little chance of advancing their careers.

Stalling or dropping housing prices, and the resulting slowdown in land sales and development, could also bring systematic risks to local governments' fiscal sustainability and the security of local government debts, all of which rely on government revenue raised from new rounds of land sales.[32]

Finally, there is the banking sector. Loans directly related to real estate made up 14 percent of all outstanding loans in China in 2005, and the ratio has increased to more than 20 percent in 2013. Among new loans, real estate related loans made up an even higher fraction, at 26 percent. Needless to say, the share is considerably higher if one were to count in other sectors heavily reliant on the real estate sector, such as steel, cement, furniture, etc.[33]

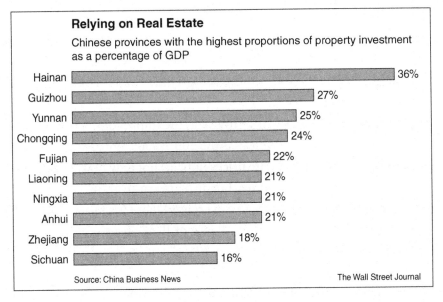

Figure 3.2

In addition, many experts conjecture that the real estate sector makes up the lion's share of the ballooning Chinese shadow banking sector and increasingly risky trust products.[34] Outstanding property trust products totaled 1.15 trillion Yuan as of March 31, 2014, accounting for 10.4 percent of all types of trusts, not even counting other property-related borrowers such as the local government financing vehicles (LGFV).[35] Therefore, it seems that the entire Chinese banking sector is in jeopardy when housing prices drop.[36] (This will be discussed further in Chapter 6 "Behind the Growth Engine.")

According to several official stress tests conducted by various government agencies, Chinese housing prices do not pose particularly concerning risks to the Chinese economy and financial stability. One agency claimed that even a 50 percent drop in Chinese housing prices would not damage the banking sector.[37]

This may reveal overconfidence. One of the major arguments suggesting that the Chinese housing sector is healthy is that, unlike in the

United States or other developed economies in which households take substantial mortgages to buy their homes, the leverage of Chinese households' mortgage is indeed quite low due to both high savings rates among Chinese households and the official requirement for higher down payments in house purchases.

This may very well be true. However, the impact of housing prices on the economy is quite complex. As the 2007–2009 global financial crisis revealed, a drop in real estate prices impacts not only household consumption and financial situations, but also government fiscal situations (as was the case for the European Sovereign Debt Crisis) and financial stabilities (as was the case of the collapse of Bear Stearns and Lehman Brothers in the United States).

As will be shown subsequently, even though Chinese households do not take out excessive debt, Chinese real estate developers are heavily leveraged on the supply side, indeed taking on far higher leverage than other industries in China and higher than real estate developers in many other countries.

Given the substantial increase in Chinese housing prices, the wealth effect from the housing boom cannot be ignored. According to the survey by Southwestern University of Finance and Economics in Chengdu, China, an average household's primary residence makes up 65 percent of household assets, far greater than the size of their other financial assets. A large part of the assets come from the 340 percent average investment return on Chinese households' primary residences.[38] If house prices were to stop rising and start dropping, Chinese households would certainly suffer some of the reverse wealth effect that has been fueling Chinese households' consumption during the past decade.[39]

This figure is far greater than that in most developed economies, and is responsible for the increased consumption in other parts of the Chinese economy. Such concentrated asset allocations indicate that if there is a drop in Chinese housing prices, Chinese households' balance sheets and consumption patterns might even be hit harder than what happened to U.S. households during the collapse of the U.S. housing bubble.

Developers at Risk

Even if Chinese households are not overleveraged in purchasing properties, Chapter 2 shows that Chinese real estate developers are certainly overleveraged, oftentimes through costly trust products.

Research based on financial statements from listed companies reveals that the debt-to-asset ratio is more than 60 percent for real estate companies, a limit widely used as financial stability for the real estate industry in general.[40] Of course, the leverage can be somewhat lowered if one takes into consideration that many real estate developers can generate a substantial cash flow once their development starts selling and they start collecting security deposits and down payments.

Nevertheless, this line of argument also exposes major risks in developers' financial soundness. If the sales of developers' new developments were to slow or come to a stall, developers' leverage would increase quickly and substantially. Given that many real estate developers also finance through other more costly financial alternatives such as subprime debt through the Hong Kong market and trust products through the domestic markets, deterioration in the housing market and developers' financial situations could quickly draw concerns and cause a sudden increase in their financing costs, adding more woes to the already troubled sector.

Chinese property trusts face record repayments of over 200 billion Yuan in 2015,[41] almost doubling the 109 billion Yuan due in 2014. At the same time as increasing repayment pressure, new issuance of the products slumped to 40.7 billion Yuan during the 2nd quarter of 2014, the lowest in the past three years. As the real estate market cools, there is growing speculation among investors that more developers, especially smaller ones, will struggle or collapse.[42]

Because of rising concerns regarding the Chinese property sector and the highly related shadow banking, China's banking regulators said in early June 2014 that they will monitor developer finances closely. This announcement confirmed existing concerns that defaults may spread after the March collapse of Zhejiang Xingrun Real Estate Co., a builder south of Shanghai, and raised questions of whether more parties may have been involved and at risk. [43]

Just as investors' expectations of housing prices change, real estate developers are shifting their expectation of the market direction as well. In late 2014, many developers were disappointed to find that, even after the government grandly loosened its curb policy on home purchases and mortgage loan availability, housing sales did not rebound much.

One apparent reason is oversupply. In many cities, statistics reveal that on average each person owns at least one piece of property.[44] As a result, it is widely expected that developers will exercise more caution in joining land auctions and developing new projects. With this shift, developers can no longer afford running promotions such as bonuses upon signing, guaranteed rental yield, and discounted financing, which were effective in generating sales. The end result is, of course, prolonged sluggish property sales.

The Shifting Tide

Optimists certainly have their reasons for hope. Consider that China will eventually reach its goal of urbanization, with the urban population making up 60 percent of national population. This translates into 816 million urban residents. This population base would require about 272–285 million units of an average size of 100 square meters (based on about 3 people per unit, currently a typical Chinese family size). This would translate into a total of 25–28 billion square meters before the Chinese urbanization movement eventually concludes. With a stock of 18 billion square meters in 2013 and an incremental supply of 1–1.5 billion square meters every year, it seems that it may take up to 10 years before Chinese cities will have enough space to accommodate the increasing number of urban residents.[45]

However, several transforming trends challenge this simple math.

First, the family size is shrinking. With the Chinese population rapidly aging, family size has already started shrinking and will keep shrinking steadily in the near future. This means that even if one were to keep the same number of urbanized families, the demand for apartment size may shrink along with family size.[46]

Second, the number of people of marrying age is decreasing. With the passing of the birth peak in 1981–1990, the birth rate has been declining from 21.5 percent in 1987 to about one half, or 12 percent, in 2002. With fewer young people graduating from college, getting married, and starting families, the demand for apartments may drop accordingly.[47]

Third, Chinese urbanization may not progress as many have anticipated. Even with the government's announcement of its resolve to further Chinese urbanization, Chinese urbanization has already shown signs of slowing down. In 2013, the urbanization rate increase by 1.16 percentage points, the slowest since 1996 (with the exception of 2008 during the global financial crisis). Compared to the 3.9 percent average growth of the urban population between 2000 and 2010, the growth rate gradually slowed down to 2.7 percent in 2013.[48]

Finally, new migrants' lack of purchasing power, especially in light of the skyrocketing urban housing prices. It is true that with the progress of Chinese urbanization, more of the population may move into metropolitan areas. However, this is nothing big or new. A large number of rural residents have already migrated to cities in the past couple of decades. Because these migrant workers have not been registered with the urban Hu Kou system, they do not show up in urban population statistics and hence cannot claim social benefits.

Most of these new urban residents already have properties back in their hometowns, and some may already have real estate properties in the cities where they work. This means that the growth of urbanization in China may have in advertently been underestimated. Given that new urban workers make relatively lower salaries in the cities where they now live and that housing prices in these cities are far higher than in their hometowns, it is not clear that these new urban residents, even if they wanted to do so, could afford to buy properties in their new locations.

In sum, the next stage of urbanization may not produce as many opportunities for the real estate sector as many people have hoped.

Shifting expectations

The even bigger challenge for the Chinese housing market, though, may be the shifting expectations.

A joke circulating among the Chinese goes like this: When a circle of business friends gather for a dinner party, they discuss what to buy for an investment in China. Among the circle of friends, everybody agrees that real estate prices are too high and real estate is no long a good investment. However, they start asking each other questions like 'What is the best investment they have made in the past decade?,' and 'Has anybody lost money in real estate investment?,' and 'Do they feel that they have bought enough properties in the past decade?' After this round of reflective questions, all agree that real estate is not only their best performing investment of the past decade, it's also the safest. Based on such surprising and seemingly perverse reasons, the friends go out to buy themselves more new apartments.

Real estate investment has been so safe that it is safe to say that everyone who has bought a piece of property in China before 2008 has made quite some money, and it would not be too far from the truth to say that those who have bought a piece of property in China before 2012 must have made some decent money.

Oddly, it is not that the Chinese real estate market has not experienced any drops or corrections. Quite to the contrary, there have been quite a few drops and dips in the Chinese real estate market since 2000. Most such market corrections resulted from government curb policies aimed at curtailing national housing prices, but there were also a few times when unexpected events occurred, such as the SARS in 2004, Bird Flu in 2005, and the Global Financial Crisis in 2008.

What distinguishes China, and Chinese investors, from the rest of the world real estate market is Chinese investors' unfazed enthusiasm for, and hence expectations of, housing prices.

At first, property buyers were quite concerned when the government announced its intention to stabilize housing prices or even to keep housing prices lower. However, after a few rounds of hide-and-seek games, property buyers became more and more confident that the government would not allow housing prices to fall. 2014 may turn out to be the watershed year. After the government relaxed the curb policy that had been in effect for the past three years, many were surprised not to see the usual feverish rebound in housing prices. Instead, weak sales and prices seemed to be lingering.

Had the market expectation finally changed?

Make the change happen

So what can the Chinese government do to persuade Chinese investors to give up their unrealistic hope for ever-increasing housing prices? Alternatively, how can the Chinese government exit from its existing guarantees to the housing market?

First and foremost, the Chinese government would have to let go of its GDP objective mentality. Given the contributions of the real estate sector and related industries to Chinese economic growth, there is hardly any possibility of stabilizing the housing market without slowing down the speed of Chinese economic growth.

To convincingly persuade investors and speculators that it would no longer guarantee the rise of the housing market, the Chinese government would first have to convince the speculators that it no longer pursues as-fast-as-possible economic growth speed. Instead, it would need to put more emphasis on improving its citizens' quality of life and satisfaction and take a more balanced approach between the speed and quality of Chinese economic growth.

In addition, furthering fiscal reform and rolling out property taxes could simultaneously solve multiple problems in the Chinese housing sector. By re-allocating fiscal income and responsibilities between central and local governments, the reform would weaken local governments' incentives to push up housing prices in order to garner greater land sale revenues.

At the same time, property taxes could provide local governments with a steadier stream of fiscal income, hence helping alleviate the growing local government debt problems in China. With property taxes, speculators' costs of carry will increase substantially, dampening speculative need for housing and abating the pace by which housing prices increase.

Finally, even though the recent anti-corruption campaign by the Chinese government proved to be an effective way to curb housing prices, especially in the higher end market, in some cities, a more transparent and accurate property registration and information disclosure system is needed to roll out property taxes and more effectively collect property capital gain taxes.

With information regarding corruption becoming public, there will be less opportunity for government officials to take bribes in the form of housing, further filling the loopholes that may create substantial shadow demand.

Notes

1. http://finance.ifeng.com/a/20140902/13046908_0.shtml
2. http://house.ifeng.com/column/news/yzdzq/index.shtml
3. http://house.ifeng.com/detail/2011_11_11/20582916_0.shtml
4. http://paper.people.com.cn/gjjrb/html/2011-11/24/content_965460.htm?div=-1
5. Some argue, though, that some of the protests were indeed staged by the developers, to put pressure on local governments for support and subsidies. http://www.zgfpbd.com/?p=5042
6. http://www.bloomberg.com/news/2014-07-01/china-developers-offer-buyback-guarantee-in-weakest-home-markets.html
7. http://www.realestate.cei.gov.cn/image/infopic/20050726g05.htm
8. http://finance.ifeng.com/a/20140521/12380519_0.shtml
9. http://tcgpggn.com/qiyedongtai/37799.html
10. http://finance.ifeng.com/a/20140521/12380519_0.shtml
11. http://finance.ifeng.com/a/20140521/12380519_0.shtml

12. http://finance.ifeng.com/a/20140521/12380519_0.shtml

13. http://finance.ifeng.com/a/20140521/12380519_0.shtml

14. http://qz.house.163.com/14/0527/14/9T8RUUQB02750A7N.html

15. http://news.xinhuanet.com/fortune/2012-03/22/c_111686393.htm

16. http://news.dichan.sina.com.cn/2014/06/07/1125025.html

17. http://www.imf.org/external/research/housing/

18. http://finance.qq.com/a/20140502/005309.htm

19. http://www.caixin.com/2014-01-21/100631353.html

20. China Consumer Finance Survey, 2014 Southwest University of Finance and Economics.

21. China Consumer Finance Survey, 2014 Southwest University of Finance and Economics.

22. http://finance.qq.com/a/20140924/009415.htm

23. http://news.163.com/14/1227/09/AEF8T54F00014AED.html

24. http://gz.ifeng.com/zaobanche/detail_2013_03/27/663677_0.shtml?_from_ralated

25. http://finance.sina.com.cn/review/mspl/20130924/222416838412.shtml

26. http://finance.chinanews.com/house/2013/05-03/4782548.shtml

27. http://cdmd.cnki.com.cn/Article/CDMD-10610-2005126356.htm

28. http://news.xinhuanet.com/legal/2008-07/06/content_8497757.htm

29. http://news.china.com.cn/2012lianghui/2012-03/05/content_24808120.htm

30. http://www.zentrust.cn/jinrongshichang/20140428/4346.html, Mohican Macro Institute, 2014

31. http://news.xinhuanet.com/fortune/2014-04/12/c_1110211930.htm

32. http://blogs.wsj.com/chinarealtime/2014/08/12/property-pile-up-which-chinese-provinces-rely-most-heavily-on-real-estate/?mod=newsreel

33. http://wallstreetcn.com/node/86419

34. http://www.bloomberg.com/news/2014-06-19/property-flops-seen-as-33-billion-in-trusts-due-china-credit.html

35. China Trustee Association, 2014

36. http://wallstreetcn.com/node/86419

37. http://business.sohu.com/20111111/n325340343.shtml

38. http://ah.sina.com.cn/news/s/2013-04-16/143247768_2.html

39. http://ah.sina.com.cn/news/s/2013-04-16/143247768_2.html

40. http://www.fangchan.com/news/2/2013-05-27/347711.html

41. http://www.yanglee.com/

42. http://www.bloomberg.com/news/2014-06-19/property-flops-seen-as-33-billion-in-trusts-due-china-credit.html

43. http://www.bloomberg.com/news/2014-06-19/property-flops-seen-as-33-billion-in-trusts-due-china-credit.html

44. China Consumer Finance Survey, 2014 Southwest University of Finance and Economics.

45. http://finance.ifeng.com/a/20140521/12380519_0.shtml

46. http://news.sina.com.cn/c/2013-10-17/100828457741.shtml

47. http://news.xinhuanet.com/newscenter/2003-08/14/content_1026863.htm

48. www.baidu.com/link?url=yMHpw-gHcHr61jma8J9wMCWj6k_h3eiaxT1vBiYnJIwq4khrokwnOEXEHGlV7n3d

4

Petition Against the CSRC

In the land of the blind, the one-eyed man is king.

—Desiderius Erasmus

Short Sales in NASDAQ

As described in Chapter 1, Carson Block of Muddy Waters Research rose to fame in 2011 by calling Toronto-listed Chinese logging company Sino Forest a "multibillion-dollar Ponzi Scheme" that was "accompanied by substantial theft."[1] After Block's research release, shares in Sino Forest fell by 82%, with prominent investor John Paulson selling his entire stake in the company at a $720 million loss.[2]

Similar practices occurred with other Chinese companies listed on NASDAQ, where some research companies and money managers started accumulating short positions in Chinese stocks.

This short-selling of Chinese companies listed on NASDAQ has triggered considerable controversy in China. Some Chinese commentators claim that the "dirty" shorting is targeted at China and may be a way for the United States to intimidate Chinese companies and the Chinese economy. Others blame the incident on short selling, arguing that short selling is responsible for almost all financial crises.[3]

As these examples illustrate, most Chinese and Chinese investors are not familiar with the practice of short sales.

Lack of Short Selling

The investors are not to blame. After its introduction to the Chinese A-shares market in China in 2007, the practice of short selling has remained very limited. Although short selling is a common practice in the NASDAQ and other Western stock markets, it has been regarded widely among some Chinese as conspiracy against China and Chinese companies. China is not alone in holding such unfriendly views about short selling and short sellers.

Regulators in many international stock markets also cite market stability as an important reason for their reluctance to encourage short sellers to play a bigger role in their markets. This prejudice against short selling has ancient roots dating back to the Amsterdam Stock Exchange, one of the earliest stock exchanges in the world, in the seventeenth century. The distaste of regulators and investors has grown so strong at times that short sellers risked being sentenced to prison under the regime of Napoleon Bonaparte.[4]

Even nowadays, short selling is not allowed or encouraged in most of the markets around the world.[5] Understandably, the major concern of regulators is that short selling may present falsehoods and lure investors to drive down the market intentionally and cause market turmoil. Indeed, this concern has been cited as one of many reasons that many countries banned short selling during the 2007–2008 global financial crisis.

However, my research with colleagues at Yale University found little support for this fear. If anything, banning short sales would make stock prices less informative about the true fundamentals of public companies. Investors with positive views can push up stock prices by buying stocks. Why shouldn't investors with negative views be allowed to push down prices through short selling? The market should not take an ex-ante view that a market rise is always a good thing. What about the rapid price rises in so many bubbles in financial history?

Apart from short selling's systematic shock to financial stocks in the global market during September 2008 (when Lehman Brothers filed for bankruptcy and the entire global financial system was in a roil), there is actually very limited evidence that short sellers caused the financial crisis or that the negative views about the financial stocks held by short sellers were far from reality. Even during the crisis, research found that the ban on short sales proved to be ineffective in preventing shares from sliding abruptly, with the exception of a few financial stocks.[6]

If anything, research shows that those listed companies that actively fight against short sellers by blaming and threatening them eventually are more likely to be found to have engaged in financial irregularities or fraud than those companies that remain tacit.

For example, Lehman Brothers accused David Einhorn of Green Light Capital of intentionally spreading negative news about Lehman Brothers in order to profit from its price drops, before the outbreak of the 2008 global financial crisis. Lehman Brothers went as far as to threaten to sue the hedge fund manager for potential losses in the summer of 2008. The result? Before Lehman Brothers even started the legal process, David Einhorn's many estimates and predictions turned out to be true, and Lehman Brothers ended up filing for bankruptcy before it could file the lawsuit against Green Light Capital.

For that matter, regulators around the world probably worry too much that short selling may cause price drops in some stocks, or even in the entire market, even though most regulators' responsibility is to ensure fair disclosure and legal compliance. Assume that there are indeed some problems with a company's fundamentals or financial disclosure; shouldn't the rest of the market thank the short sellers for uncovering these problems and sharing their findings with the market?

On the other hand, if regulators are correct in worrying that some short sellers may get it wrong in being negative about a company and driving down the company's stock price (sometimes intentionally), then it may help to think about the counterparties in those transactions. Smart investors who accumulate such stocks at low prices after aggressive short selling may benefit handsomely from the short sellers' actions and may want to thank the short sellers for making the stocks so attractive and available.

This is consistent with common folklore on Wall Street that "slumps make the perfect buying opportunities." For example, one of the most successful hedge fund investors in 2009, David Tepper from the Appaloosa fund, made most of his money by correctly betting on the rebound of stocks and bonds of financial companies whose prices were beaten down by short selling during the 2008 market collapse. As long as there is a market, there will be price volatilities. For every trade, while some investors are losing, someone else must be profiting. The government should watch from the sidelines and let the market determine which investors make the correct bets.

Regulators and investors in China are even more concerned with the idea of short selling than investors in most other countries. Most participants in China have a deep faith that a rise in the market is a good thing, whereas a drop in the market is a bad thing. This is in part reflected in the mission of the market watchdog, the Chinese Securities Regulatory Commission (CSRC). According to a statement by the Cabinet, the CSRC should "foster the development of Chinese capital markets."[7]

In response, the CSRC feels that it is obligated to keep the stock market rising, even when it comes down to critical next step reform in the Chinese stock market. As a result, like stock investors in the West who have believed in the "Greenspan Put," many Chinese investors have a similar, if not stronger belief in the "CSRC Put."

Many Chinese investors believe that the Chinese government will not allow the stock market to drop by too much, thus causing investors so much loss that it might endanger the harmony of society. For some extended periods of time, Chinese investors staged protests in front of the branch office of brokerage firms, the stock exchanges, and even the headquarters of the CSRC, to beg the regulators to provide more bullish news and regulatory measures to boost the market or prevent it from further sliding. Such implicit guarantees by governments turn out to be an important reason that many Chinese investors choose to participate or stay in the Chinese A-shares market.

Some U.S. researchers also argue that the difficulty with shorting technology stocks was at least partly responsible for the internet bubble in the late 1990s[8] and that the lack of a short selling feature in the real estate market is one major reason that real estate is far more likely to experience bubbles than any other asset class.

In this sense, a bull market may not necessarily be a good thing, and a bear market may not necessarily be a bad thing. Allowing short sales also facilitates comprehensive information and views to be incorporated into asset prices, producing a more accurate and less volatile asset price. Unlike many regulators' belief that short sales destabilize the stock market, short selling may indeed be a key *stabilizing* force of financial markets most of the time.

Lack of Derivatives (futures and options)

Another mechanism that can counter abrupt market rise and bubbles is derivatives trading. Similar to short sales, derivatives (futures and options) trading helps investors with negative views or information share their information with the market through trading. After having made preparations for almost a decade, China did not roll out futures products on the stock market index until 2009.

In a way, the Chinese financial market's experience with derivatives back in 1995—the time of the infamous "3/27" in the nascent Chinese treasury futures market—was responsible for the reservations about derivatives. Because a brokerage company intentionally manipulated the price of treasury futures, it created tremendous volatilities in the then very young derivatives market in China. Many investors suffered losses from the incident, causing the government to step in, bailout the company, and eventually shut down the treasury derivatives market for more than a decade.

Another factor contributing to Chinese investors' lack of confidence in derivatives is that many Chinese companies, not too experienced with derivatives or risk management related to trading derivatives, have suffered considerably from trading derivatives in the international market. China Aviation Oil, a leading Chinese SOE in the field of energy, lost hundreds of millions of dollars when trading oil futures in the international market in 2004.[9] In addition, Chinese State Reserve of Copper was reported to have lost hundreds of millions of dollars over its trade on copper futures.[10]

More recently, Citic Pacific, a subsidiary of the giant state-owned holding company Citic Group, lost over 100 billion Hong Kong dollars during the 2008 global financial crisis over highly speculative trading of complex derivative accumulator contracts. Many other Chinese companies and highnet worth individuals have also lost tremendous amounts of money when trading against international financial institutions over exotic derivative products.[11]

All these incidents have led Chinese government officials and regulators to believe that derivatives are "Weapons of Mass Wealth Destruction," therefore to ban Chinese companies from even some very basic hedging with derivatives and be hesitant about developing a Chinese-based derivatives market. Such attitudes toward derivatives, however understandable, come at the hefty cost of ignoring how much derivatives can help set asset prices accurately and ward off excessive volatilities during regular market conditions. Without such tools, overly speculative sentiment is allowed to go on for too long with little restraint, directly causing the market to be susceptible to boom and crash bubble patterns.

Similar to short sales, a major fear with the derivatives (i.e. index futures and treasury futures) is that they will drive down the stock market. Therefore, regulators were not willing to launch this product during a bull market lest it spoil the market. Unfortunately, the regulators were even less motivated to roll out index futures in a bear market because they worried that the index futures could crush already weak market nerve and drive the market even lower. Because of this mentality, a critical instrument for hedging and risk management had to wait for a decade before it could help equilibrate the market.

What may have helped in triggering the roll out decision was the Chinese A-shares market during 2006 and 2008. The Chinese A-shares composite index rose from about 1,000 points in 2006 to 6,100 points in 2008 before it crashed back all the way to 1,600 points. Many investors, especially less sophisticated retail investors, had poured money into the market only when it was about to peak and lost out tremendously during the phenomenal bull market.

Interestingly, this was a rather global phenomenon. Research in the United States and many other global stock markets indicates that retail investors, about whom market regulators are highly concerned, suffer considerable losses from entering the market at the wrong time during some of the greatest bull markets in stock market history (i.e. the internet bubble in the late 1990s and the market run right before the 2008–2009 global financial crisis).[12] Hence, it seems that regulators' concern may be misplaced: a bull market is not necessarily going to help investors, just as a bear market may not necessarily hurt investors.

When there is a ready mechanism, such as index futures and options on index futures that allow some investors to express their negative views on the market's prospect and short sell against the market, the market is far less likely to witness bubbles forming in the first place. My colleagues at Tsinghua University and I have done research to show that additional supply through short sales, like derivatives creation, proved to be effective in limiting bubbles in the Chinese warrants market, which suffered considerably from bubble-like speculations between 2005 and 2007.[13]

Excessive listing requirement

The Chinese regulators' intention to help markets rise is not limited to secondary market trading, but also reflected in the listing requirement in the Chinese A-shares market.

Consider Alibaba, Chinese e-commerce giant, who went public at the New York Stock Exchange and set a record for the largest IPO ever in U.S. history in September 2014. While the Chinese cheered at the company's impressive performance in international markets, many also raised the question of why Alibaba chose to list its shares in the United States instead of China, where its business and customers are.

The short answer to this question is that Alibaba cannot.

The listing requirements at the Chinese A-share market set by the CSRC clearly forbid certain types of companies to list on the market, including most Chinese giant internet companies such as Alibaba, Baidu, and Tercent. This is disappointing to both the Chinese financial market and Chinese investors, who are left with not-so-great "high growth" companies listed on the CHINEXT market, many of which have cost investors distressing losses. This listing requirement explains why so many Chinese companies decide to list their shares in overseas markets, even at the cost of a relatively lower level of investor recognition and valuation.

Setting financial requirements for IPO companies and investigating the companies' fundamentals may seem to be a diligent way of protecting investors. As a matter of fact, this screening inadvertently leads investors to blindly believe in the qualities of the listed companies and to invest in them with blind confidence. Consequently, investors are indeed more likely to suffer from their irresponsible investments due to the regulators' helpful intentions.

On the other hand, the requirement for companies to reach a certain financial status before they can file for IPO provides unnecessary and indeed perverse incentives for companies to aggressively manage their earnings and cook their books. Numerous studies around the globe have shown that aggressive earnings management, a practice to boost a company's short-term earnings at the expense of long-term earnings potential, is detrimental to long-term investor returns.[14] However, because of the listing requirement and resulting elevated valuation in Chinese IPOs, investors in other countries have never suffered the amount of losses Chinese investors have from companies with worsening earnings and dropping share prices right after their IPOs in the A-shares market.

Closed for cross-border capital flow

Another regulation that is indirectly related to the implicit guarantee in the Chinese capital market is the control over capital accounts. Under the current regulation on foreign exchange, capital can flow freely under current accounts, but not capital accounts—accounts that are generally associated with financial activities and investments.

Unlike the deregulations in the current accounts, which dealt with trade-related activities about a decade ago, capital accounts remain tightly regulated in China. For example, one would have to get the approval of the State Administration of Foreign Exchange (SAFE) before one could invest in China or withdraw one's investment in China if the amount is over $50,000, the quota that each Chinese is entitled to exchange freely within any calendar year.

This regulation has created a series of problems in the Chinese economy,[15] ranging from ballooning foreign reserve to excessive monetary supply stemming from sterilization (releasing RMB into the economy as a result of mandatory buying of foreign currencies from trade surplus).[16]

One of the implications is Chinese investors' pent up demand for domestic investment opportunities. Because Chinese capital is not allowed to flow into the international financial market, Chinese investors and households are forced to settle for the sub-optimal international asset allocation and invest excessively in some less attractive domestic companies and real estate projects. This way, the capital flow constraint serves as a form of implicit guarantee for domestic investors in the less attractive investments, with almost inexhaustible capital coming from sterilization operations by the PBoC.

This, in part, explains why the Chinese A-shares market trades at higher valuations than most other international financial markets, sometimes for the very same companies.[17, 18] For example, studies show that the same shares by the same companies listed in the Chinese A-shares market often enjoy much higher valuations than their counterparts listed in Hong Kong, and the premium can sometimes be as high as 100 percent. That is, the share price of the same company listed in Hong Kong only trades at about 50 percent of the value of their counterparts listed in Shenzhen or Shanghai.[19, 20]

With more opening up of the Chinese capital market, the introduction of index futures and stock options, and increasing arbitrage through the underground RMB exchange market, discrepancies are gradually converging, and the market has started to witness fluctuations of the spread around zero in the past few years.

This development suggests that the government's implicit guarantee for the stock market through capital regulation is gradually phasing out. This also paves the way for a direct trading mechanism called "Shanghai Hong Kong Stock Connect," rolled out in 2014. The new trading mechanism will allow Chinese domestic investors and international investors to trade stocks through their brokerage accounts in Hong Kong or Shanghai listed at the other exchange. Hopefully, with more free capital flow across the border, the implicit guarantee for the Chinese A-share market through capital control will eventually disappear, and with its disappearance, restore the long overdue market-based transparent pricing mechanism to the Chinese A-share market.

From the investor's perspective

As a direct consequence of the apparent guarantees the Chinese stock market receives from regulators and the government, investors in the Chinese A-shares market suffered from some of the worst performance among global stock markets between 2009 and 2014, despite the fact that China remained one of the fastest growing economies in the entire world, given its herculean size.

This contrast is epitomized in the IPO process. On one hand, China boasts some of the world's mostly richly priced IPOs, and listed companies enjoy some of the highest first-day run ups in their share prices in the world. On the other hand, investors in Chinese IPO transactions have been complaining for years about the excessive valuation, excessive oversubscription, and massive earnings disappointment problems in the Chinese IPO process.

For example, even during the down market between 2012 and 2014, most IPOs in China were priced at over 40 times price-to-earnings ratio, even though the secondary market traded at about 20 times price-to-earnings ratio for most already listed stocks. As a result, many IPO companies raised much more capital than they originally planned for and used such capital from excessive oversubscription to make financial investment not related to their main businesses.

Given the strong motivations behind such high valuation and over-subscription, aggressive earnings management is commonplace in the IPOs in Chinese A-shares. As a result, of the 270 stocks listed in 2011, a quarter (65 companies) reported decreased earnings right after their IPO and dozens even reported losses, right after passing the rigid listing requirement set by the CSRC.[21]

Facing such disappointment in their IPO subscription, more and more Chinese retail investors question the validity of the IPO approval system and demand the CSRC reform. This may seem to be contra-dictory coming out of the mouths of the same investors who complain about the high pricing of IPOs yet display great enthusiasm in purchasing the IPOs at the same time. Taking a closer look, one can probably understand why reforming the IPO process has become a herculean task that top officials face at the CSRC.

On one hand, investors feel that the market is generally being over-valued and that they do not have a strong interest in investing in either the primary or secondary market. On the other hand, there are not many investment alternatives that investors can choose from within Chinese borders. Because of the capital flow constraint, Chinese investors cannot access the international equities market and so have to focus their attention on choosing the more promising stocks. As the old saying goes, "In the land of the blind, the one-eyed man is the king." If Chinese investors cannot access the international equities market, then the most promising stocks within China's border are like the one-eyed man in the land of the blind. Though flawed, these stocks reign within their own kingdom.

But the real problem is actually more complicated than that. First, the IPO process is the first time that companies debut in front of investors. Therefore, the serious information asymmetry problem makes it hard for investors to judge the true quality of the IPO companies. Hence, it is not always easy to identify the "blind" from the "one-eyed" in the Chinese IPO market.

In addition, a stock's performance right after the IPO cannot predict the stock's long-term performance. Therefore, investors not only have to know which IPO stocks to buy, but also when to sell these stocks, a skill that most investors unfortunately lack.

Finally, because the supply of IPOs is limited and IPO firms bring better short-term returns than the rest of the market, investors still have strong demand for IPO stocks, causing expensively priced Chinese IPOs to perform among the best IPOs in the entire world.

To address this problem, the CSRC has adopted some measures that mirror the Ministry of Housing and Construction's policy in its attempt to stabilize Chinese housing prices. To curb housing prices, Chinese Ministry of Housing and Construction at certain points gives orders to developers not to sell new properties at prices higher than a certain level.

Not surprisingly, such temporary measures force some high-end property offers to stay out of the market and keep the prices in check. But it has happened often that once the pricing restriction is lifted, prices of these high-end housing projects rebounded much more than the rest of the market, again suggesting the ineffectiveness of a short-term policy that does not solve the long-term misallocation of resources and distortion in market prices.

Similar results happened with the CSRC's policy on IPO stocks. By putting a short-term cap on first-day IPO price gain, the CSRC managed to achieve its goal of pushing down the first-day price run on the IPOs. However, going beyond the first day, the market witnessed much stronger price run ups in the weeks following, largely compensating for the foregone gains in the first day of trading due to the return cap.

Unrealistic expectations of PE investors.

Phenomenal returns at the IPO have created a wide range of problems. To name a few, the sudden run-up in the newly listed stocks has become such an apparent and easy way to make some quick money that Chinese investors, individuals and institutions alike, have been trying every possible way to invest in so-called "pre-IPO" investment projects: investments in companies that have high likelihood of having their shares listed and turning dust into gold during the IPO process.

This process is so "magical" in creating millionaires and billionaires that private equity investment firms, which typically specialize in privatizing and restructuring companies through mergers and acquisitions in the West, focus almost exclusively on investing in companies that are very close to going through the IPO process in the near future in China. A popular joke goes like this: "At every banquet table in China, there is a partner from a private equity investment firm who is working and helping integrate resources and obtain approvals so that a pre-IPO company can successfully navigate through the IPO listing approval process."

The attraction of such deals is so strong that in the 2009–2011 period, two proverbs loomed popular in Chinese society. The first is mass PE (in Chinese, literally "everyone is invested in a private equity deal"), a description of the mania for pre-IPO investment. The second, with more negative connotations, is PE corruption (literally, private equity corruption), which is widely used to refer to government officials' involvement in helping companies get their shares listed so that the officials can profit from such deals personally.[22, 23]

Separation of the primary and secondary market

Another problem with exorbitant valuation at the IPO process is that such excessive pricing precludes investors in the secondary market, mostly retail investors, from the opportunity of investing in the IPO companies for the long term.

Granted, there is prevalent international evidence that IPO companies in general underperform in comparison to otherwise similar companies that have been listed before.[24] This pattern is particularly serious in China. Because of the pent up demand for IPOs (due to loose monetary supply and pent up demand for investment opportunities) and artificially depressed supply (due to the IPO application and approval process), the IPO overpricing problem is most notably problematic and leads to long-term underperformance of IPO stocks.

Many retail investors are unaware of this pricing mechanism and buy stocks in secondary markets right after an IPO at unreasonably high price levels, such that it would take them forever to recoup their investment principal. PetroChina, one of the largest companies in the world and one of the largest SOEs in China, listed its shares for over 40 Yuan during the market peak of 2007. Soon after its IPO and the market crash, the share price slumped and has been trading at around 10 below 20 Yuan ever since, leading many who invested near IPO with considerable losses.

Thus, even with IPO stocks' long-term underperformance around the world, their valuations in China are still considered unbelievably high. Even with declining share prices and dwindling valuation, IPO stocks still pull up the valuation level of the entire Chinese A-shares market, which in part explains why the Chinese A-shares market trades at much higher multiples than most other stock markets all over the world, and higher than their counterparts listed in Hong Kong.

Short-term investment and excessive volatility

Yet another problem arising from phenomenal IPO performance is related to investors' investment horizon. As more and more investors realize that pre-IPO may be the best, if not the only way to make big money in the Chinese A-shares market, investors, including many institutions, forget all about the long-term value investment mottos and turn their attention to shorter and shorter horizons, speculating on quick money.

It is rational if one understands that almost all IPOs are overpriced. So it may only be a matter of time before such overpriced stocks fall and cause disappointing losses to their investors. Keeping such logic in mind, many institutional investors that are supposed to be long-term investors choose to speculate on the ups and downs of stock prices in the very short run, hence making the investment horizon of the whole market even shorter.

This lack of long-term commitment and research, in turn, becomes a self-fulfilling prophecy that ignores the stocks that would otherwise enjoy promising long-term potential and investment returns. This shortsightedness in investment, partly due to the implicit guarantees for short-term investment gains in IPO companies and ignorance of long-term impact, further increases the speculative sentiment in the Chinese A-shares market. Shortsightedness is therefore responsible for the unpredictable performance swings of the "Monkey Market," a market that goes up and down all the time without a predictable direction.

Investor protection?

The CSRC argues that the very reason it sets up the very strict IPO requirements is to protect investors from buying "bad apples" and suffering considerable financial losses. Unfortunately, as good as the CSRC intentions are, the protection of investors can only go as far as making sure the disclosure is fair, timely, and complete, and making sure that retail investors are not taken advantage of by more sophisticated institutional investors.

Any attempt to further protect retail investors by artificially installing new requirements and price caps can only prolong the process of distortion and mispricing of stock prices. Even worse, once investors, especially retail investors, sense that the government and regulators intend to support the market and their investments, they will smartly take on far more risks than they should or otherwise would, even though they understand little about investment.

A similar example in the West is the famous "Greenspan Put," named after Alan Greenspan, former U.S. Federal Reserve Chairman. Because Greenspan had been actively engaged in monetary policy to boost the stock market, or at least avoid its correction, investors of all types and from all over the world believed that the "maestro" had a magical formula that could sustain one of the greatest bull markets in U.S. stock market history. Exactly because of the Greenspan Put that gave investors false hope and confidence in the stock market, speculative investment escalated in the late 1990s, eventually culminating in the boom and bust of the famous internet bubble.[25]

To salvage the aftermath of the internet bubble, Greenspan continued his active monetary policy to boost asset prices. Again, this approach, originally thought to be ingenious, unleashed tremendous liquidity. This excessive liquidity quelled the returns on safe assets, such as U.S. treasury bonds, and induced capital to flow into risky assets, such as the global real estate market and fixed income securities tied to that market.

Just before the market celebrated the Fed Chairman's chivalrous move that helped steer the United States and the world economy around the internet bubble fallout, creating billions of dollars of wealth, the 2007–2008 global financial crisis arrived. The crisis once again reminded investors and regulators that economic policies can only do so much through distortion of the financial system and economy, and only for so long. The market will eventually find a way of revealing itself, sometimes with vengeance and compounded interest.

Investors have to learn from their own experiences. This is particularly true for Chinese investors. With a long gap in the history of the Chinese capital market, many Chinese investors have had very limited experience with the stock market. To make matters more complex, the high volatility of the Chinese A-share during the past decades has made a few Chinese investors ostensibly rich in a very short period of time. These legendary investor examples motivated other investors to believe that they too could amass a fortune quickly.

Because of the ban on any form of gambling activities in mainland China, anybody with an appetite for taking financial risks turns their eyes to the stock market. According to some industry surveys,[26] however, many Chinese investors lack the basic investment knowledge or skills needed to make sound investment decisions. For example, a large fraction of investors in the Chinese warrants market (similar to the single name stock option in the United States.) and Qualified Domestic Institutional Investors (mutual funds that specialize in investing in securities outside China) do not even know what derivatives and overseas mutual funds are or what they invest in.

Partly reflecting this phenomenon, the Chinese Survey of Consumer Finance reveals that Chinese households have been making some really disappointing investments under the auspice of the government's protection. Among the 8 percent of households who do choose to participate in the Chinese A-shares market (with about 15 percent of each households' financial assets invested), only about 20 percent of them reported investment gains during the past five years, whereas the remaining 80 some percent of households reported investment losses. This means that these 80 some percent households would have been better off putting their money into cash or savings accounts.[27]

As a result, bank deposits and cash make up more than 75 percent of Chinese households' financial assets, reflecting a lack of interest or trust in the Chinese A-shares market.[28] It is worth noting that, because of the protection from the regulators, investors fall into the false impression that investment does not require skills or education. The same survey shows that more than half of stock market investors did not finish a college level education. So, if anything, it seems that the investor protection engineered by Chinese regulators managed to have accomplished one thing: to encourage uneducated risk taking and speculation.[29]

From the listed companies perspective

IPO process and delistings

Because the corporate bond market has been underdeveloped and close to nonexistent in China, IPOs and the Seasoned Equity Offering (SEO) become the dominant sources through which companies finance themselves. The reason some companies enjoy access to the capital market, whereas others do not, lies in the pre-IPO screening process conducted by the CSRC, the market regulator.

Needless to say, any pre-IPO screening by a regulator or stock exchange can serve the purpose of verifying the legitimacy of a company and protecting the investors. However, the nuances lie in what investors believe the screening process has achieved.

In the West, the screening process only ensures that the company filing for IPO has satisfied the minimal requirement for listing shares and submitted all required documents. What the screening process does not certify, however, is the accuracy of the information or the valuation of the company seeking financing. That job is intentionally left to the underwriter and the syndicate behind the IPO deal. Investment banks, through their reputations and road shows, are expected to carry the responsibility of convincing potential buyers of the value of the listing company and its valuation.

However, things work differently in China. Chinese companies would have to seek approval from the CSRC and stock exchange before they can start the road show process. In addition to verifying the legitimacy of required information, the CSRC also forms committees to review the companies' business prospects and financial soundness. This due diligence on investors' behalf can substantially change investors' expectations and judgments about the listed companies. Many investors, especially retail investors who are not very savvy with the IPO process, wrongfully believe that the listing companies not only meet the listing requirements, but also are sound investment choices as warranted by the CSRC.

Their argument is simple and, truth be told, there is some validity to it. They argue that since it is so difficult to go through the IPO approval process at the CSRC, those companies that have succeeded in the IPO application process must be good companies. Otherwise, how would this particular company stand out among so many others that have not managed to list their shares? Such blind confidence in IPO companies, and the pent up demand for IPOs due to limited investment channels in China, explain the rich valuations for Chinese IPO companies.

Once listed, the companies' incentives shift completely. Because the demand for investment is so strong and the fact that there is little risk of being delisted, many listed companies, or the controlling shareholders behind such listed companies, become more interested in raising more capital from the stock market without properly rewarding their shareholders. This explains why dividends and share repurchase are far less common than they are in most other international stock markets.

Because it is so difficult and costly to get a company's shares listed in China, a listed company does not have to worry about facing the consequence of being delisted. Without delisting, listed companies can probably enjoy shell value, at the very least. Because many qualified companies cannot get listed, or cannot get listed quickly, listed companies facing potential delisting penalties may become attractive acquisition targets to unlisted companies. By simply succeeding in the listing process, listed companies have already managed to create value to their shareholders by creating a shell status coveted by so many other companies. At some point, a listed company with losses in continuous years can fetch market capitalization of greater than 2 billion Yuan, reflecting its tremendous shell value.

In sum, the difficult listing and delisting processes artificially suppress the number and value of listed companies available to investors in China. Because investors in the Chinese A-shares market can only choose from a limited number of similarly overpriced alternatives, all Chinese companies may enjoy artificially elevated rich evaluations. This may in part explain the discrepancies between the performance of the Chinese economy and that of the stock market. The next question is then what the listed companies have done with investors' money.

Diversification into Real Estate Development and Shadow Banking

An interesting feature of the financial reports of Chinese companies is that they obtain an increasingly large share of their profits from other incomes after their IPOs. If one were to plough through the fine print of the financial reports, it would become clear that two sources make up the majority of such other income: real estate development and investment income.

There is a longstanding debate regarding whether conglomerate business groups (such as General Electric) can generate a higher value, or at least a higher business valuation, than otherwise more specialized companies. Unlike their international counterparts, many Chinese listed companies are relatively young and still going through a period of fast expansion.

That being said, the core competency of each company is probably limited in a few rather concentrated areas. The concerning fact about Chinese companies is that, all of a sudden, they have all become experts in real estate development. Even if some listed companies do not have substantial involvement in specific real estate project development, almost all Chinese listed companies report profits from making loans to other companies that can only obtain financing by borrowing from the listed companies at a higher rate. Most of these borrowers are in the business of real estate development.

On one hand, it reflects the widely reported financial repression in China, in which many small- and medium-sized enterprises have had difficulties in accessing the capital market or capital altogether. On the other hand, the profit-maximizing listed companies smartly spot and grab such opportunities. As long as the listed companies can finance (much) more cheaply from their exclusive IPO and SEO process, they are more than happy to lend out their cheaply financed capital and earn some easy interest and dividends as long as their prized listed company status warrants.

Lack of Dividends and Share-Repurchase

This also explains why few Chinese companies repurchase their own companies' stocks, another interesting aspect of the Chinese stock market and listed companies. The matter has become so important that, soon after taking office, the then Chairman of the CSRC, Mr. Guo Shuqing, publicly pleaded to listed companies to repurchase their shares.

However, even with encouragement from regulators, few companies whose share price fell below its book value per share responded. When it became clear that his plea had fallen on deaf ears, Mr. Guo Shuqing went on to require Chinese listed companies to pay a minimal level of dividends back to their shareholders.[30]

This is in stark contrast with the recent trend in the Western capital markets, where more companies choose to pay out to their shareholders through the means of share repurchasing.[31]

Academic research finds that companies engaging in share repurchasing can outperform otherwise similar stocks by 7–8 percentage points in the upcoming year. A major reason behind this outperformance is the company's way of effectively communicating with the stock market. By buying back its own stock, a listed company sends a clear and loud signal that its management believes the company's shares are being undervalued by the market. By buying back its shares, the company intends to reveal the true value of the company and boost shareholder value.

Not only do listed companies in China pay less in dividends than their Western counterparts, they also pay most of the dividends in the form of stock dividends, instead of cash dividends. Further, some of dividend payments take place at the same time as right issuance, which collects more money than repurchases payout.[32] That is, listed companies obtain additional financing through their shareholders at the same time as they pay out to their shareholders, reducing the net amount truly paid out to investors.

One potential explanation for listed companies' lack of incentive in rewarding their investors can also be traced back to the implicit guarantee provided in the IPO process. As long as listed companies can access a precious channel for financing through the stock market, which thousands of other companies cannot, and as long as listed companies do not face the risk of delisting, why would listed companies have any incentive to cater to their shareholders and make them happy?

Of course, it may also be that, even at seemingly low prices to outside investors, management still does not believe that the company is being undervalued. Share prices reflect management expectation of the company's future operation and value. Maybe management is indeed quite content: thankful to the rich valuation at IPO, even the seemingly low share price may still exceed the true value of the company.

On the other hand, it is an open secret in the Chinese stock market that controlling shareholders in Chinese-listed companies use related party transactions, such as price transfers and profit transfers, preferred dividends payments and right offerings, and loans to private companies with the listed company's assets, as collateral to transfer wealth away from listed companies and the A-share stock market into their own pockets.[33] Such practices generate a strong incentive to retain free cash flow within the listed company instead of paying it back to other shareholders.

This lack of connection between company fundamentals and investor returns eventually disillusions investors who have a long-term investing mentality and undermines investor confidence in the Chinese A-shares market. Many Chinese investors' long-term ideals have been crushed by the cold reality that companies with good fundamentals do not reward investors.

Perversely, it is often those companies lacking fundamental support and those relatively easily manipulated by insiders or controlling institutional investors that generate the most attractive short-term returns. This, in turn, explains why Chinese companies are not motivated to pay out dividends or perform share repurchase to engage long-term investors as much as their international counterparts.

Chinese regulators have been trying very hard to improve the practice of corporate governance in the Chinese A-shares market in the past decades. Many blame the poor performance of the Chinese stock market on the practice of poor corporate governance.[34] Perhaps many corporate governance problems in China can trace their roots back to the strict listing requirement and near nonexistent delisting penalty, another form of implicit guarantee by the Chinese government. Should more companies be allowed to go public and face the risk of being delisted, many of the problems discussed in this chapter will go away quickly by themselves.

Notes

1. http://dealbook.nytimes.com/2011/08/26/canadian-regulators-order-sino-forest-executives-to-resign/?_php=true&_type=blogs&_r=0
2. http://en.wikipedia.org/wiki/Sino-Forest_Corporation#cite_note-nyt-7
3. http://finance.sina.com.cn/focus/ChinesecompanyinAmericastockmarkekt/
4. Bris, Goetzmann, and Zhu, 2007, Efficiency and the Bear: Short Sales and Markets around the World, Journal of Finance, 62–3, 1029–1079.
5. Bris, Goetzmann, and Zhu, 2007, Efficiency and the Bear: Short Sales and Markets around the World, Journal of Finance, 62–3, 1029–1079.
6. http://papers.ssrn.com/sol3/papers.cfm?abstract_id=486264
7. http://money.163.com/13/0722/19/94DLCCM400254ITV_all.html
8. Can the market add and subtract? Mispricing in tech stock carve-outs, Lamont and Thaler, 2003, Journal of Political Economy, 2003, 111, 227–268
9. http://finance.sina.com.cn/hy/20130601/172315666216.shtml
10. http://baike.baidu.com/view/1063724.htm
11. http://finance.qq.com/a/20140616/001895.htm
12. http://web-docs.stern.nyu.edu/salomon/docs/assetmanagement/S-AM-01-05.pdf
13. Liao, Li, Zhang, and Zhu, 2014, Security Supply and Asset Prices, working paper.
14. http://onlinelibrary.wiley.com/doi/10.1111/0022-1082.00079/abstract
15. http://economia.icaew.com/opinion/october-2014/chinas-financial-floodgates
16. http://www.frbsf.org/economic-research/publications/economic-letter/2012/december/external-shocks-china-monetary-policy/
17. http://baike.baidu.com/view/2867871.htm

18. http://www.hsi.com.hk/HSI-Net/HSI-Net

19. Greg Stuard Hunter and Deng Chao, Chinese Stock Buying Frenzy Sweeps into Hong Kong, Wall Street Journal, 2015 April 9th.

20. http://www.reuters.com/article/2015/04/08/china-hongkong-stocks-connector-idUSL4N0X52QH20150408

21. http://www.nbd.com.cn/articles/2012-03-03/638246.html

22. http://www.ft.com/cms/s/0/e20f271a-3879-11e2-bd7d-00144feabdc0.html#axzz3oyPj8lj2

23. http://blogs.wsj.com/privateequity/2013/1%4/china-corruption-pushes-private-equity-to-the-edge/

24. http://www.cbsnews.com/news/why-ipos-underperform/

25. http://www.amazon.com/Maestro-Greenspans-Fed-American-Boom/dp/0743204123

26. http://wenku.baidu.com/view/4f620c10a8114431b90dd87c.html

27. http://wenku.baidu.com/view/4f620c10a8114431b90dd87c.html

28. http://news.hexun.com/2013-01-10/150023967.html

29. http://finance.sina.com.cn/zl/china/20140325/152418607856.shtml

30. http://www.bloomberg.com/news/articles/2013-01-08/china-to-require-30-company-dividend-payout-to-lure-investors

31. http://www.cfapubs.org/doi/abs/10.2469/dig.v33.n1.1204

32. http://www.mckinsey.com/insights/corporate_finance/the_value_of_share_buybacks

33. http://www.sciencedirect.com/science/article/pii/S0927538X08000474

34. http://www.sciencedirect.com/science/article/pii/S1043951X99000061

5

Alternative Financial Innovations

Business has only two functions: marketing and innovation.
—Milan Kundera

THE GROWTH OF THE MUTUAL FUND COMPANY TIAN HONG astonished even Chinese observers accustomed to blazing growth speed as it grew into the largest Chinese mutual fund company (as measured by assets under management) within merely a year. Such leap frog growth is due in part to both the interaction between the internet and finance and to interest rate liberalization.

Starting in the early summer of 2013, Alibaba, the largest electronic commerce company in China, started marketing Yu'e Bao, a money market mutual fund managed by Tian Hong, to hundreds of millions of clients who used Alibaba's online marketplace and payment function.

Over of the course of less than one year, Yu'e Bao managed to attract more than 100 million investors and catapulted Tian Hong, Yu'e Bao's manager, into the largest mutual fund management company in China and third largest money market mutual fund in the entire world.

According to Alibaba, these services were originally aimed at providing short-term money management services to Alibaba's clients who had outstanding balances with the company from their daily operations.

The convenient settlement rule that allows investors to subscribe and redeem fund shares during the same business day provides considerable flexibility to many clients, most notably small online vendorson Alibaba. Originally concerned with the risk and hassle of management, Yu'e Bao revolutionized the way many small investors manage their investments.

In addition to its convenience, what makes Yu'e Bao really attractive is the product's high investment return at its inception. Compared to a deposit savings rate of about 3.5 percent during 2013, the Tian Hong fund generated investment returns of 6.5 to 7 percent during the same period.

In no time, Yu'e Bao became the poster child of the tremendous success from the marriage between internet technology and finance. To replicate Tian Hong's success, many electronic commerce companies and internet companies have also adopted similar strategies to market financial products through their cyberspace network, hence the birth of a fancy new phenomenon in China, "internet finance."

While small vendors celebrated their access to better wealth management services and investment opportunities with internet finance products, some argue that the birth of Yu'e Bao did not simply coincide with the credit crunch in June 2013, but directly led to it. During the credit crunch, Shanghai Interbank Offered Rate (Shibor), a benchmark for the interbank lending rate in China, surged to as much as 30 percent per year due to banks' liquidity shortage and the systematic credit crunch throughout the economy. So where did the money go? Banks and regulators alike believe that internet finance products and interest rate liberalization have motivated many savers to move their savings away from banks into such new investment opportunities.

So how did internet finance manage to pull the rabbit out of the hat by delivering investors returns when banks could not? And how did it manage to sell money market mutual funds to so many retail investors, a task that baffles the CEOs of Chinese mutual fund companies?

The short answer is that Tian Hong, like many other internet finance products, has successfully managed to be several things at the same time.

First, with its strong client base through Alibaba, Tian Hong successfully promoted the idea of "money market fund" among many small investors. By setting a minimal threshold for investment and easy redemption policies, Tian Hong managed to attract potential clients who have been historically turned away by traditional financial institutions, such as banks and mutual fund companies, because of their small accounts, high capital turnover, and unit service cost. This huge population segment—hundreds of millions with a small amount of money to manage—have all of sudden found an investment service that is open and suitable to them. In some sense, Tian Hong has managed to jumpstart the investment awareness of money management for millions of Chinese investors.

Second, Tian Hong offers much higher investment yield over the banks. Tian Hong generated returns of almost 7 percent during the late part of 2013. Such returns are almost twice as high as bank deposit rates and have really shown investors where the money is. Additionally, Alibaba has managed to convince its investors that Yu'e Bao is just as safe an option as bank depositing. Such investors' peace of mind has certainly made the transition away from traditional bank savings very palatable.

Finally, with the help of internet technology, the Yu'e Bao customers only need to make a few taps on their cell phones to complete their fund transfers instead of having to wait in line at bank branches, which is a big step up in customer service and interface friendliness.

At the same time as Yu'e Bao's ascent to celebrity, many have started to question whether such "high-yield, no-risk" investments can truly exist in reality. Yu'e Bao traces its roots back to money market funds. Money market mutual funds, believed by many investors to be as safe as bank deposits in the United States and other Western countries, have indeed proved to be reliable.

Since money market funds' inception in 1971, there have been few instances where Net Asset Value (NAV) per share has fallen below one dollar, meaning the point at which investors in such funds would lose investments and yield. During the 2007–2008 global financial crisis, due to the bankruptcy of Lehman Brothers and many financial products held or marketed by Lehman Brothers, several U.S. money market funds filed for bankruptcy themselves, not only costing their risk-averse investors considerable losses, but almost wreaking havoc in the U.S. credit market. As can be seen from such instances, even though many investors believe money market funds are as safe as bank deposits, they really are *not*.

Given that no money market fund has ever defaulted in China, and also given the reputability of Alibaba, many investors believe that the Tian Hong fund is not only safe, but probably safer than any other money market mutual fund available. Given its size and influence, investors in Yu'e Bao confidently believe that the Tian Hong fund, Alibaba, and the Chinese government cannot afford to let them experience losses, which partly motivates investors to pour even more money into this product.[1]

How did money market funds manage to generate much higher returns than small retail investors? The answer is closely related to Chinese interest rate liberalization. In China, all banks have to follow savings deposit rates for retail customers, which are strictly regulated by the PBoC and CBRC. As a result, there is little price competition among banks for retail savers' money.[2]

In contrast, there is open and fierce competition over savings interest rates for savings over 10 million Yuan (termed "agreement savings"), where the savers and banks can negotiate with each other over interest rates. The bank with the most attractive interest rate typically wins the client's money, generating much higher returns than the regular savings by retail investors.

Of course, a typical catch to such an attractive savings rate is that the savers often need to commit to the bank for 1 to 2 years. In this sense, these agreement savings are more like long-term investment instruments, much like certificates of deposit in the West.

By attracting short-term capital from its clients and investing in long-term agreement savings, Tian Hong manages to generate returns that cannot be achieved by traditional bank savings. But at the same time, Tian Hong makes itself look a lot like a Structured Investment Vehicle (SIV), which were once so popular among U.S. and European banks before the 2007–2008 global financial crisis.

Since 1988, SIVs operated by borrowing from the short-term credit market (normally through commercial paper) and investing in longer term higher-yield investment opportunities, such as the collateralized debt obligations (CDOs). Even though they do so mostly off their balance sheets, banks use their own credit to endorse the credit worthiness of SIVs in order to obtain more attractive borrowing rates. During their peak, over 30 SIVs held over $400 billion in assets, and such instruments have generated generous returns for the banks in return.[3]

With the collapse of the U.S. sub-prime market and the freeze in the U.S. credit market, most SIV investments ended up losing considerable value and creating turmoil in the U.S. credit market. As a result, every SIV had collapsed by the end of 2008, not being able to survive after the 2009 market rebound.

The SIV experience exposed similar risks in Yu'e Bao. When there is excessive liquidity in the economy, many chase higher-return products with implicit guarantees and false peace of mind. But when there is an eventual tightening in the economy (liquidity risk), the consequences can often be disastrous or fatal, especially to those who have gotten so used to easy financing assumptions.

Secondly, SIV creditability derives mostly from their parent banks' creditability. With the banks' balance sheet damaged and its own reputation tarnished during the 2007–2008 global financial crisis, it should come as no surprise that SIVs went belly up during the peak of the global financial crisis.

Of course, with its IPO in the U.S. market in 2014, Alibaba has become one of the largest companies in China. Therefore, it should have a lot of resources to back Yu'e Bao up. However, as reflected in the 2008 financial crisis, only cash is king during crisis periods—there is no motivation for Alibaba to bail out Yu'e Bao should things go sour with Tian Hong's investment.

Much of the high investment returns of the U.S. SIVs came from investing in seemingly safe and high-returning securities, such as sub-prime securities, before the crisis. The risks of such sub-prime securities did surface and cost the SIVs their dear lives.

Similarly, although the agreement savings in China seem much safer than those sub-prime securities before the 2007–2008 global financial crisis, the recent defaults in bonds and trust products of Chinese companies in 2014 have warned about Chinese banks' asset quality and contingent liabilities. Also, let us not forget that most of the sub-prime securities were AAA-rated by leading credit rating agencies, a coveted rating that even Chinese sovereign debt does not enjoy at the moment.

Of course, some also argue that Yu'e Bao's success is partly because it has taken an unjustifiably favorable position when competing with banks' savings.[4] For starters, Yu'e Bao does not have to set aside capital for reserve requirements, which gives it a sizeable advantage in terms of the cost of capital. Also, with its huge number of small investors, Yu'e Bao can practice a same day purchase redemption cycle fairly easily, which can greatly reduce its liquidity cost. Finally, the marketing of money market funds is not subject to the regulation of the CBRC, which is often more prudent when it comes to savings-like products.

Of course, as many similar products come to the market and the development of Chinese interest rate liberalization, Yu'e Bao's yield has gradually come down and will eventually fall below 5 percent one year after its inception, and below 4 percent eighteen months after its inception. Nevertheless, such alternative ways of financing and investment expose again how much financial repression there is in the Chinese economy and how much financing and investment demand by SMEs and small household investors is not well met.

With such a burst in investors' demand for higher returns, and relatively poor knowledge of risks and investment, many choose to ignore the risks in their investments, a common recipe for financial calamity that would not only hurt the financial sector, but also the entire economy and social stability.

Given that it is commonplace for investors in some mutual funds or trust products to petition in front of their mutual fund companies or banks (distributors) after they suffer from investment losses, it is conceivable that the hundreds of millions of investors in Yu'e Bao would do the same.

If it really comes down to default or losses at the largest fund in China with the largest number of retail investors, it will certainly have the attention of the government. It is probably safe to predict that most investors in Yu'e Bao are under the impression that the government has to bail them out should anything happen to their investments.

Peer to peer lending and its derivatives

CreditEase

CreditEase, one of the largest peer-to-peer financing companies in China, was founded in 2006, with early stage investments from leading institutions such as Morgan Stanley, IDG, and Warburg. It is estimated to have more than 40,000 employees and to have facilitated billions of Yuans by the end of 2014.

Unlike trust products, which are under the regulation of CBRC, P2P companies like CreditEase faces virtually no regulation. Part of the reason is that P2P companies historically target households with less than 1 million Yuan, a hurdle for most trust products and wealth management products, to invest.

Unlike a regular P2P business, which averages about 10,000 Yuan per transaction, CreditEase started the experiment of raising a small amount of money online and then investing the raised capital into bigger and higher return fixed-income portfolio products offline. Through such innovation in business model, CreditEase's average transaction value is about 100,000 Yuan, ten times as big as the traditional P2P business.

Such a difference may seem trivial to regulators, but has proven to provide companies like CreditEase unparalleled competitive advantages over traditional P2P business models that directly match borrowers and lenders. In some ways, CreditEase is more like a fixed-income investment advisor and not a P2P company. Some of CreditEase's competitors argued that, "Unlike traditional P2P companies that do not undertake investment risks themselves, CreditEase indeed takes responsibilities for its own investment returns and losses, and therefore is not a P2P company at all."[5]

By pooling lenders into different investment products with different returns, risk profiles, and maturities, CreditEase claims that it is very effective in diversifying the client's capital and risks and generating higher returns for its investors. However, with no third party custodian verification and lack of disclosure about how each individual transaction is matched and placed, CreditEase's business model evolves into something that is closer to bank lending or shadow bank lending (such as wealth management products and trust products) than its originally claimed way of doing business.

As long as there is enough liquidity coming to its big pool of capital, CreditEase can reasonably easily move capital across different products to ensure the safety of most of its products. But exactly because of the ability to move capital across products within the same pool of capital, it is difficult for investors and regulators to truly understand the returns and risks of each individual product. It is reported that CreditEase has related-party transactions with many other companies and accounts, most of which are controlled by CreditEase's founder and CEO, Mr. Tang Ning.

Lack of disclosure and regulation leads many to wonder how CreditEase and other like companies manage their accounts prudently. Given that the funds are not being managed by a third-party custodian, there is no knowing if the money has been channeled into the company manager's personal accounts.[6]

New P2P Model

CreditEase is just one of many Chinese P2P financing companies in the West that go beyond the traditional P2P model of directly matching borrowers and lenders online. As a matter of fact, many Chinese P2P companies owe their success to a new Chinese model of online-offline collaboration (raising capital online and investing offline). Such innovation helps Chinese P2P in two ways.

First, it helps borrowers and lenders meet and conduct transactions online while managing their raised money offline. In some ways, this creates a regulatory vacuum because it is hard to trace how the money has been invested, or where the money has been kept, offline. The flipside to such opaqueness is the 15 to 20 percent annual returns these P2P platforms have managed to generate during the past few years.

Secondly, instead of letting lenders choose their own borrowers, some Chinese P2P companies make such lending and investment decisions for lenders by providing capital on their website, therefore acting more like investment advisories or asset management companies. With such blurring between businesses that have to be regulated and those that do not, some successful Chinese P2P businesses boast an assets under management (translation volume) of over 10 billion Yuan every year and workforces of over 10,000, far greater than their counterparts in developed economies.

With its success, the Chinese version of peer to peer lending has also attracted increasing regulatory concern and induced increasing risks, some of which have already started surfacing. Mr. Wang Yanxiu, a CBRC official, announced that 150 out of 1,200 P2P companies on record defaulted in 2014. Many companies, he claims, do not have the necessary capital or risk management capabilities to handle their business. To make things worse, many companies promise higher returns and provide implicit guarantees to their customers without properly disclosing risks and detailed project information in their business prospectus.

Delinquency and Risk Management

One challenge that faces most peer-to-peer financing companies—at least those in the West—is the management of delinquency and default. According to Prosper.com, one of the earliest companies in the U.S. peer-to-peer world, the delinquency rate is 1.55 percent even for customers with the highest credit ratings. On the other hand, the delinquency rate can be as high as 29 percent for the riskiest borrowers.[7] Such delinquency rates require the company to set aside about 15 percent of its capital as reserve and drive down the company's return on equity by 10–15 percent.

Unlike many customers at Prosper.com who are trying to gain a cheap extension on their overdue credit card payments, many Chinese resort to peer-to-peer financing for business related purposes. With a fast expanding economy and credit base, and booming entrepreneurial activities, it is conceivable that Chinese borrowers have better prospects of repaying their debt. The critical assumption by borrowers and lenders alike here is, however, that the Chinese economy remain booming and the credit market remain unprecedentedly loose, as it has been since the 4 trillion stimulus package in 2009.

For example, CreditEase has long been thought of as a successful implementer of risk management in the Chinese P2P business. Mr. Tang Ning, the founder and CEO of CreditEase, once proudly claimed that not a single user on CreditEase has lost a penny on their platform.[8]

That is, until the economic slowdown and housing price stall of early 2014. Starting in early 2014, several incidents of default surfaced in several of CreditEase's loan products. Thousands of CreditEase lenders filed collectively on April 9th, 2014, and an 800 million Yuan loan made by CreditEase to a dysfunctional real estate developer went into default.

With the cooling off of the Chinese housing market and the depreciation in the developers' collateral real estate assets, CreditEase failed to repay its lenders on time. While CreditEase assured its investors that it was working with debtors to reclaim the collateralized assets, some suspect that this may have just been the tip of the iceberg in regards to the outstanding debt; CreditEase made risky investments in areas such as real estate development and coal mines. "With interest rates as high as 22 percent per annum, many companies forget about risk management and bottom lines and make aggressive loans in order to make their exorbitant fees," a person familiar with the matter commented.[9]

Right after this incident, CBN reported another event in which CreditEase provided financing to a HuaRong PuYin Fund, which turned out to be a fraud scheme that ended with the project's borrower and direct controller fleeing the country. It is estimated that CreditEase had borrowed more than 200 million Yuan from its lenders to finance the HuaRong project, and many of its lenders were not paid for several months after the event.

To appease its investors, CreditEase paid for some lenders in this particular product to salvage its tarnished reputation. However, this bailout indicates to many investors that P2P lending is actually safe, and perversely encourages lenders to more frequent risk taking, which could signal future disaster ... Therefore P2P lending inadvertently creates another form of implicit guarantee in the economy[10]

Another reason to be concerned is that there are no clear and uniform criteria for defining delinquency. Some companies use "overdue 60 days" as a criteria for delinquency, but it is not uncommon that some other companies define delinquency as 90 or even 120 days. Because such peer-to-peer lending companies stay off of the regulatory radar screen, it is not clear how informative the self-reported delinquency rate is in evaluating the companies' cost of capital.

This may help explain why there may be a wide gap between the delinquency rate that companies estimate and the actual rate. Prosper.com indicates that the 13 percent delinquency rate they originally estimated before debts mature turned out to be far lower than the real delinquency rate—25.44 percent by the time all debts mature. This example makes people wonder whether the delinquency that CreditEase and similar companies estimate for themselves is being (seriously) understated by their quickly expanding loan size and where the raised capital has been invested.

People have started questioning whether CreditEase and some other P2P companies are trying to become "too big to fail."[11] By expanding its business and investor base at such an astonishing speed, many wonder what would happen if a large P2P company were to default on some of its products. If too many investors are being impacted by a series of correlated default events, can the government afford to stay on the sidelines? Or will it be forced to step in and bail out the P2P company and its investors, even though it is not within any regulatory purview?[12]

CBRC official Wang Yanxiu stated that 150 of 1,200 P2P companies defaulted in July 2014, and argued that an entry barrier and better information disclosure is urgently needed for managing the risks in the P2P industry. Wang also emphasized that many P2P businesses provided guarantees on the returns of their offered products, even though they lack the funding or the legal status to provide such guarantees. He highlighted that such guarantees risk eventually leading to company defaults and investor losses.[13]

Copper financing

On March 7th, 2014, the copper price suffered from its biggest single day drop in the previous two years. China is the world's largest consumer of copper and represents 40 percent of global copper demand. Copper is used in construction, power lines, and refrigerators, among other things, so it is often taken as a gauge of industrial and business activity.

While weak Chinese manufacturing and the resulting demand have been used to justify the slide in copper prices in the past couple of years, the price drop on March 7th coincided with another significant event in China: a Chinese solar technology company defaulted on its corporate bonds, the first default ever in the Chinese corporate bond market.

Copper is used as collateral by many companies and investors in China in an effort to work around strict lending standards enforced by Beijing. Chinese companies typically obtain a letter of credit to import copper. By selling the copper or using the copper as collateral to take out a loan, the companies often invest in higher yield assets before paying back the loan three to six months later, according to a *Wall Street Journal* report.[14]

It is fairly common for companies to use copper as collateral for borrowing money in China, and as a matter of fact, this is the primary reason why many Chinese companies import so much copper in the first place. With a letter of credit of up to 6 months, the importers typically put down 15–30 percent of the margin for the trade and obtain full transaction lending value from the banks. Because of the differences in investment returns over borrowing rate, and the RMB appreciation, many trade companies use such capital to invest in high-yield short-term investment products or even speculate in the Chinese real estate market.

Falling copper prices do not bode well for companies that engage in such copper financings. Lower prices will force borrowers to post more copper as collateral, or to sell more copper, to raise the same amount of capital. To do so, the companies would trigger another round of sell-off, which could push prices further down.

In order to maximize the copper's collateral value, it is also common for companies to use the same collateral to borrow from several banks, increasing the total amount borrowed from banks. This may even involve collusions between the trade companies and the port that holds the inventory to circumvent or deceive the banks into lending based on collateral that has already been previously pledged (many times) to other creditors.

In early June 2014, Citic Resources, a subsidiary and listed company of the investment giant Citic Group, disclosed that DeCheng, a company that it has business dealings with, used the same collateral to borrow capital many times greater than the value of the copper that DeCheng put down as collateral.[15]

In the wake of such events, Citic Group announced that it had business related to copper financing in Qingdao Port and was looking into whether similar problems happened in its own business or those of its clients. At the same time, other leading international banks, such as Standard Chartered, BNP Paribas, and ABN Amro all announced that they also started investigating to determine their risk exposure from copper financing.[16]

Fortunately, the size of the loss at Citic Resources is not that alarming. However, what really rattles many investors' nerves is that DeCheng is only a fairly small copper trading company in Qingdao Port, and Qingdao Port is not considered the largest port with copper inventory. The Shanghai Duty Free Zone has about 750,000 tons of copper, ten times

122 CHINA'S GUARANTEED BUBBLE

more than what is being held in Qingdao. It is believed that 85 percent of the copper being held in these ports are primarily used as collateral for borrowing money.[17]

According to the estimates by Goldman Sachs, the total amount that been financed through commodities since 2010 is probably over 1 trillion Yuan. According to Jonathan Cornish at Fitch Ratings, China's outstanding credit liabilities have increased from 130 percent of GDP in 2008 to over 220 percent of GDP in 2013. Cornish believes that the nontraditional financing platforms and channels, such as copper financing, have been the major force fueling the rapid growth of Chinese debt during this period.[18]

The use of copper and other commodities with high value-to-density ratios such as gold and nickel not only puts some pressure on the Chinese banking system, but also creates upward pressure on the exchange rate of CNY.

As a result of this implication, China's State Administration on Foreign Exchange (SAFE) decided to pass new regulations aimed at ending such financing deals in May 2014. SAFE acknowledges that some companies have been aggressively using copper collateral to take out financing sometimes 10–30 times the size of the collateral value before the letter of credit expires, typically in 6 months.

To prevent such financing activities, SAFE now requires banks to reduce the scale of their loans denominated in foreign currencies and reduce Chinese banks' foreign exchange loan-to-deposit ratio to 75–100 percent from the relatively loose requirement of 150 percent. This new guideline would require banks to set aside more foreign currency reserve deposits for taking out the same loan, thereby increasing the financing costs for banks to make foreign exchange loans and letters of credit.

In addition, SAFE asked trade companies to provide detailed information on their transaction records and collateral information. A trade company is required to reduce the size of its letter of credit if its balance sheet goes far beyond its transaction volume or collateral size. This new requirement will pressure these companies to forego their upcoming letter of credit and reduce their holdings of collateral accordingly.

Many expect such a move to not only impact international copper prices and bank bottom lines that have big exposure to copper-related letter of credit issuance, but also Chinese monetary supply and even economic growth. For example, Goldman Sachs analyst Max Layton estimated that "hot money" through commodity financing deals and the gray market may have accounted for about one third of the growth in the Chinese monetary supply in 2012.[19] Much of the "hot money" inflow has been invested into speculative areas such as real estate and wealth management products, which further fuels Chinese credit booms and asset bubbles.

This directly explains why the Chinese government is not willing to shut down this channel of "hot money" inflow completely. A sudden stop in foreign capital inflow may lead to a gap in Chinese financing needs and availability of low cost capital through commodities financing. As previous crises have shown, an unexpected halt in financing could not only bring speculation and asset bubbles to an end, but also bring catastrophic shocks to the financial sector and a country's economy. Hence, the Chinese government chooses to gradually close the commodities financing channel and tailor its risk exposure to such financing deals.

Unfortunately, such a gradual move is also considered to be accommodative, understanding that the Chinese government is implicitly guaranteeing that the market will not be allowed to fall abruptly because of its dire consequences.

Iron ore and other commodities financing

Similar to copper financing, there has been considerable financing carried out through the iron ore trade. On April 18th, 2014, the China Banking Regulatory Commission (CBRC) required all banks to look into the financing activities through iron ore trade.

This ruling came not too long after the deregulation of the iron ore trade requirement toward the end of 2013. Even with the apparent slowdown in Chinese economic growth and real estate price escalation, the amount of iron ore imported jumped unexpectedly by 19 percent compared to the same period in 2013.

Many suspect that the jump in imports came as a result of demand for collateral financing. According to a leading Chinese business media outlet, the total inventory of iron ore at major Chinese ports exceeded 110 million tons, more than 30 percent higher than the 75 million tons at the same time in 2013.[20] This argument becomes especially appealing after subsequent reports on the glut in iron ore stock piling in China and the considerable drop in iron ore prices.[21]

Similar to copper financing deals, trade companies may then use the iron ore to obtain a letter of credit of up to 70 percent of the value of the collateral. Such letters of credit typically require an interest rate of 3–5 percent, far lower than the interest rate one could obtain by investing in trust products or wealth management products offered by various banks, which are widely regarded as "safe."

Some even argue that, similar to the situation in international copper prices, the trend of decreasing the iron ore price itself foretells of further weakening in iron ore prices. The logic works as follows: The drop in iron ore prices decreases the value of iron ore, given any pre-fixed amount of iron ore. The drop in the value of iron ore, in turn, decreases their value as collateral and the amount that can be financed through the iron ore.

Put differently, the trade companies that use iron ore to finance would have to buy more iron ore in order to command the same collateral value as before. This will not only increase the banks' concern over why the company may require so much iron ore, but also increase the shipping and storage cost of iron ore for the company (for the same amount of collateral, a larger shipment of iron ore would be required). Next, lower iron ore prices would reduce iron ores attraction as a useful financing tool, and therefore reduce use of iron ore as a financing tool, which would further weaken demand and iron ore prices.

As regulators are alerted, many banks have stopped making loans on iron ore collateral or substantially increased the margin requirement from the current 10–20 percent to the new level of 30–50 percent.

According to some estimates, an increase of 10 percent in margin requirement can result in a shortage of 2–3 billion of collateralized capital in the market.

To make things even worse, as many letters of credit were about to expire near the middle of 2014, a lot of companies had to liquidate their holdings of iron ore in response to a disappointing market environment and dropping iron ore prices. With the competition among companies to "fire sell" their iron ore, a stampede may become inevitable, which will depress iron ore prices even further.[22] So starts the vicious cycle!

Some believe that the iron ore industry is indeed relatively safe compared to financing based on other collateral. For one, the financing cycle for iron ore is typically two months, much shorter than with other collaterals.

However, regulators and investors still worry that capital financed through iron ore has been invested into areas with low returns and poor liquidity, such as real estate, related trust products, and wealth management products. Given the stagnation in real estate prices, these investments previously believed to be safe and liquid may face serious liquidity problems moving forward. This, in conjunction with the dropping prices in iron ore and increasing demand for margin, may push debtors into difficult distress not previously thought possible.

In addition to the fluctuation in iron ore prices, another layer of the implicit guarantee adds more salt to the wound. In addition to the profits coming from interest rate differentials between financing costs (through letters of credit) and investment returns (trust products and wealth management products), companies have traditionally benefited from another implicit trend, the appreciation of CNY.

The average appreciation rate of CNY against USD is over 3 percentage points per year during the past eight years. Consequently, to those who borrow letters of credit in USD and invest in China, this has become another implicitly safe cushion of 3 percent investment return, regardless of the investment return from the trust products or wealth management products.

Unfortunately, this trend is about to change too, and it is happening at the worst possible time facing the iron ore trade industry. The CNY has depreciated by over 4 percent since the start of 2014. Given that many companies have gotten so used to the notion of endless CNY appreciation, many have not taken any precaution in hedging against the fluctuation of the CNY exchange rate. As a result, all of a sudden the iron ore price, the interest rate, the margin requirement, and the exchange rate all started working against the industry, causing a close-to-collapse Minsky moment in China, according to some.[23]

Slowing economic growth, chronic overcapacity, and rising debt service problems in key industries are becoming more common, raising the risk of chain defaults involving suppliers and purchasers. Overcapacity recently prompted a senior executive in the Chinese Iron and Steel Association, Li Xinchuang, to say the problem was so severe it was "probably beyond anyone's imagination".[24]

Unlike the copper financing deals, which normally involve hedging about copper futures price fluctuation, iron ore financing deals rarely involve such a hedging element with iron ore prices. As a result, there is considerably more selling pressure when there is a sharp drop in iron ore prices, and the selling pressure itself may result in some further decrease in iron ore prices.

Further, the iron ore spot market is far less liquid than the copper market, and the futures market is less developed. Therefore, many trade companies are less prepared for the price fluctuation and hence suffer more and have stronger incentives to liquidate their positions. As an example, Chinese banks reported billions in non-performing loans related to failed steel and ore financing deals in the first half of 2014.[25]

Mutual Guarantees by companies

In addition to the above innovations in obtaining additional capital, businessmen across the nation, though most notably in the Zhejiang province, have come up with a strategy to grow bigger by providing explicit guarantees to each other.

Such guarantees started out as ways to confront the small- and medium-sized enterprises' difficulty in obtaining bank loans. Because sometimes companies do not have the necessary collateral to qualify for a loan, companies provide guarantees to each other when taking out loans, promising to make up the payment should the guaranteed company fail to come up with its own payment.

Normally, when a company attempts to apply for a loan from a bank, the bank would require the company to provide collateral. Based on the total value of its collateral, the bank would often grant a loan up to about 50 percent of the value of the collateral and require the company to secure guarantees from another 3 to 5 companies before it makes the remaining 50 percent of the loans.

Hence, the practice of mutual guarantee has been an important supplementary way through which private companies can obtain their bank loans. With this practice becoming more common among lending companies themselves, almost all companies in Zhejiang are involved in the practice of "mutual guarantee" to different extents.

Originally, these types of guarantees have proved to be valuable or even critical in helping SMEs obtain bank loans. However, businessmen quickly find out that it is more profitable to use the capital to make investments than it is to expand their own businesses.

The traditional export industries in the Zhejiang province, clothing, shoes, eye glasses, and electronic appliances, have felt considerable squeeze from increasing international competition and rising domestic labor costs since mid-2010. In response to such challenges, more Zhejiang provinces have turned their attention and focus to increasingly speculative investment areas such as real estate, natural resources, stock market, and high-yield lending.

Needless to say, some speculations are highly risky and do not work out well. However, things changed after the 2009 stimulus package. The influx of unprecedented liquidity makes the meager returns from traditional investment (bank savings) negligible, and it is almost certain that prices of all assets will skyrocket in light of such credit boom and strict constraints on cross-border capital flow.

Consequently, savvy Zhejiang merchants have increased their stakes in speculation by borrowing more aggressively from banks and investing in riskier areas that are bound to do well in the credit boom. Partly to diversify each other's risks and partly to further increase their risk exposure, Zhejiang businesses started engaging in active guarantee dealings, and many borrowed more than they could handle.

According to a survey of the lending market in Wenzhou, conducted by the PBoC in 2012, only about 35 percent of 110 billion Yuan in loans in 2011 was used for real business operations. The remaining 65 percent was used for investment and speculation. Many people familiar with the matter believe that both the total amount of lending and the fraction being put into investment and speculation was considerably underestimated in the PBoC report.[26]

There is no doubt that the practice of mutual guarantee provides much needed credit enhancement for small- and medium-sized enterprises when they are trying to engage in business expansion. However, the consequences can be rather dire if the companies use borrowed capital to make risky investments. The expansive monetary supply and global recovery have boded well for almost all speculations. Nevertheless, with the tapering off of quantitative easing by the U.S. Federal Reserve and the slowdown of Chinese economic growth, the risks in many highly speculative areas such as real estate development, trust products, and local government debt have surfaced and been aggravated.

Banks play an inexcusable role in expanding the size of mutual guarantee. To boost each bank's balance sheet, bank managers have strong incentives to ask companies to apply for loans of greater value than the companies really need. The banks would then use the additional money to make loans to other companies, sharing part of the additional interest income with the original loan applicant.

During this process, the original loan applicant implicitly provides guarantees of the safety of the capital should anything happen to the company that borrowed from the additional amount. With increasing scrutiny over the banking sector's lending practice and savings-to-loans ratio, more and more banks use such practices to circumvent regulations on loan size and continue to expand their balance sheet through lending.

With mutual guarantees, it is no longer a single company that is affected by a bad investment. Those who provide guarantees to the company's loan will inevitably have to shoulder the losses as well.

Many companies have been affected by the dropin prices in many speculative asset classes (real estate, iron ore, etc...). To make things even worse, many manufacturing companies have found making money through speculation so fast and easy that they have switched their focus away from their traditional manufacturing to more innovative ways of making money. Now that the investment and speculation arm of their business has gone sour, they have suddenly realized that the traditional bread and butter of manufacturing has already lost its competitiveness and can provide little support in stabilizing the situation.

Notes

1. How Safe are Money Market Funds? http://qje.oxfordjournals.org/content/128/3/1073.abstract
2. To avoid such regulations, most banks run frequent promotional events, with valuable gifts and overseas travel packages, to lure savers' deposits. Such programs typically run towards the end of each month, quarter, and year, when liquidity is relatively tight and savings base is assessed by regulators.
3. The Financial Crisis Inquiry Report (PDF). National Commission on the Causes of the Financial and Economic Crisis in the United States. 2011. p. 252.
4. http://finance.ifeng.com/a/20140313/11881567_0.shtml
5. HE, Yingyan, Global Entrepreneur Magazine, December, 2002 (I).
6. HE, Yingyan, Global Entrepreneur Magazine, December, 2002 (I)
7. https://www.prosper.com/downloads/research/dynamic-learning-selection-062008.pdf
8. http://www.wangdaizhijia.com/news-more-10550.html
9. http://finance.sina.com.cn/roll/20140508/122719042218.shtml

10. http://finance.sina.com.cn/money/bank/bank_hydt/20140523/021719198689.shtml

11. http://finance.qq.com/a/20140419/006172.htm

12. http://finance.qq.com/a/20140419/006172.htm

13. http://finance.sina.com.cn/money/bank/bank_hydt/20140815/135020024790.shtml

14. http://online.wsj.com/articles/china-metal-probe-weighs-on-copper-outlook-1403341855

15. http://money.163.com/14/0612/23/9UIVHQLN00252H36.html

16. http://cn.nytimes.com/business/20140612/c12banks/

17. http://finance.sina.com.cn/money/future/fmnews/20140606/000019328151.shtml

18. http://cn.nytimes.com/business/20140612/c12banks/

19. http://www.bloomberg.com/news/2014-03-18/goldman-says-chinese-commodity-financing-may-unwind-in-24-months.html

20. http://www.p5w.net/futures/zhzx/201405/t20140519_601993.htm

21. http://www.mining.com/copper-iron-ore-imports-defy-china-weakness-78229/

22. http://www.p5w.net/futures/zhzx/201405/t20140519_601993.htm, China Business Network, May 19th, 2014.

23. http://www.macrobusiness.com.au/2013/06/chinas-minsky-moment/

24. http://finance.ifeng.com/a/20140405/12062883_0.shtml

25. http://finance.sina.com.cn/money/bank/bank_hydt/20140829/030420154473.shtml

26. http://www.nbd.com.cn/articles/2012-07-04/664703.html

6

Behind the Growth Engine: The Great Slowdown

The New Normal is a period in which economies grow very
slowly as opposed to growing like weeds.

—BILL GROSS

WITH ITS AMAZING ECONOMIC GROWTH SPEED, CHINA HAS undoubtedly become an increasingly important economy in the world. China overtook Great Britain, France, Germany, and Japan to become the world's second largest economy, all within a matter of a decade.

China's economic ascent has brought fundamental changes and increasing demand to the rest of the world, and its impact can be felt in almost every corner of the globe. Chinese tourists have been on shopping sprees for merchandise ranging from luxury handbags to baby formula powders, lifting the share prices of one company after another.

At the same time, Chinese corporations and high net worth individuals are snapping up international brands, companies, and mansions at a pace that was only last seen during the 1980–1990 Japanese real estate bubble. Chinese immigrants have flocked into many prime areas of major metropolises and lifted prices to such levels that only other Chinese could afford.

The global commodities market, which provides limited supplies of raw materials ranging from coffee and cocoa in agriculture, to copper and aluminum in natural resources, has gone through fluctuations that are highly related to the world's expectations of Chinese economic progress.

Even at the slowed pace of a projected 8 percent GDP growth in the coming decade, China's economy will still be growing at twice the speed of most other developed economies. China's relatively smooth navigation through the last financial crisis certainly has assured global investors of its ability to manage its domestic and international matters during global turmoil.

With such speed and consistency, fewer people now doubt that China will one day surpass the United States and become the world's largest economy, sooner rather than later. Even based on a relatively conservative projection of 7 percent annual growth rate, China's economy is forecast to double and overtake that of the United States in the coming decade to become the largest economy in the entire world.

As the uncertainties disappear regarding China's economic growth speed and the size of its economy, more and more questions are turning to the *quality* of its growth.

Along the path, what becomes clear and almost certain is that Chinese economic growth is slowing down. Although people had been saying this during China's blazing economic growth in the past decade, China has proven such forecasters wrong again and again. Right after the global financial crisis, China astonished the world with its colossal stimulus package and miraculously pulled its economic growth back to an impressive rate of over 10 percent a year. With such marvelous turn around in economic speed, China contributed considerably to the global economic recovery after the 2008 global financial crisis.

The rest of the world was shocked to find that, bucking all negative international influences, Chinese growth rate picked up after the 2007–2009 financial crisis thanks to the grand economic stimulus package launched in 2009–2010. At the same time, because the 2009–2010 economic stimulus packages were so unprecedented, the blazing economic growth afterwards should *not* be used as a benchmark to evaluate or forecast future growth.

If anything, it is now becoming almost clear that, exactly because of the 2009 -2010 economic stimulus package, China will not be able to pull off another economic stimulus plan of similar magnitude. Therefore, China's economic growth probably cannot go back to the 10 percent per year rate it had in previous years.

There is nothing wrong with the slowdown in Chinese economic growth, per se. After all, the growth that China has achieved over the past three decades is unparalleled and one of the greatest in recent human history.

The key question facing China going forward is *how* the economy slows down and whether China can maintain economic growth at a slower and more balanced pace. To answer that question, it helps to take a closer look at how three drivers behind economic growth in any nation—namely exports, consumption, and investment—evolved in China over the past decades. Better understanding of the sustainability of each driver behind Chinese economic growth can help predict its speed going forward.

Disappearing export advantage

Consumption, investment, and export—the three major drivers of economic growth—have taken interesting turns in the past 30 years of the Chinese economic growth miracle. Some 20 years ago, "made in China" was still a relatively novel term. Nowadays, it has become a synonym of "the world's factory."

Twenty years ago, exports were a major contributor to Chinese economic growth. More recently, however, investments have become the single most important force driving the Chinese economy, and the contribution from exports has diminished to second.

The most recent data on Chinese trade confirms this pattern. China's overseas shipments declined by 18.1 percent in February 2014 from a year earlier, continuing the trend downward during the course of the past 12 months. This biggest drop in Chinese exports since August 2009 has not only cast China's future economic growth into further question, but also has led many people to worry about economic recovery in the rest of the world. After all, ever since China became the "world's factory," its export statistics have been sometimes taken as barometers of global demand.

This was not the first time that Chinese exports dipped in history. The Southeast Asian financial crisis in 1997–1998 and the global financial crisis in 2007–2008 both witnessed a weakening of Chinese exports. What sets this time apart is the prolonged duration of the slowdown in Chinese exports.

Labor cost, the single most important factor for turning China into the world's factory, is now becoming even cheaper in other countries. According to the U.S. Congress, China's labor costs increased by 11.4 percent per year between 2000 and 2013. In 2000, China's labor cost was at 30 percent of Mexico's. By 2013, however, China's labor costs were 50 percent higher than Mexico's, more than 168 percent higher than Vietnam's, and more than 5 times higher than Cambodia's. If China's income per capita were to double to more than $10,000 per year by 2020, Chinese competitiveness based on cheap labor would disappear completely over time.

In addition to increasing labor costs and an aging population, another noteworthy trend is that younger generations'—chiefly, Millennials—attitude toward work has shifted fundamentally during the past decade. Now that many families have broken the poverty barrier and have started leading materially decent lives, Millennials display far less interest in working as hard as their parents. Instead, they have become more interested in pursuing their individual dreams, causing further drop in China's labor force and pushing up labor costs accordingly.

Multinational companies have already been noticing these trends and have been moving their operations away from China. For example, 40 percent of Nike's global sales were produced in China in 2000.

In 2013, China's share of production dropped to 30 percent, whereas its neighbor Vietnam now commands 42 percent of Nike's global production.

Moving operations further inland is an alternative that many international and domestic countries have been adopting. However, research shows that the gap between wages in eastern and inland areas is shrinking quickly, with the differential in many industries smaller than 10 percent. This means that within a matter of one or two years, the inland salaries will soon catch up with those currently in the Eastern area, deterring many companies from moving operations further inland. Instead, many have decided to move their operations out of China altogether to a country with much lower labor costs.[1]

Stalling labor productivity

One key bottleneck to Chinese economic growth is labor productivity. According to a large number of studies on this topic, Chinese labor productivity has been stagnating since the early 2000s. Put differently, many people believe that Chinese economic growth has been accomplished through increasing factor inputs. Such factor inputs may include the inputs of labor and capital, as argued by classical economic theory, and environment and population health, as felt by firsthand experience.

According to a report by the World Bank (2012), China's labor productivity in 2011 was eight times greater than in 1980 and about two times greater than in 1990. However, put in a global context, China's labor productivity was about 1/12 of that of the United States and 1/11 of that of Japan during the same period. To many observers' surprise, even after 30 years of growth, China's productivity is still lower than that of India, Thailand, and Morocco.[2] A recent comparison between China's and India's economic growth points out that even though the two countries have similar populations, the size of China's labor force is about twice that of India.[3]

Lagging labor productivity is one aspect of Chinese economic growth that needs further improvement in quality, in addition to quantity. China's economic growth in the past thirty years, especially during the past decade, can be clearly felt through statistics and household quality of life. However, as the growth reaches a temporary bottleneck, the problems that have been covered by the high speed growth have gradually started surfacing.

With labor productivity staying tempered, China's economic growth relies more on increased inputs. Cheap labor and excessive infusion through monetary policies and credit expansion have been two major reasons for China's economic growth during the past decade. Now that China's labor costs have increased and labor's marginal propensity to work has decreased, China has started feeling the pinch in its exports. Exports have been the driving force of Chinese economic growth for the past couple of decades, thanks largely to China's supply of cheap labor. However, things have changed, and the world realizes that "cheap China" has come to an end.

Starting in 2008, more and more multinational companies have decided to move their production centers away from China to countries with cheaper labor. Of course, similar movements are taking place within China too, with corporations moving operations from the more developed and expensive eastern areas of China to the less developed and still cost-attractive middle and western areas. Nevertheless, it is almost certain that with Chinese labor costs increasing in the coming decade, China will gradually lose its advantage in low cost labor.

Domestic consumption yet to grow: Lack of value

With exports gradually losing steam, the Chinese economy will have to be jumpstarted by boosting domestic consumption. Because the transition of the Chinese economic growth model depends heavily on increased household consumption, the growth of consumption will hold the key to Chinese economic growth in the coming decade.

According to some projections, if Chinese household consumption can grow at 8–9 percent annually, then China's economy can keep its growth pace of 6–7 percent per year before reaching its target per capital GDP of $10,000 and overcoming the "middle-income trap."

On the surface, this should not be a problem.

During the past decade, almost every major international metropolis and tourist destination has started feeling the purchasing power of Chinese consumers. Flagship stores by luxury brands such as Louis Vuitton and Prada in Paris and Milan have been hiring increasing numbers of Chinese-speaking employees to serve the increasingly large Chinese clientele.

To ensure elegance and order on the sales floor, some stores have set a limit on the number of customers admitted at any time, and many of the customers waiting in lines outside the stores are Chinese. Some observers even report that some Chinese customers spend hundreds of thousands of dollars on luxury handbags and watches within a couple of hours, as if they were grocery shopping in the neighborhood fresh market.

This is a bit intriguing because Louis Vuitton and Prada both have an increasingly large number of retail stores in China. As a matter of fact, the sales of these two brands, and those of many other luxury brands, have surpassed 30 percent in growth per year during the past decade. So why would Chinese customers still line up in foreign cities to buy these products?

This reminds me of one of my personal experiences at the Los Angeles airport when I was returning to China. At the boarding gate, I saw a group of tourists picking up their duty free purchases. One of ladies who apparently had bought too much couldn't carry all her purchases and had to seek her friend's help. Surprised by how much she had bought, her friend asked, "Why did you buy so many things?" The lady replied, "The more I shop, the more I save. Look how much money I have saved!"

"Shop more and save more" has become a motto for many Chinese visitors and consumers who make purchases overseas. According to surveys by the *Wall Street Journal*, the same luxury products sell at far more expensive prices in China than in any other leading country in the world.[4] Part of the reason for these high prices is the to companies' international pricing strategies: they intentionally set the prices higher in China to exploit its large population and strong demand for luxury goods.

In addition, China's tariffs and taxes are also responsible, making some of the higher-priced products even more expensive. It is commonplace that the same item can easily sell for twice as much in China as in the United States. In some extreme cases, such as with baby milk powder or luxury cars like the BMW 7 series, the difference can be as much as three to five times the price.

Apple's flagship product, the iPhone, is another interesting example. Even though almost all iPhone parts are made in China, the price of an iPhone in China is much higher than in the rest of the world. Additionally, the free iPhone promotion at contract signing run by many international wireless carriers is nonexistent for Chinese consumers.

The price difference is so great that almost all Chinese will choose to load up on consumer goods while traveling overseas. What is more, some people who travel frequently across Chinese borders choose to specialize in "dai gou," buying products from overseas on commission. There was a highly controversial case in 2013 in which a flight attendant working for a leading airline company was charged with smuggling cosmetic products and selling them at the leading Chinese C to C website Taobao, backed by Chinese internet giant Alibaba.

The court ruled that the flight attendant had been evading taxes on over 1 million Yuan and sentenced her to 11 years in prison (which was later reduced to 3 years). The sentence stirred a lot of controversy, partly because the public felt that because the price difference was so big, most people were doing the same.

So the follow up question is, how can the Chinese afford to spend so much even though the country's per capita income is only about one tenth that of developed countries like the United States and Japan?

Another question that begs to be answered regarding Chinese overseas spending is why Chinese consumers are so interested in buying so many luxury handbags and watches.

As seen in many anti-corruption cases, luxury gifts are often not bought for personal use, but bought to be used as gifts to government officials. In one extreme case, the head of the safety inspection bureau of Shanxi province was found to be wearing many different luxury watches over time, which led prosecutors to investigate. The investigators found that the official had an astonishing 83 luxury watches of different brands and models, in addition to over $1 million in cash from bribery.

Culture certainly has something to do with it as well. After being repressed for so many decades, many Chinese feel that they can finally earn some money and enjoy a better lifestyle. In closely knit Chinese communities, as in many other East Asian countries, to succeed is to let other people see that you have succeeded. As a result, conspicuous consumption of luxury cars, handbags, and watches is particularly attractive to Chinese consumers.

This seems to be in stark contrast with the above-mentioned challenge that the Chinese economy is facing—that Chinese households are spending too little. How can these seemingly contradictory observations be reconciled? The secret may lie in the key question of wealth distribution.

Lack of resources

Consumption contributes about 50 percent of the Chinese GDP, far lower than the 70 to 80 percent range witnessed in major developed economies. Even when compared to the other BRICs (Brazil, Russia, and India), it becomes puzzling why consumption makes up only such a small fraction of the Chinese GDP. With a closer look, however, it becomes apparent that the major difference stems from differences in household consumption. U.S. household consumption makes up about

70 percent of the U.S. GDP, almost twice as much as the 35 percent in China.

So why do some consumers spend beyond even a Westerner's imagination, whereas some don't spend enough? Disposable income and income distribution are two key explanations.

First, as in many other countries, Chinese households have to pay their taxes before they can spend. According to some studies, Chinese corporate and household income tax rates are among the highest around the globe.[5] With the relatively low threshold for income tax in China, almost all workers are taxed, with little chance for a refund. Hence, taxation, especially high income taxation, has become a reason that Chinese households do not have as much to spend as China's GDP suggests they should.

Further, the GDP can only reflect a nation's wealth, but not how the wealth is being distributed. According to official statistics published by the PBoC, China's Gini coefficient, a gauge for measuring income distribution, is 0.48, higher than that of the United States and most developed countries. A higher reading indicates greater inequality in income distribution. A survey conducted by Southwest University of Finance and Economics (SWUFE) puts the Chinese Gini coefficient at 0.61, one of the highest in the entire world. Although it is hard to determine which number is more reliable, inequality in income distribution can indeed explain the discrepancies between the previous anecdote and the official statistics, indicating that some people really spend a lot while others don't.

Finally, China's housing boom has created tremendous wealth for those who own more than one property. However, it has also become an increasingly heavy burden on those who have not had the chance to buy property. Saving up to buy an apartment has gradually become the minimal requirement before young men can propose to their beloved. Because buying a property is not technically classified as consumption, such a strong need to save unavoidably prevents household disposable income from being spent.

Lack of confidence

Social security has been found to be an important safety net that may provide citizens with greater confidence to spend and consume. With the development of the Chinese social security system and the social security fund, Chinese have started benefiting from the growing social security system. At the same time, with the transitioning nature of the Chinese economy, the drastic shift in Chinese demographic structure due to the high birth rate during the first 30 years of the republic's history, and the subsequent one-child policy, many people are worried that the Chinese social security system will soon face the underfunding problem that has already been harrowing many developed countries, especially those with quickly aging populations.

The current Chinese national social security system only covers urban citizens, leaving out rural citizens, who are the majority of the country's population. Leading administrators of China's social security fund publicly admit that, with a relatively low starting assets under management (AUM), the Chinese social security fund management faces a serious challenge of underfunding.[6] Reports suggest that local social security accounts face similar, if not even more serious, underfunding problems.[7] This uncertainty regarding the social security system can understandably hold back some households' willingness to spend, but it also leaves room for future improvement in the social security system to further boost Chinese consumption.[8]

Another important safety net is the health care system. After experiencing almost a decade of reform, many people believe the Chinese health care system is in need of another major overhaul to ensure the quality of health care services and the sustainability of health care providers. Longer life expectancy, the one-child policy, fast changing social values, and the improvement of medical technology with related increasing costs all motivate households to save more and spend less. Similar to the social security system, the health care system is viewed with uncertainty, thus holding back household consumption. But it may also turn into a major force pushing consumption forward if reform in the health care system succeeds.[9]

Anti-corruption, Anti-growth?

The Communist Party's Anti-Corruption Campaign has received wide popular acclaim and support in China since its inception in December 2012. What came as a surprise, though, is that some people claim that anti-corruption was responsible for the slowdown in Chinese economic growth in the ensuing two years.

On the surface, there seems to be some connection. The anti-corruption campaign has reportedly sent chills through industries such as luxury retailers and upscale restaurants. Hard liquor and French vintages, which are widely used at official banquets, also suffered from much weaker demand. Sales of Guizhou Maotai, an indispensable drink at Chinese government and military banquets, have experienced much slower growth than during the two-year period right before the anti-corruption campaign.

BMW, the luxury auto maker from Germany, sold 86,224 cars in China in the first quarter of 2013, up 7.5 percent from a year earlier. This otherwise encouraging sales growth was deemed "greatly disappointing" compared to a 37 percent jump in the same period of 2012. Sales of Volkswagen's Audi, widely considered as the "official purpose" vehicle of the Chinese government, rose a mere 14 percent to 102,810 cars, compared to a 41 percent gain in 2012.

Sales of luxury handbags and watches, two popular items used in gift giving, also experienced an apparent dent. Sales of Prada in Greater China fell more than 10 percent, and that of Swiss watches fell by an even bigger 25.6 percent in the first quarter of 2014 following the anti-corruption campaign started in the last quarter of 2012.[10]

Five-star hotels also suffered as officials and companies canceled big-budget banquets and conferences. State media reported that in

2014, more than 50 five-star hotels asked for a downgrade to four stars in hopes that this would attract more official events.[11] What's more, in response to this campaign, many state-owned enterprises and even privately-owned companies cut expense budgets for their annual conferences and retreats.

Even Macau, the casino capital of China and reportedly a popular destination for Chinese tycoons and the officials they woo, felt the pinch. Macau's casino revenues fell for the first time in a few years in June 2014. The travel industry also lags because of stricter requirements for overseas travel for government officials and state-owned enterprise executives.

These situations coincided with slips in China's retail sales growth, leading many observers to conclude that the anti-corruption campaign caused a decline in overall retail sales and might have even endangered the country's overall economic growth.[12] However, the decrease in retail sales is not confined to luxury retail, but spread across the board. This decline may be more reflective of lesser government-led investments than weakening household consumption, as some economists argue.[13]

From an investment driven to consumption based growth model

Indeed, with neither exports nor consumption showing promise in boosting economic growth in the short term, the Chinese government has no option but to turn to the third driver of economic growth: investment.

Compared to exports, investments take effect primarily within China and therefore have more direct impact in boosting the economy. In addition, investments take effect mostly at the corporate level and hence do not have to depend on millions of households to respond. Thus, investing can increase Chinese economic growth more directly. Furthermore, because government at various levels has more control over investments and capital formation, investments are relatively easier to control than the other two drivers.

Of course, even the Chinese government itself acknowledges the limitations and complications of depending on investments to boost the Chinese economy.

First, there is the problem of decreasing investment returns. Return on invested capital (ROIC) dropped from about 20 percent during the pre-crisis period to less than 15 percent during the few years after the 2008–2009 financial crisis. With overcapacity in many sectors of the economy, many economists predict that the ROIC will keep decreasing in the near future.[14] To some, the decreasing return on invested capital is indeed a logical outcome, given the staggering labor productivity and ever increasing size of investments.

Government investments did not seem to fare much better. As the World Bank's "China 2030" report discussed in 2012, even though Chinese state-owned enterprises report operating efficiency and investment returns far lower than their international counterparts, the size of state-owned enterprises was allowed to grow considerably during the past decade.

Another major area receiving considerable investment since 2008 is the government's infrastructure projects and housing developments. Over the past few years, Chinese local governments have been making aggressive infrastructure investments to build new cities or new industrial parks, hoping to generate more revenue in the future from selling off local land at higher prices.

The curb policy on real estate since 2010, though still far from being effective in curbing or lowering housing prices, has already shown its impact on local governments' investment returns. Because most infrastructure projects take a long time to pay off and generate only meager returns, staggering housing prices have forced many local governments to rely heavily on LGFVs to raise capital and keep existing projects alive.

Because investments have a unique feature of temporal mismatch, many local governments are enthusiastic about using them to boost short-term growth at the expense of ballooning debt levels in the long run. Once it became a public secret that local government officials could jumpstart local economies and their own careers by borrowing from the future, the GDP growth tournament motivated almost every local government official to borrow and build more.

One consequence of this extensive borrowing and investment is the "ghost city" phenomenon that has appeared in many international reports.[15] In the case of Ordos, the entire new city area was close to being completely abandoned several years after all the construction had been finished and properties sold.

The reason was that, despite the fact that many Chinese households already had a satisfactory primary residence, they were still lured by the irresistible opportunity to make quick money from real estate speculation. Such investing can be so speculative that Ordos' housing prices almost doubled in 2011, only to fall back to their original level a couple of years later when it became increasingly clear that few people were willing to live there and that the coal-mining capital was hit hard by slumping global coal prices. Similarly, many other Chinese cities, such as Tianjin, Yingkou, ChangZhou, GuiYang, are well-planned and well-constructed, yet abandoned.[16]

At the same time that ROIC has been decreasing, the cost of financing for making such investments has been climbing steadily. To fuel a new round of investments, the government and certain corporations have to raise more capital. With the Chinese traditional banking system reaching its limits as required by the Basel II Accord, more developers and local governments have to turn to more nascent and innovative forms of financing, namely the shadow banking system discussed earlier in this book.

Even with government implicit guarantees, the cost of loans from shadow banking is easily twice as high as that of bank loans, and sometimes even many times higher. With stalling housing prices, many borrowers soon find that it is difficult to repay their debt with the cashflow generated from their investments. Without any alternative, some borrowers have had to turn to trust companies and wealth management products to borrow even more at higher borrowing rates. This constitutes the classic "Ponzi borrowers" situation in Hyman Minsky's framework of debt crisis.[17]

The ghost cities are just the tip of the iceberg of overcapacity in the Chinese real estate sector and many other sectors. If the Chinese do not buy into real estate, many other sectors of the Chinese economy will undergo fierce price wars and become unprofitable and financially unviable (as you will see in Chapter 7).

After realizing the dire consequence of the mass stimulus package and the ensuing growth from irresponsible investment manias, the Chinese government became far more careful with investments when the economy inevitably slowed down again in early 2014. Instead, the Chinese government launched a series of targeted "mini-stimulus" or "smart-stimulus" fiscal, monetary, and administrative packages whose sizes and investment targets were better controlled by the central government.

These mini-stimulus packages have certainly addressed many of the problems of previous mass-scale stimulus packages. Not surprisingly, however, such moderate stimulus measures only brought a moderate boost to the economy. China's growth recovered only marginally at 7.5 percent in the second quarter of 2014, after a disappointing first quarter of 7.4 percent growth, which is below the ideal growth target set by the Chinese government. Concerned that China might not reach its annual growth target of 7.5 percent, some observers fear another round of massive investment-led stimulus packages, which have gradually become the only hope for many who have been investing rampantly in anticipation of such massive investment stimulus measures.

Why so fast?

So why does the Chinese economy have to grow at such a pace?

It is apparent that exuberant economic growth has been promised to the entire country by the Chinese Communist Party. Deng Xiaoping, in his humorous and seminal speech, advocated to the Chinese living through the Cultural Revolution that "regardless of the color of the cat, he who can catch the mouse is a good cat." In other words, whoever can create jobs and wealth for the society should be valued and respected.

At that time, this new notion drastically shifted the population's ideology and turned the population's attention to economic growth. By leading its billion citizens to better lifestyles, the Chinese Communist Party has convinced the population that it can lead the nation into a new era of revitalization and supremacy.

At the same time, economic growth is closely tied to another closely-watched gauge of the economy—the unemployment rate. The tens of millions of Chinese graduating from college along with other young people entering the workforce need a booming economy to find jobs and build their careers. Economic stagnation and high unemployment has set off protests among younger people in other parts of the world, which eventually shook the ruling regimes. The Chinese government certainly does not intend to repeat the consequences felt in Egypt or Libya.

Once a GDP growth target is set, the GDP growth tournament has started. According to research done by the National University of Singapore, a local government official's chances of getting promoted increase by 8 percent if their local area's economic growth is 0.3 percent greater than the national average.[18] Local government officials, understanding the importance of local economic growth to their careers, try their best to speed up their local economies. Because local officials only have a short tenure at any post, and because until recently local government officials were not evaluated on the amount of debt accumulated during their tenure, most local officials opted for boosting the local economy through heavy borrowing and investing.

The real estate sector is a direct beneficiary of this mentality. The pro-growth mentality was indeed very powerful and instrumental when the economy was at a relatively low point and when the labor force's creativity and entrepreneur potential had been suppressed for so long during the Cultural Revolution.

However, after three decades of rapid growth, the Chinese economy is at a new crossroads as the old "the faster the better" growth model is reaching its limit and displaying its weaknesses.

As a direct beneficiary of the old growth model, real estate exemplifies the challenges that many other sectors of the Chinese economy are now facing. After years of heavy investment and households' overconfident expectation of further housing price appreciation, Chinese real estate and related sectors combined contribute more than 20 percent of Chinese economic growth.

With China's housing prices at levels much higher than those in even some developed economies, and with real estate related investment becoming the most important driver of the Chinese economy, Chinese policymakers are now facing the impossible choice between housing affordability (a social task) and GDP growth speed (an economic target). So far, the government has managed to keep economic growth at an acceptable pace at the cost of housing prices resuming their upward trend. However, with growing dissatisfaction with skyrocketing housing prices, and uncertainty about the Chinese housing market's prospects, not only is the Chinese economy and banking sector cast into question, so too is the fate of other areas of Chinese daily life—such as education, employment, and even marriage—deeply impacted.

In this regard, a slowdown in Chinese economic growth speed is a necessary thing for China to overcome the growing pains resulting from fast growth. Maybe only at a slower pace will Chinese corporations and households be able to form more realistic, and therefore more sustainable, goals for their investments. A slower pace can also help China turn its attention away from the speed of its growth and towards the quality of its growth.

According to an announcement by the Chinese government, China will focus more on economic growth that can bring satisfaction to its population, which signals a very promising shift in target. In addition, topics such as environmental protection, education, health care, income distribution, and the social security system should all receive more attention, which will not only add more stability to Chinese economic growth, but also more sustainability.

Sustainability is so important because all economic growth forecasting relies on the assumption of sustainable growth. In this sense, sustainability is more important than speed in regard to China reaching its goal of becoming the world's largest economy and achieving its per capita goal of $10,000 GDP by 2020.

Not too many countries in the world have ever claimed the title of the largest economy in the world, and even fewer have done so by planning. China's neighbor Japan is an exception. Even with its much smaller surface area and population size, Japan surprised the United States by briefly overtaking it as the world's largest economy in the late 1980s. Unfortunately, because Japan did not manage to ensure the sustainability of its growth, it experienced lost decades by failing to address problems during its period of fast economic growth. China should probably start thinking about this issue soon, as well.

With China's increasing economic size, growing labor costs, decreasing return on investments, and deteriorating environment, it may be about time for the Chinese government to start paying more attention to the sustainability of its economy.

In the end, economic development is a marathon instead of a 100-meter dash. Economic growth should not be just a number, and it should be favorable to all citizens. With China's economy keeping its fast growth pace, it is probably time for China to think about how to make this economic growth better benefit, and be appreciated by, its citizens, or, to borrow President Xi's words, "to help each Chinese to fulfill his or her China dream."

Notes

1. http://www.voafanti.com/gate/gb/www.voachinese.com/articleprintview/2423968.html
2. http://finance.sina.com.cn/china/20120524/022412133289.shtml

3. http://www.stats.gov.cn/tjsj/qtsj/gjsj/2010/t20110630_402735801.htm

4. http://online.wsj.com/news/articles/SB1000142412788732447400457844090260265834

5. https://en.wikipedia.org/wiki/List_of_countries_by_tax_rates

6. http://news.sina.com.cn/c/2013-03-01/143826397583.shtml

7. http://acftu.people.com.cn/GB/14132733.html

8. http://business.sohu.com/20140521/n399855429.shtml

9. http://www.ftchinese.com/story/001052976

10. http://ineteconomics.org/blog/china-seminar/anti-corruption-slowing-down-overall-retail-sales-china

11. http://money.cnn.com/2014/0½8/news/economy/china-anti-corruption/

12. http://ineteconomics.org/blog/china-seminar/anti-corruption-slowing-down-overall-retail-sales-china

13. http://www.economist.com/news/china/21610316-weighing-economic-impact-anti-corruption-campaign-anti-graft-anti-growth

14. http://stock.sohu.com/20130907/n386084982.shtml

15. http://content.time.com/time/photogallery/0,29307,1975397_2094492,00.html

16. http://www.bbc.com/news/magazine-17390729

17. http://en.wikipedia.org/wiki/Hyman_Minsky

18. http://epaper.oeeee.com/A/html/2013-03/31/content_1832133.htm

7

An Abundance of Overcapacity

Going too far is as bad as not going far enough.

—Confucius

To halt economic slowdown during the 2008 global financial crisis, the Chinese government launched an unprecedented 4 trillion Yuan investment stimulus program. Many people believe that the true amount of the stimulus was in the range of 20–30 trillion Yuan,[1, 2] making the stimulus package similar size to the U.S. Federal Reserve's asset purchase plan (quantitative easing).

Unlike in the United States, in which much of the generated liquidity moved toward every corner of the global economy, China's humongous stimulus package was contained mostly within the country, since the RMB is not an international currency and since China has a capital account flow restriction. This has caused serious problems with inflation and asset bubbles within China and has spread so that the Chinese choose to invest and emigrate instead (for example, to the West coasts of the United States and Canada, Australia, New Zealand, Dubai, and other major metropolitan areas all over the world). One direct consequence of the 4 trillion Yuan stimulus package is that housing prices more than doubled in most Chinese cities within a few years.

Another direct consequence of the fixed asset investment boom came a little later. By the end of 2011, overcapacity had become a closely watched situation in China. With the recent economic slow-down in 2013, more people have started asking more questions related to overcapacity, such as how severe overcapacity is in China's manufac-turing industry, how the overcapacity problem has become so serious so suddenly, and what solutions China has to address such a serious issue.

Based on official data on production capacity, many economists are worried about overcapacity across many industries in China. According to the Bureau of Statistics, the capacity utilization rate is 72 percent, 73.7 percent, 71.9 percent, 73.1 percent, and 75 percent, (translated into at least 30 percent overcapacity industry wide) for steel, concrete, electro-lytic aluminum, flat-panel glass, and ship building, considerably lower than the international average.

Even with existing high capacity, many experts expect that more ongoing and new investments will generate another round of capacity expansion in the next few years.[3] The overcapacity problem in certain industries has become so dangerous that China has started a national ban on new investments in the coal-chemical, steel, cement, polycrys-talline silicon, wind turbine, flat-panel glass, ship building, electrolytic aluminum, and soybean-pressing industries.[4]

When one takes a closer look at these industries, the problem of overcapacity is indeed startling. China's national demand for steel in 2012 was about 320 million tons, and the existing capacity was over 470 million tons, with a few more major steel mills still being con-structed as of this writing.[5] Similarly, China's national demand for elec-trolytic aluminum is about 7.2 million tons, and the existing capacity is close to 11 million tons.[6]

Even with the construction spree and housing boom, the Chinese cement industry experiences 30 percent overcapacity. With the recent curb policy in the housing market and the decline in local governments' infrastructure momentum, the overcapacity problem in the cement industry may very well worsen in the near future.

It is worth noting that the overcapacity problem is not confined to a few limited sectors, but is prevalent throughout almost the entire

Chinese economy to varying extents. In addition to the usual suspects in overcapacity, mostly in raw materials, some new, and once promising, industries are now feeling the pinch of overcapacity as well.

The automobile industry, once believed to be the propelling force of the Chinese economy, reports overcapacity in the range of 50 percent (10 million capacity vs. an average annual demand of about 6 million vehicles).

The photo voltage and wind turbine industries, designed to be China's strategic priorities in the coming decade, both report overcapacity of more than 40 percent. Both industries have felt considerable pressure in the past few years after increased use of shale energy in the United States and gradually cooling energy prices.

Of course, statistical methods and strategic bluffing to deter future entrance may explain part of the overcapacity, but they fail to explain the extent of the problem. According to a recent research report by UBS based on statistical analysis, field surveys, and interviews with corporate executives, the Chinese industrial capacity utilization rate (the fraction of production capacity that has been utilized) has declined continually since 2007. Whereas the industrial capacity utilization rate was close to 100 percent before 2007, the current utilization rate has dropped to about 70 percent. Put differently, in aggregate, there is an average of 50 percent overcapacity in the Chinese industrial sector.[7]

Such overcapacity, or capacity overhang, can have a serious impact on the Chinese economy. First, with such sudden jumps in capacity in so many industries, competition intensifies and corporate earnings drop rapidly. For example, the Chinese solar panel industry reported a reasonable 30 percent gross margin in 2010. With the massive industry capacity expansion and cut-throat price wars, gross margin in the solar panel industry dropped to 10 percent in 2011 and further down to 1 percent among Chinese solar manufacturers listed overseas.[8]

Similarly, just five years ago electrolytic aluminum used to be a highly profitable industry with a capacity utilization rate close to 100 percent. But the industry's high profitability and strategically important status motivated investors to pour in so much money within so little time that the updated capacity utilization rate was down to 60 percent (an overcapacity of 67 percent) merely three years later.

Such deterioration in corporate earnings is quickly and clearly reflected in investment returns and the asset quality of banks that make loans to such industries. Likewise, after five continuous years with an annual growth rate of more than 100 percent in solar panel manufacturing, almost all major Chinese banks have had some exposure to the industry. Now that many companies in this industry have started losing money, some banks are worrying about their loans and investment in bonds issued by the companies.

Failed investments limit capital needed for progress and upgrades in an industry. Moreover, they undermine the confidence of banks and investors, deterring future investment and restricting future growth in these industries. Hence, even though short-term excessive investment and speedy growth may seem attractive and appropriate, they may inadvertently create the ceiling for future investment and growth.

Next, we'll examine two industries closely to get an up close and personal look at the overcapacity problem.

Renewable Energy Industry

In addition to the potential default event mentioned in Chapter 1, another noteworthy and distressing event that attracted considerable attention in early 2014 was the Chaori 11 Debt (Security code 112061.SZ). The Chaori 11 debt failed to come up with its due payment, making it the first bond that defaulted in the history of the People's Republic of China.

Shanghai Chaori Solar Technology, the issuer of the debt, had suffered losses in the past three consecutive years. The company's revenues dropped 66.3 percent compared to the previous fiscal year and it faced the risk of being delisted based on the Shenzhen Stock Exchange's listing rules.

According to the latest financial reports before the default, Chaori had total assets of 6.27 billion Yuan and total liabilities of 6.55 billion Yuan, resulting in a debt-to-asset ratio greater than one. As a result, more than 100 cases have been filed against Chaori, demanding a total of 2.38 billion RMB in debts. Some of the creditors have started the process of filing bankruptcy reorganization. In addition to its publicly traded debt, Chaori owes about 1.48 billion Yuan in bank loans, 1.33 billion Yuan of which was overdue by the time Chaori defaulted on its bond.

What is more worrisome to many observers is that this may be only the tip of the iceberg for the Chinese solar panel industry. WuXi SunTech, JiangXi Saiwei, and Yingli, major players in the industry, have already been facing strong headwinds, surviving with government support since 2012.

SunTech Technology, once the largest solar panel integrated manufacturer and service provider, sought bankruptcy protection in the spring of 2013. Shi Zhengrong, once the richest man in China and the symbol of the Chinese alternative energy industry, faced an outcry from 529 creditors demanding repayment of their debts.

According to a Bloomberg analysis,[9] the Chinese new energy industry (solar, wind, hydraulic) faced the maturity of over 4 billion Yuan in debt by June 2014, which is ten times as much as the amount one year previously. Further, the total amount of debt due by the end of 2014 summed up to 7.7 billion Yuan. The solar panel industry is not alone in facing increasingly large amounts of maturing debt. CICC, a leading Chinese investor bank, surveyed a wide range of Chinese enterprises and projected that 2014 would be the year of the greatest default risk in Chinese financial history since the liberation.

Given rising crude oil prices since the early 2000s, countries all over the world have been betting heavily on finding alternative energy sources and technologies. Given the lack of economic viability in most new technologies, green technology investment has always been a sensitive and sometimes shaky investment area in many countries.

In China, new energy has been listed as one of the top priorities for development in the 11th and 12th five-year plans, and therefore received considerable, and even unbridled, attention and investment in some provinces and regions. To kick start the development of this industry, many local governments provided substantial incentives to researchers and entrepreneurs to start new businesses in this field.

As in many other industries that are considered strategically important, local governments commonly provide tax exemptions and rebates for new energy enterprises to attract investment. To compete for the limited amount of promising business, many local governments will even provide land and fiscal subsidies to attract investment into renewable energy. Moreover, some local governments use their fiscal budgets to purchase such products directly in order to boost sales and facilitate IPO for these companies.[10]

As a result, new energy technology has enjoyed breakneck growth in the past decade. However, with the drop in energy prices and the reduction in subsidies on new energy technologies by many developed countries due to the 2007–2008 global financial crisis, the economic viability of these industries is open to question.

The bankruptcy of a major player in any industry can trigger the so-called fire sale problem and have profound impact on the entire industry. If some distressed companies are forced to sell off their assets or equipment, or slash their prices in order to boost sales and to raise much needed liquidity, it may create a glut in supply of both materials and discounted end products, causing even greater trouble to the competitors still in operation.[11]

Such dire situations are not limited to the solar panel industry. The wind turbine industry, once believed by many people to be the Chinese answer to energy shortages for the entire world, faces similar or even tougher challenges. Huarui Wind Electrics, once one of the largest wind electronic companies in China, reported on April 30, 2014 that its operating revenue for the 2013–2014 fiscal year was 3.66 billion Yuan, an 8.87 percent drop from the previous year. More concerning, its net profit in

2013–2014 was a loss of 27.6 million Yuan, a decrease of 319.96 percent compared to the previous year. This is the second year that Huarui faced losses (the net loss for 2012–2013 was 0.66 billion Yuan). If Huarui were to report another year of loss, it might face the risk of being delisted by the Shenzhen Stock Exchange.[12]

What happened to the new energy industry is not an isolated case. Many Chinese companies in strategically important areas have been accustomed to low financing cost and ease in accessing bank loans. In fact, cheap lending and government investment or support for investment have been major reasons why so many companies and industries have been able to grow fast in China after the 4 trillion stimulus package in 2009.

According to some incomplete statistics by the CASS,[13] Chinese companies owed a total of approximately 10 trillion Yuan in bonds that are due by the end of 2013. Among this 10 trillion, about some 60 percent (over 5 trillion) was concentrated in the interbank market (NAFMII). So the consequence of default by some companies is not limited to any specific bank, but can affect the entire banking sector.

Given that only a select number of financial institutions are allowed to invest in the NAFMII market, the transactions taking place there can transfer default risks from one institution to another, but not out of the Chinese banking system. With the looming interest rate liberalization, most experts anticipate interest rates, both savings rates and lending rates, to increase.[14]

Such an interest rate hike will pose considerable risks to companies that have catapulted their growth in the past year under the belief that liquidity would remain abundant and interest rates would remain low for a prolonged period of time. Once this implicit assumption is violated, some fear that many Chinese industrial sectors that depend heavily on easy lending will face financial constraints. The depletion of future funding sources will not only jeopardize the financial soundness and credit worthiness of these highly leveraged companies, but also the speed and quality of Chinese economic growth.

These negative shocks, in turn, may induce government at different levels to bail out distressed companies. These bailouts, similar to those engineered during the 2007–2008 global financial crisis, are aimed at protecting distressed companies, industry sectors, and local economies in the short run. Unfortunately, as the incidents in the West reveal, these bailouts also provide implicit guarantees to companies troubled by their previous irresponsible borrowing and investments, and may encourage similarly irresponsible investment decisions in the future, leading to the next crisis.[15, 16]

As a result, implicit guarantees can distort the risk of default. The risk of default is not linear and is hard to predict, even for industry experts, depending on varying economic situations. A distortion in credit default risk and risk in general would encourage the entire economy to take unwarranted risks, creating bubbles and ensuing busts.

Railway Debt and Soft Budget Constraints

Another example of the implicit guarantees behind Chinese industrial policy is the high speed train system in China. Implicit guarantees, coinciding with the emergency mood during the 2007–2008 global financial crisis, led to the rather astonishing explosive growth in the Chinese high speed train system. According to incomplete statistics, a total of over 1 trillion Yuan in debt was taken out by the Ministry of Railway right after the launch of the 4 trillion stimulus package in 2009.[17]

To put the investment spree in the Chinese railway system into perspective, investment in the railway system stood at 337 billion Yuan in 2008, almost twice as much as that of 2007. The railway infrastructure investment increased further to 600 billion Yuan in 2009 and to over 700 billion Yuan in 2010 and 2011.[18] In addition to investment in infrastructure construction, it is estimated that another 100 billion Yuan was spent to purchase locomotives and carts.

To finance this burgeoning growth, the Ministry of Railway had to take on increasing debt during the same period, from 0.67 trillion Yuan in 2008 to 1.68 trillion Yuan in 2009. This debt to asset ratio of 0.56 would scare away any private company's investors if the company failed to show promising earnings increases.[19]

However, the debt incurred by the Ministry of Railway seemed to defy such market logic and kept increasing through 2010. The logic behind such high indebtedness is probably twofold. First, the Ministry of Finance is a part of the Chinese government. With its more than $4 trillion in foreign reserves and large assets in SOEs, the Chinese government is considered to be a very reliable debtor in the world. Consequently, even if the investment made by the Ministry of Railway cannot stand on its own, the Chinese government will not sit on the sidelines should there be a default in the Ministry of Finance's debt repayment.

Secondly, there is also the classic problem with any lending and bank loan. Once the debt has reached an unhealthily high level, the creditor's optimal decision becomes more complicated. To cut the debtor loose may result in a rapid deterioration of the debtor's financial situation and ability to repay, which would be like the creditor shooting itself in the foot. Instead, if the creditor could wait and coordinate with the debtor to reorganize outstanding debt, there is a chance that the debtor could manage to turn around and repay its due liabilities. If things work out as wished, the creditor might be able to recover not only its principal, but prolonged interest as well.

Of course, if the situation keeps getting worse, the creditor may run the risk of losing even more from the loan. But at the very least, the problem would not surface in the short term, the timeframe of greatest concern to the management team of many companies. This is especially true of public companies concerned with the vigilant watch of institutional money managers and Wall Street sell side analysts who focus on short-term profitability far more than on long-term sustainability.

With the its escalating debt-to-asset ratio, the Ministry of Railway has no option but to finance through means other than bank loans or debt issuance. However, many private sector investors balked at the idea of investing in Railway projects, let alone with the alarming leverage in the existing Ministry of Railway's balance sheet.

Such aversion by private investors should come as no surprise to those who are familiar with infrastructure investment. Similar to other infrastructure investment products, railway investment lies somewhere between a profit-maximizing private investment and a safety net public investment. Because railway investment requires considerable up-front investment and uncertainties in routes and terrain selection, it is not a top choice for investors in today's financial world.

Given that equity financing does not attract private investors' interest, the Chinese railway system seems to have no alternative but to finance through issuing debt. According to the classic pecking order theory in modern corporate finance, debt financing has the advantage of low financing costs and a relatively easy issuing process. Of course, the flip side of the story is that debt financing poses stronger controls on the debtor than is suitable for every company.

Once a company's debt rises to a heightened level, investors become worried about the company's financial soundness and highly suspicious of the company's ability to repay its debt. Given a large and increasing debt base, even the financing costs every year can eat into the company's profits.

Even worse, if the company cannot generate enough cash flow to repay its debt interest or principal (debt coverage), the company may run into financial distress. Default would hurt not only the company's stock and bond prices, but also endanger the company's ability to refinance in the future, which may be even more devastating. According to Thomas Friedman, the *New York Times* columnist, "There are two superpowers in this time, the United States and the credit rating agency. One destroys a country with bombs and the other with credit rating downgrade. I do not know which is more powerful."

Nevertheless, the Ministry of Railway has managed to expand its balance sheet (debt) exponentially over the past years without being checked or stopped. One key development in the Chinese railway system is that it successfully managed to solve the financing problems that have hindered the development of many other socially beneficial infrastructure projects all over the world.

The key innovation is the implicit guarantee that the railway system borrowed from the Chinese central government. In August 2011, the DaGong credit rating agency, one of the largest and most influential Chinese credit rating agencies, gave the Chinese railway system a AAA rating, its highest rating.

This announcement caused considerable controversy because the public had come to realize that the Chinese railway system was struggling with a debt-to-asset ratio of close to 60 percent, the widely used alarm level. In addition, the same agency downgraded the U.S. debt a notch lower, from A to A-, a few months earlier. Thus, even before the downgrading, Dagong considered the U.S. Treasury to have a greater default risk than the Chinese railway system.[20]

The explanation is simple. Dagong argues that the Ministry of Railway is part of the Chinese government, and therefore its debt shares a similar risk profile to that of Chinese sovereign debt.[21] Second, it postulates that the railway system's operating cash flow will improve over time, therefore enhancing the railway system's repayment ability. Further, the railway system has considerable assets that it can use for future financing.

Setting aside the financial status of the railway system, Dagong's argument crystalizes the concept that the Chinese government provides valuable implicit guarantee to lower-level government, state-owned enterprises, some preferred private enterprises, and investors in real estate, shadow banking, and stock markets.

Even if some industry sectors suffer from daunting debt problems and financial distress, some investors and investment agencies are smart enough to see through the corporate veil and understand that all liabilities taken out by such companies will eventually trace their credit worthiness back to that of the Chinese central government. With the growing Chinese economy and powerful foreign reserve, there should be almost nothing to worry about in any specific investment projects, as long as the central government will eventually step in and bail out the company.

The same logic applies to local government debt. Under the general incentive framework that encourages faster economic growth

(GDP growth), local government all over the country has every incentive to boost local investment, which accounts for about two thirds of the economic growth nationwide.

Two factors implicitly aggravate this incentive mechanism. First, local government is under the impression that the central government will step in and bail out the troubled local governments. Such a mentality is behind the irresponsibly excessive investment into many areas, eventually leading to overcapacity. Even though it only takes Game Theory 101 to understand that tremendous investment into the same industry at the same time will unavoidably result in overcapacity and eventual distress,[22] each local government is not as concerned with the worst-case scenario because they are under the impression that the central government will not let its local subsidiaries fall.

Local officials' limited tenure at any (local) government position is another reason that officials have short-term incentives at the expense of long-term ideals. As long as local government officials can manage to boost the short-term economic growth and get promoted to a higher position, they don't have to concern themselves with mounting debt, which will be left for successors to handle.

Consequently, it should come as no surprise that all local governments actively engage in a "heads I win, tails you lose" borrowing and investment spree, which can greatly enhance economic performance in the short run and sweep the long-term risks under the carpet. Both distorted incentive systems mentioned above were in place during the tremendous stimulus program of 2009, which made the problem even worse.

How did we get here?

Of course, overcapacity is a phenomenon that is not uncommon among the world's economies. What makes the Chinese experience unique is how Chinese industries reached such excessive overcapacity in such a short period of time.

Three forces probably have worked closely together and eventually led to China's serious overcapacity problem.

Government level

Clearly, China's government, both central and local, should take major responsibility for the overcapacity problem. With central planning of strategically important industries every five years, the central government literally encourages local governments to focus their investment in a few select areas. This encouragement from the government and the corresponding favorable investment policies in such sectors are very likely to induce waves of highly concentrated development into a previously neglected or underdeveloped area.

Of course, with strong motivation to boost local GDP growth, a local government would not easily pass up opportunities to make major investments, especially opportunities under the guidelines from the central government. With guidelines on strategically important sectors from the Cabinet and the National Development and Reform Committee (NDRC), local governments would have a rather easy time getting approval and funding for big investments in unusually large projects.

Unfortunately, because all local governments try to enjoy these "free passes" from the central government, and all try to outdo one another in following the central government's guidelines for promoting a few select industries at the same time, uncoordinated investment booms can quickly turn a previously underdeveloped and highly profitable industry into an industry with cut-throat price wars and overcapacity of more than 100 percent. In some sense, this is similar to the prisoner's dilemma in game theory, the lack of basic knowledge and coordination in local government leads to disappointing and sometimes disastrous outcomes for some strategically important sectors.

Finally, as was the case right after the 4 trillion Yuan stimulus campaign, sometimes it is the financier, most of the time the large state-owned banks that push for such reckless investments. Because state-owned banks are expected to carry out loans consistent with national strategic plans, many banks provide strong incentives for local government to invest aggressively in projects in similar industries, all at the same time. These industries will quickly become haunted by overcapacity, primarily because many other banks and local governments have been thinking along the same lines.

Corporate level

Of course, corporations have to take their own share of responsibility in creating such severe overcapacity problems in China, often times under the government's explicit or implicit guarantees.

Expectations for economic stimulus and everlasting expansive business cycles

If a corporate manager expects the economy to keep expanding, it is in his own interest to invest rationally for greater capacity. Over the past 30 years, the Chinese government has proven its power in engaging in counter-cyclical monetary and fiscal policies and stimulating the economy whenever needed. This successful practice has gradually formed a widely accepted expectation among Chinese executives that the Chinese economy will expand forever.

Under this expectation, companies would compete for capital and for investments in order to catch up with the increasing demand in an expansive economy. With this mentality, increasing capacity may very well seem rational. Further, given that borrowing and investing takes less management effort and know-how than research and development, Chinese companies prefer to turn to investment and expand capacity in order to win competitive advantages through price cutting.

The encouragement and guarantees that Chinese local government provided to select sectors mirror other forms of government guarantee from as early as the seventeenth century, during the tulip bubble in the Netherlands. Throughout the Tulip Mania, the Dutch government allowed parties in tulip transactions (mostly forward contracts on tulips) to pay the government a fee of 3.5 percent of the total value of the transaction to have the government annualize the contract. This is, in essence, the government providing a guarantee that the investors' losses will not exceed 3.5 percent. This would, of course, give investors even stronger incentives to gamble on the prospect of tulip appreciation during the Tulip Mania.

Another analogy is the more recent adoption of the credit default spread (CDS), a major culprit behind the 2007–2008 global financial crisis. By offering insurance to investors who bought risky fixed-income assets related to the U.S. real estate sector, insurance companies and financial institutions used CDS to create a market in which the investment loss in gambling in the subprime market could be successfully managed and insured. Doing so helped reduce investors' risk aversion and solidified their confidence in the U.S. real estate bubble.

Expectations for asset price appreciation

The Chinese monetary supply increased from 13.8 trillion Yuan in 2000 to 40.3 trillion Yuan in 2007 (tripling in 7 years), and further to almost 120 trillion Yuan in 2013 (ten folds in a decade). The speed of monetary supply far outstrips that of Chinese economic growth. A direct consequence of this is an asset bubble, or at the very least, very fast asset appreciation.

If a corporate manager expected the monetary supply to keep rising at such blazing speed, he would expect asset bubbles and serious inflation going forward. Under such expectations for asset and product prices, it is in the company's interest to invest as early as possible, and as much as possible, before the next round of asset price booms. Again, so many investments that were thought of as very aggressive early on turned out to be well timed and highly profitable because of asset bubbles. Such successful experiences boost the confidence of many investors to make aggressive fixed-asset investments, as large and as fast as possible.[23]

Expectations for "too big to fail" and governmental bail out

Finally, there is a clear "too big to fail" sentiment behind the feverish investment style in China. Some simple statistics from the Fortune 500 largest companies in the world tell a very compelling story about how fast Chinese companies have grown over merely the past five years.

The number of Chinese companies ranked on the Fortune 500 companies list increased from 29 in 2008 to 54 in 2010, 61 in 2011, 79 in 2012, 95 in 2013, and finally to 100 companies in 2014. Such speed of ascent undoubtedly sets a record for the fastest growth of companies in the world.

One potential reason behind such fast growth is the consolidation among Chinese SOEs. Almost all Chinese ranked companies are SOEs, most of which are in regulated and semi-regulated areas such as natural resources, energy, transportation, and communications. Following a string of high-profile mergers and acquisitions among SOEs, required by the SASAC in order to create some of the largest companies in the world, many Chinese SOEs are motivated to expand their size so as not to acquire or be acquired by other SOEs. As a result, governmental guidelines for creating bigger SOEs through M&A and consolidation created the peculiar incentive systems behind the fast growth of Chinese companies.

It is worth pointing out that SOEs are not the only companies motivated to expand. Private companies, to many peoples' surprise, also share a "too big to fail" mentality. Private enterprises in China fully understand the power of governmental support and explicit and implicit guarantees from central and local governments.

To obtain this support, a visible public image and powerful bargaining chips (usually in the form of local employment or technological innovation) are critical. Apparently, the bigger an entrepreneur grows his company, the more visible and powerful he becomes in the eyes of the government. Even if something indeed goes wrong with the company, as was the case of Wenzhou City in Zhejiang province in 2010, it is the largest and most influential companies that are more likely to attract governmental attention and be bailed out by the government. As many enterprises that have lived through that tough period have learned firsthand, the incident in Wenzhou in 2012 made an ever more convincing case for companies to grow as big as possible and as fast as possible.

Financial market level

The Chinese financial system also shoulders some undeniable responsibility for overcapacity. China's bank-dominated financial system allocates the majority of its credit based on assets and collateral size. Following this credit rationing policy, bigger projects and enterprises are far more likely to be favored and serviced by the Chinese financial sector.

Because bank loans dominate the corporate financing channel and prove to be far cheaper than equity financing and debt financing in the capital market (which is only available to a select group of enterprises with excellent credit ratings), companies find that advantages in accessing loans and financial systems can quickly turn into very powerful competitive advantages and profits when it comes to industry consolidation, mergers, and acquisitions.

Therefore, the next steps in financial reform—the liberalization of interest rates and lowered entry barriers to setting up banks and other forms of financial institutions—can hopefully reduce companies' motivation to have better and cheaper access to the financial market and to impress banks with the size of their balance sheet.

Also, with a multitude of ways to finance, such as the corporate bond market and the market for corporate control, some companies may learn that there are costs, sometimes considerable ones, as well as benefits, which come along with increasing a company's size.

Bankruptcy: Lack of Exit

Another question about the overcapacity problem is why there haven't been more exits taken through bankruptcy and acquisition, eventually eliminating overcapacity.

The concept of bankruptcy has never been a familiar one in Chinese society, and the Chinese have never been open to this option. As a matter of fact, the concept of bankruptcy has always been taboo in China. Most officials, businessmen, and even scholars consider bankruptcy disgraceful and try to avoid bankruptcy as much as possible. Partly reflecting this attitude, the number of bankruptcy cases filed every year in China is very small, sometimes even less than the number of cases filed in much smaller countries such as the Netherlands or Belgium.[24,25]

Granted, bankruptcy must be tough on enterprises and the entrepreneurs behind the companies. During the slavery period, people who failed to repay their debts ran the risk of being forced into slavery. Only 200 years ago, debtors were forced to enter a debtors' prison to make sure that they would repay their debt. Some 100 years ago, it would have been hard to imagine that a debtor could negotiate with creditors on how to repay a debt and even walk away from some debt liabilities. Nowadays, it has become commonplace for creditors and debtors to work out an optimal plan to restructure the debtor's liabilities.

In this sense, the bankruptcy procedure has become friendlier to debtors now than it was centuries ago. Nevertheless, in addition to personal freedom and financial losses, bankruptcy also carries stigma wherever it goes. This stigma has been considered an important moral and emotional factor in guiding corporate and household investment decisions, and may explain why the Chinese are so reluctant to let bankruptcy happen.[26]

Notwithstanding, Chinese officials and businessmen have to realize that bankruptcy carries a very important price signal that cannot be conveyed otherwise. Only through bankruptcy can the capital market distinguish firms that are financially viable in the long run from those that are not. Because short-term financials and stock performance can be relatively easily manipulated, the market needs another way to express its information about the long-term prospects for a company. A company's credit risk or default risk provides this important pricing mechanism.

With bankruptcy as a realistic threat to irresponsible companies, default risk becomes a powerful disciplinary tool to motivate companies and their management to balance their short- and long-term objectives.

Only when a company is fully aware of its long-term risks from excessive borrowing and high leverage can it proactively manage its liabilities and adjust its management style accordingly.

Bankruptcy, like death, is critical in eliminating unhealthy businesses and operations to make room for new and more vibrant companies. Also through bankruptcy, future companies learn about the balance between growth and stability, between returns and risks. This "natural selection" process may prove itself to be important in helping the best companies thrive in the business world.

Taking a closer look at the bankruptcy procedure, one probably would agree that the bankruptcy process is not only beneficial to creditors with high stakes, but also valuable to the bankrupt companies and their employees. Creditors can, of course, reclaim part of their capital and put the capital into some safer or better investment that can generate greater returns. With the dissolution of a failed business, its assets may be auctioned off to the highest bidder, who may be able to put the equipment and facilities to better use and generate greater profits.

Executives and professional workers can move their human capital to better companies and restart their careers. For young and inexperienced workers, bankruptcy provides new opportunities, or at least catalysts, to think carefully about their career paths. When employees are still young, it is much easier for them to transfer to another industry and start another career.

Of course, various parties have to comply strictly with the Bankruptcy Law of 2006 during the bankruptcy process. Given that bankruptcy is a rare and critical corporate event, and considerable interest and wealth have to be negotiated on and re-allocated through the process, a fair and equitable process is critical to protect the interests of all stakeholders.

In particular, law enforcement has to make sure that major shareholders or real controllers of the companies (normally the executive officers of the company) provide accurate information, act in good faith, and do not enrich themselves at the expense of other stakeholders during the bankruptcy process.

Of course, there are clearly priority claims that need protection during the bankruptcy procedure. Before creditors and shareholders can get paid, all owed taxes and legal fees have to be paid. In addition, employees' salaries and vendors' payables have to be dispatched before creditors can be paid. This is especially important in China because it can effectively deter a company's strategic incentive to file for bankruptcy in an attempt to shirk debt. (The company's incentive is to shirk debt, which is the case in the rest of the world as well.)

Once the basic laws and rules have been set, the government should try to stay out of the bankruptcy liquidation or negotiation process and not interfere with the bankruptcy procedure. The key element of bankruptcy is to let the market determine the value of the company and the value of a bankrupt company's assets.

If the government is too involved and intends to bail the distressed company out of bankruptcy as a short-term solution, it may create a much bigger problem in the future. The research on bailouts and nationalization of private companies in the West has provided ample evidence of the limitations of government helping fundamentally flawed industries and companies.[27,28]

To stimulate or not, this is the question

The recent overcapacity problem that challenges the current Chinese government is really nothing new to China, but rather is an intensified version of the problems and challenges that have been happening in China over the past couple of decades.

Government-led investment areas and favorable policies have proved to be very useful and were welcome at the beginning of Chinese economic reform, when China was trying to get away from the old central planning economic paradigm and transition into a market economy.

By injecting liquidity and making promises on investment returns, one can unleash the entrepreneurship that has been repressed and restore key price factors that have been distorted. With incremental

relaxation on entrance into new areas of the economy, and incremental capital through monetary supply and bank loans, the economy received the much-needed ointment that helped lubricate the cogs of a
huge economy. Step by step, these incremental reforms culminated in
the Chinese economic growth model witnessed by the entire world in
the past decades.

However, as China quickly navigates through reforms in many areas,
one key area that begs for deeper reform is the financial markets. Because
of the tremendous influence of the financial markets in most leading
economies, it is critical that reforms be undertaken with great caution.

At the same time, the nature of financial reform is challengingly
endogenous. By not engaging in deeper and faster reform, one can get
away from short-term risks and shocks to the financial system and economy. What one cannot manage, however, is getting rid of such risks and
shocks altogether in the long haul. Sometimes, putting reform off into
the future is similar to sweeping dirt under the carpet. This problem is
not solved, just postponed.

Unlike other parts of the economy, where sometimes problems are
transitory and may be able to correct themselves over time, misallocation and risks in the financial sector cannot take care of themselves.
As long as China exercises controls over capital flow and as long as the
Chinese domestic interest rate and exchange rate of the RMB are being
regulated, market forces cannot meaningfully equilibrate the market.
If anything, such risks may accumulate and compound in a corner that
seems to have been neglected or not addressed. However, without fundamentally reforming the Chinese financial system, it will not be long
before such risks come back with a vengeance to haunt us again.

What is really worrisome in the Chinese financial system is the mis-
guided expectations investors and corporations form regarding the government's power and guarantees. By bowing to short-term shocks and
providing stimulus whenever the economy slows down or runs short of
liquidity, the government has been sending a consistent yet dangerous
signal to the market that it is willing to do anything to make sure that

the economy grows at tolerable speed, which has been 8 percent in the past decades.

Let us forget about how magical an 8 percent annual growth rate is (an economy will double its size every 9 years with an annual growth rate of 8 percent) for a moment and just imagine how local governments, financial institutions, and corporations would respond to such a message.

Local government officials clearly understand that they need to grow GDP as fast as possible to get promoted and advance their careers. Therefore, they are more than happy to see that the central government stands by its economic growth mandate with real arsenals from the central bank and Ministry of Finance.

A direct result of this sentiment is the GDP growth tournament, in which local government officials are motivated not only to grow their economy at full steam, but actually beyond full steam so as not to lose to other competing regions. The short-term benefit is of course burgeoning economic growth, especially right after a mini-crisis, because local officials feel stronger pressure to show how closely they have followed the central government's footsteps.

In the long run, however, things are very different. To reach short-term growth targets, most local governments take the path of least resistance and increase local investment. To find investment opportunities, all local governments follow the same industry planning enacted by the NDRC and invest in similar industries, causing overcapacity to loom alarmingly serious in many industries, even in some rather new industries.

To finance these investments, local governments have to either auction off some of their land reserves or finance through borrowing. To maximize their land auction revenue, local governments have every incentive to boost local land value, resulting in exorbitant housing prices throughout the country. To finance through borrowing, local governments need to use LGFVs and other increasingly innovative platforms to borrow more new debt to cover existing debt, before interest rates become so exorbitantly high that future borrowing is no longer feasible.

Even worse, during these investment frenzies, local companies believe that the local government will bail them out during hard times. This belief was reflected in the high-profile bankruptcy case of SunTech from Wuxi, JiangSu province. During such corporate distress, the corresponding local government believed that the provincial government would bail out the company and lower-level government. (A similar case is that of another large solar energy company, Saiwei of JiangXi province.) At the same time, the provincial governments themselves believed that the central government would bail them out (as was the case in the real estate in bubble Hainan province during the early 1990s, and again in 2013–2014).

With implicit encouragement and guarantees from upper-level government, every individual in the economy has incentives to take more risks than is prudent. The remaining question is how long can this mentality and investment boom last.

In this regard, the overcapacity problem is merely a reflection of the seriousness of the overleveraging problem in each individual industry sector, and altogether in the Chinese financial sector. The source of the problem lies in the excessive investment that has been made to create overcapacity.

Notes

1. http://www.ftchinese.com/story/001049441?page=1
2. http://bbs.tianya.cn/post-develop-1569824-1.shtml
3. http://finance.21cbh.com/2014/5-10/3OMDAzNzFfMTE2MTA3OA.html
4. The State Cabinet, Oct, 17, 2013, "Guidance on solve the overcapacity problem"
5. http://money.163.com/13/0416/00/8SHRUOM9002524SO.html
6. http://news.cnal.com/industry/2013/10-24/1382575927350766.shtml
7. How severe is the over-capacity in China, UBS Global research, Jan 13, 2013.
8. http://news.xinhuanet.com/energy/2012-10/29/c_123883520.htm
9. http://www.bloomberg.com/news/articles/2014-09-04/clean-energy-defaults-seen-amid-record-china-debt-loads
10. http://finance.ce.cn/rolling/201406/28/t20140628_3057065.shtml

11. http://onlinelibrary.wiley.com/doi/10.1111/0022-1082.00040/abstract
12. http://www.cs.com.cn/ssgs/gsxw/201409/t20140913_4511139.html
13. http://news.cnfol.com/130724/101,1277,15604416,00.shtml
14. As reflected in the interest rate offered by many money market mutual fund products such as (Yu'E Bao) and banking wealth management products, This process has already taken place.
15. Andrews, E, A 'Moral Hazard' for a Housing Bailout: Sorting the Victims From Those Who Volunteered, New York Times, 2008, February, 23.
16. Johnson, S. and J. Kwak, Lehman Brothers and the Persistence of Moral Hazard, 2009, Washington Post, 2009, September 15th.
17. http://news.ifeng.com/mainland/special/tiedaobuxinzheng/content-3/detail_2011_04/20/5860136_0.shtml
18. Reports on Chinese Railway Locomotive Industry, 2010-2011,
19. http://news.ifeng.com/mainland/special/tiedaobuxinzheng/content-3/detail_2011_04/20/5860136_0.shtml
20. http://www.reuters.com/article/2013/10/17/idUSL3N0I71YW20131017
21. http://news.xinhuanet.com/fortune/2011-08/13/c_121855478.htm
22. The concerted industry sector planning certainly does not help when it comes down to which industry each local government should invest into.
23. http://m.ftchinese.com/story/001048086
24. http://www.sciencedirect.com/science/article/pii/S092911991300062X
25. http://onlinelibrary.wiley.com/doi/10.1111/j.1540-6261.2008.01325.x/full
26. Fay, Hurst, and White, 2002,http://www.jstor.org/stable/3083362?seq=1#page_scan_tab_contents
27. M Beesley, S Little child, Privatization: principles, problems and priorities Lloyds Bank Review, 1983
28. http://www.cabdirect.org/abstracts/19811874006.html?freeview=true

8

From Fortune 500 to Truly Internationally Competitive Companies

One of the great mistakes is to judge policies and programs by their intentions rather than their results.

—Milton Friedman

WHEN *FORTUNE* MAGAZINE PUBLISHED ITS 2012 LIST OF Fortune 500 companies, China, with 79 companies, ranked 2nd among all countries on the list. One year later, the number of ranked Chinese companies increased to 95. The number reached 100 in 2014, setting another new record for mainland China companies and also reducing China's distance from the United States, the longtime global leader in this category. While many Chinese business people are excited about further growth in the Chinese corporate sector and about their increasing status with their international counterparts, others are concerned.

As some of these skeptics point out, most of the leading Chinese companies on the mainland come from monopolistic or semi-monopolistic industries where entry barriers are high and competition is limited. Secondly, the rankings of many of these large companies would drop if companies were ranked by their profits instead of their revenues, the common standard used by *Fortune* magazine.

These concerns echo some of the comments made by the World Bank in 2012 on the sustainability of Chinese economic growth over the next two decades. Based on their research, the World Bank and the National Development and Research Center of China (NDRC) both recommended that, to make Chinese SOEs more competitive, their sizes should be limited, their growth model modified, and their dividend payout increased.[1]

These recommendations seem to be shared by the common people. More and more college graduates target SOEs as their ideal employer. SOEs provide great job security and easy advancement, given their monopolistic power in the market place, according to many. "Even though the nominal salary is not as high, SOEs provide unparalleled benefits, and the work is not that demanding," states a college freshman.[2]

At the same time, private enterprise owners are voicing their worries that SOEs crowd out growth potential for private enterprises, many of which start with disadvantages in resources, financing, and government support. As the SOEs grow even bigger, private enterprises find that opportunities are becoming limited in their development, and oftentimes it is difficult to keep up with the mighty resources that SOEs can command and squander.

Private enterprise owners are not the only ones who are concerned. Senior officials from the State-owned Assets Supervision and Administration Committee (SASAC) admit that, with the increase in SOE sizes, the operational efficiency and profitability of SOEs have not improved accordingly.

So what has gone wrong? One of the answers may lie in the corporate strategy for SOEs. With the SASAC's objective of reducing the number of SOEs, the remaining SOEs have not only become bigger, but also more complex. By acquiring some other smaller SOEs, the remaining SOEs have ventured into more sectors and businesses that they were not originally familiar or experienced with.

Investors, in general, are not keen on such diversifications. Reviewing the corporate strategy of Western firms in the past three decades, scholars find a clear trend in companies from America, Europe, and Japan: they all show a pattern of becoming more focused in their lines of business. The number of conglomerate companies, defined as companies with at least five major lines of businesses, has decreased steadily over the past three decades. In contrast, the number of specialized companies, whose revenues come from no more than three lines of businesses, has increased at the very same time.[3]

Corporate managers have quoted operational performance and stock market performance as major motivations for the above trend. Investors tend to favor companies with clear business models and competence to excel in their chosen business models. For example, Warren Buffett, the investment oracle from Omaha, is famous for sticking with his investment philosophy of picking simple businesses with clear competitive advantages in the long run.

A recent incident reflecting this trend is the announcement of a split in News Corporation. As one of the largest global media companies in the world, News Corp. has been facing challenges in how to manage its stagnant traditional publishing business, in contrast with the fast growth of the video and internet businesses. Although the publishing business still commands the majority of the corporation's assets, its contribution to profits has been decreasing steadily, to about one third of the corporation's profits. To make things more urgent, the publishing business faced an investigation due to illegal eavesdropping, which not only blemished the company's public image, but also shook investors' confidence in the business and caused its stock price to underperform.

To revive growth and restore investors' confidence, Rupert Murdoch decided to split the company in two, with film and TV assets going to 21st Century Fox and the publishing business staying with News Corp. This decision was greeted by the market with great enthusiasm, and News Corp's share price shot up by about 30 percent within a week of the announcement.

So, would such a decision to split up business areas work in China? The answer is yes, according to some of my research. I conducted a study that divides all companies included in the Shanghai and Shenzhen 300 Composite index into groups based on whether the companies are diversified, or focused, in terms of lines of business. I then compared the operational performance and stock performance of those that have more diverse business lines with those that have more focused business revenues. I found that, consistent with investors' preferences in the West, more focused investors performed better, both in operational efficiency and stock prices, than the more diverse ones.[4]

So why do investors prefer more focused companies?

First and foremost, many investors believe that capital markets are more efficient in allocating capital than are average companies. As a result, investors prefer to see a listed company distribute its cash flow back to its investors and let investors decide whether they want to go along with company's investment plans for the future. Given that corporate managers are influenced by agency problems and shortcomings in their own behavioral patterns, investors sometimes prefer to avoid complex businesses where internal markets play too large a role.

Corporate governance can be another issue. According to extant research, corporate managers have a tendency to retain and squander companies' cash flow (free cash flow) for their own benefit. For example, researchers find that companies with more corporate jets have poor corporate governance and stock performance.[5] As the size of the company grows, the increased resources and cash flow at the management's disposal concerns investors.

Finally, if investors prefer to diversify across different sectors of the same companies, more specialized, divided companies would give investors greater flexibility in choosing the best player within a given industry than the choices offered by conglomerate companies.

Of course, China is still going through a stage of fast economic growth, and the size of Chinese companies is bound to increase with the economy. However, it is important to point out that increasing the size of a corporation does not necessarily require the parent company to put all its subsidiaries within the same group. Flexible corporate structure, such as a parent holding company, may be more effective in increasing the parent company's asset size and market capitalization, if this is what the parent company pursues.

Several modern corporate finance tactics, such as spin-off, split-off, or carve-out, are available to Chinese companies when they consider restructuring and improving their investor relationships. Successful examples, such as the split of News Corporation and of Marathon Oil, prove that such restructuring tools can effectively improve corporate performance, at least in the short to medium run.

Some of the senior managers of SOEs are concerned that splitting up a parent company may result in a decrease in the parent company's asset size or in a loss of corporate control. The lessons from more developed capital markets suggest that, as long as the valuation and transaction are carried out at fair market value, the restructuring of SOEs should be able to attract increased capital from investors and improve the core competence of existing SOEs. At the same time, investors would value each business line of the same company more, now that they can understand the company better.

Only when an SOE is open to such restructuring possibilities can it set up an effective monitoring mechanism over its respective lines of business and truly make each of its chosen businesses strong and competitive on its own. The success of an SOE relies on the success of each of its businesses, and the success of the Chinese economy relies on the success of each of its SOEs.

Can SOEs keep driving Chinese economic growth in the coming decades?

Of course, a closely related question about Chinese SOEs is whether they can help China maintain its blazing economic growth in the decades to come. When the pace of Chinese economic growth slowed considerably in the first half of 2013, more questions arose about what would drive Chinese economic growth in the coming decades. While analysts seemed to reach a consensus that the government has to let the market play a greater role in setting key factor prices and interest rates, there has been considerable debate on which type of enterprises, state-owned as opposed to privately-owned companies, would be more instrumental in helping China successfully switch its economic growth model and sustain its economic miracle.

At first look, the SOEs have clear advantages. First, the largest companies in China, measured by total assets and total market capitalizations, are SOEs, and many of them rank among the largest companies in the entire world. Second, some of the SOEs enjoy monopolistic or oligopolistic power in some key industries, such as energy, natural resources, telecommunications, and transportation, with no competition in the near future. Furthermore, with their strong market power, some SOEs have expanded out of their traditional areas of operation and into more lucrative areas such as real estate development and broadly defined financial services.

However, if history and international lessons can serve as useful benchmarks, there are probably more issues than meet the eye. Given the complex objectives of SOEs, profit making has never been their expertise. Chinese SOEs are no exception. Even though the days have passed in which the Chinese railway system had its own police force, it remains very common for SOEs to run their own hospitals, middle schools, restaurants, and catering businesses. Because SOEs are expected to do more than bring the best returns to their shareholders, SOE management inevitably faces the challenge of juggling multiple objectives. Given that profit maximizing is no longer the sole, or even the major, criteria by which SOEs are evaluated, it becomes difficult to measure how SOEs can contribute to Chinese economic growth.

To make things more complex, most senior management at SOEs is also part of the Chinese civil servant system. Many senior managers at SOEs hold greater political aspirations than commercial ones. SOE managers may care more about the size of the company than the profits, and more about the speed of growth than the quality. That can be partly reflected in that, recently, almost all of the largest profit losers in the Chinese A-share market are SOEs or subsidiaries of SOEs.

Another important concern that international scholars and policymakers share about SOE structure in general is corporate governance. Because the state is the clear dominant shareholder, other shareholders may lack the power or incentive to monitor the company and its senior management. The lack of monitoring in SOEs may further lead to governance problems such as corporate empire building, executive compensation and perquisites, tunneling, or even fraud and stock market manipulation.

Separately, some of the largest trading losses in Chinese companies, such as the trading debacles at China Aviation Oil (CAO) and the Citic Pacific company, also centered around SOEs. These incidents again highlight the importance of balancing various stakeholders at SOEs and underscores that SOEs are not particularly good with internal checks and balances.

If one were to look around the world, one would find that the trend in SOEs in the past decade has been to privatize. By introducing private capital into previously state-owned enterprises, many developed and developing economies, such as Great Britain, Japan, and India, have enjoyed the benefits of letting the market exert greater influence on SOEs.

Moreover, the SOEs will eventually face the challenges that the Soviet Union faced before its collapse. Because it is very costly for a central planner to collect and verify information, the market force always has an advantage in providing incentives to find out information and better allocate resources than in a state-controlled environment. As a result, even if the SOEs can provide a much needed short-term boost to Chinese economic growth, the real trillion dollar question may be whether the SOEs can sustain their contributions to China's economic growth. And if not, what would be the best way to reform the SOEs?

SOE's Crowding Out

As more Chinese SOEs enjoy higher rankings and increasing power in the global business arena, as evidenced by blockbuster acquisitions and improved Fortune 500 rankings, Chinese small- and medium-sized enterprises (SMEs) have been experiencing increasing difficulty in accessing capital, especially during the credit crunch of 2013.

Some experts worry that the increase in SOEs is "crowding out" SMEs. *Crowding out* is a term that economists use to evaluate government-led investment and expenditure projects. Economists point out that although government investment and expenditure can create new demand and bolster the economy in the short run, these run the risk of replacing the original demand provided by the market and SMEs. Exactly because of the influence of the government, the private sector may find it harder to compete or operate in the market and decide to quit, leaving the private sector a smaller market share in the economy. Hence the term *crowding out.*

In order to properly assess the impact of the crowding out effect, it is imperative to have a fair and comprehensive way of evaluating economic policies. Witnessing growth in a certain sector of the economy is undoubtedly encouraging. However, one has to be aware of the equilibrium influence stemming from such growth and evaluate whether the growth comes at too great a price because it is being shouldered by other parts of the same economy. Focusing on piecemeal benefits and failing to integrate social welfare gains or losses may indeed jeopardize the sustainability of every member of the economy.

The fast development of large Chinese enterprises, especially SOEs, is certainly encouraging and laudable. At the same time, one has to realize that as the SOEs gain greater influence on the economy, they are causing centralization in a growing number of industries. Even more concerning, many large enterprises leverage their advantages in regulated sectors and encroach on other originally competitive industries. With their advantages in resources, personnel, and access to the capital markets, such large SOEs gradually crowd out the SMEs that originally flourished in the market.

To make matters worse, because of their operational stability, large companies are far more favored by banks when it comes to loan approval, even at a lower interest rate. Hence, the expansion of large enterprises makes it harder for SMEs to finance. This exemplifies how the development of large enterprises can profoundly yet indirectly undermine SMEs.

Another important lesson is that the crowd out effect largely depends on whether the economy is already operating at a near-capacity level. If not, then the government's investment and expenditure may prove effective in creating additional demand and stimulating the economy. However, if the economy is already operating at a near-capacity level, as is the case in many Chinese industrial sectors, then the government's stimulus may not be as effective as wished for.

Instead, the government's investment and expenditure may directly crowd out the products and services that were originally provided by the private sector, without being able to create any additional demand to stimulate the economy. The net outcome of such government actions may be merely a transfer of business from the private into the public sector, which is often associated with undesirable outcomes such as increased prices, decreased competition, and worse service quality.

Such consequences are particularly unwelcome in China right now, as international lessons show that SMEs are very important in ensuring a country's economic growth, full employment, innovation in technology and business, and urbanization, the very key goals that China is trying to achieve through its economic growth model transitions.

Therefore, while it is commendable that more and more Chinese companies are achieving enviable Fortune 500 rankings, these rankings come at a price. The equilibrium principle of economic thinking should be kept in mind. An artful balance between the SOEs and SMEs may be key in driving sustainable growth in both sectors and in the entire economy.

High corporate leverage

On January 4, 2014, the President of China Railway, Bai Zhongren, ended his own life. The press has speculated that his suicide was connected to the staggering 84.8 percent debt-to-asset ratio that his company faced.[6]

What is alarming is not just the sheer high level of indebtedness, but also the speed at which corporate debt has ballooned in China in the past few years. For example, the Chinese Overseas Freight, another major SOE, observed its debt ratio jump from 58.7 percent in 2010 to 74.8 percent in 2012.

According to statistics published by WIND on all Chinese listed companies, the level of debt of Chinese listed companies in 2013 increased by more than 10 percent from 2012, and more than 25 percent from 2011.[7] Of all companies listed in the Chinese A-shares market, about 10 percent of listed companies reported a debt-to-asset ratio of over 70 percent, a number widely considered to jeopardize a company's financial soundness. This high level of debt is particularly concentrated in the real estate and manufacturing sectors.[8] For example, the debt-to-asset ratio for all real estate companies is 60.7 percent, also higher than the 60 percent benchmark for a 'healthy' level of debt.

It is worth noting that this high level of debt is not limited only to companies controlled by private parties, which are often believed to experience difficulty securing bank loans or debt issuance. Indeed, many SOEs, even larger SOEs directly administered under SASAC, face the highest debt levels. The problem has become so dire that Zhou Xiaochuan, the governor of the PBoC, acknowledged in the Bo'Ao International Forum of 2014 that leverage at Chinese corporations is "alarmingly" high.

How high is the Chinese corporate leverage ratio? According to statistics from the PBoC, the Chinese nonfinancial corporate leverage ratio was 106 percent in 2012 and increased to 110 percent in 2013. These figures are far higher than 49 percent for Germany, 72 percent for the Unites States, and 99 percent for Japan. The Chinese leverage ratio is even higher than that of many other Asian countries that arguably share similarities in their developmental stages and social structures.[9, 10]

Since the stimulus package in 2009, the Chinese nonfinancial leverage ratio has been continually increasing. On one hand, the softening in the economy starting in 2013 has made it harder for corporations to increase profits and weakened their ability to repay their debts. On the other hand, many companies surveyed by the PBoC complained about deteriorating financial situations along the entire industry value chain.[11]

Of course, there have been ups and downs in the Chinese corporate leverage ratio in the past, depending on macroeconomic situations and monetary policy. Chinese corporate leverage has remained high for the longest period in the past two decades, and nonfinancial corporate leverage increased steadily from 54 percent in 2007 to 60 percent in 2012. In some extreme cases, the increase in debt repayment liabilities has outpaced that of profit increase, putting a lot of pressure on corporate operations and performances.

By examining detailed data from Chinese listed companies, it becomes clear that not all sectors in the Chinese economy suffer from a high corporate leverage ratio. As a matter of fact, heavily industrial sectors such as petroleum, steel, coal and charcoal, and construction equipment experienced particularly sharp increases in leverage. In contrast, many service-intensive sectors, such as food and restaurant, traveling, and apparel, underwent some decreases in their leverage ratio. Most companies in heavily industrial sectors are SOEs, which explains why 80 percent of the liabilities are concentrated in SOEs. The trend continues as this book is being written.

According to data from the Chinese Ministry of Finance,[12] Chinese SOEs' total assets were $91.1 trillion and total liabilities were $59.3 trillion in 2012, with a leverage ratio of 65 percent—higher than that of the private sector. Among total SOE debt, the liabilities of centrally controlled SOEs stand at $31.8 trillion (a 12.6 percent increase from 2012) and local SOE liabilities stand at $27.6 trillion (a 15.6 percent increase from 2012).[13]

SOEs generated $46.5 trillion in revenue in 2013, more than doubling the $21 trillion in 2008. However, a closer look at the data reveals that SOE's profits have been increasing at a much slower pace than their revenues, at only 5.9 percent in 2013. At the same time, the financial costs at SOEs have increased at a much faster pace than their profits, growing from 3.2 percent of profits in 2009 to 33.5 percent in 2012, and remaining in the double-digits since then.

One major reason that financial costs have outpaced corporate profits in the past four years is that SOEs lack alternative financing channels. With the Chinese stock market trailing the performance of most other markets around the world, the financing channel originally established to help solve the SOE debt problem during the downturn of the early 1990s business cycle cannot help much now. Even after the SOEs successfully managed to go through the IPO process (with much help from central and local governments), investors in the A-shares market became wary of SOEs, given their deteriorating performance.

This has forced SOEs to turn to debt financing, mostly through bank loans. Fortunately, the Chinese banking sector remains dominated by state-owned banks. These state-owned banks prefer to make loans to SOEs because they understand that making loans to SOEs typically exempts them from being criticized for making bad loans. Banks also understand that the state government would stand behind the SOEs should their loans go sour. Therefore, when the 2009 stimulus package was rolled out, state-owned banks were motivated to lend aggressively to SOEs, leading to ballooning debt for SOEs in the following few years.

Nonfinancial drivers

From a purely financial perspective, a company will only make an investment if the return on investment is higher than the company's cost of capital (i.e., the interest rate on its loans from banks). However, several studies have pointed out that the return on investment is clearly lower than the cost of capital (benchmark lending rate) for average SOEs.[14]

This pattern is most notable among listed companies. Since 2008, the listed SOEs have been witnessing deteriorating return on investment capital (ROIC). At the same time, their leverage has been climbing steadily. According to some simulations, SOEs' profits could cover financing costs in 2009, as long as their financing cost was no higher than 27 percent, a fairly comfortable safety margin for an average company.

However, this safety margin dropped sharply to only 11.5 percent in 2012, reflecting both the ballooning size of debt and the mounting financial costs due to increasing financing costs. In contrast, the safety margin remains comfortably high at 35.8 percent for non-SOE listed companies.[15]

So there are clearly some nonfinancial considerations that shape SOEs' financial decisions. SOEs themselves are, of course, primarily responsible. During the last wave of consolidation, mergers, and acquisitions, almost all SOEs were motivated to grow bigger, at a faster pace, so as not to be acquired by their sister companies. As SOEs expanded, they naturally found their investment returns decreasing and their debt increasing.

Unlike privately-owned companies that would worry about deteriorating leverage, the dual roles of SOEs, as both government branches and as enterprises, induce SOEs to stick closely to the SASAC's guideline to become bigger and (presumably) stronger. SOEs understand just as well as state-owned banks, their counterparts in the financial sectors, that the SOEs' distressed debts (the state-owned banks' nonperforming loans) are all implicitly guaranteed by the Chinese government. Should something bad occur, in the end all of the liabilities would be taken care of by the Chinese government.

Of course, there is a closer and more direct tie between SOE debt and the government. Part of the rapid increase in Chinese SOEs' leverage is due to the local government GDP growth tournament. Because all Chinese local government officials are evaluated by GDP growth in their respective regions, "growing by borrowing" has become the quickest and easiest way for many governments to boost their economic growth speed. As long as a local government can provide enough incentives and implicit guarantees for companies to invest, the companies, mostly SOEs, are more than happy to kill two birds with one stone by expanding their own business and providing a favor to local government officials.

This push towards high speed growth comes not only from the local government, but sometimes from the central government as well. When the Chinese central government faced economic slowdown in the past couple of decades, it typically engaged in countercyclical expansive fiscal and monetary programs. SOEs, including state-owned banks, have become the most powerful channels through which the Chinese government can effectively push through its investment-driven development model.

During the 2008 global financial crisis, almost all countries in the world increased governmental leverage to bail out and help private sectors troubled by irresponsible borrowing and unhealthily high leverage. However, China is exceptional in the sense that the Chinese central government's leverage did not increase much in the same period, even in light of the $4 trillion stimulus package. The secret? It is probably that local governments (through LGFVs and local SOEs) and SOEs, both those under SASAC's direct leadership and those under local government's leadership, increased their leverage substantially, instead.

Government guarantee

Lying at the core of SOE's increasing and concerning debt level is the long-standing soft budget problem that harrows most SOEs, particularly those in socialist countries under Soviet governance. On one hand, SOEs shoulder some governmental responsibilities, such as providing infrastructure, social welfare, education, and even government debts.

On the other, however, SOEs enjoy many benefits from close ties with government.

For example, most SOEs, especially those under direct leadership from SASAC, enjoy access to easy and cheap bank loan financing. Put differently, government at different levels absorbs some of the SOEs' liabilities and financing costs. Of course, when some SOEs really get into trouble, the government invariably bails them out from their own governmental budgets.

A clear example is that of the LGFVs. Because Chinese local governments are forbidden to raise debt directly, they set up LGFVs to raise debt for them. These LGFVs come into existence with explicit guarantees, financial support, and implicit guarantees for repayment from local governments. According to statistics from earlier in this chapter, SOEs probably make up 90 percent of Chinese corporate bonds, and a big proportion of these debts supports local governments' debt and infrastructure investment. In the more transparent corporate bond market, the bonds issued by LGFVs make up about 20 percent of total publicly traded corporate bonds in China. Almost all the LGFVs that issued these bonds are directed to help local government with their administrative responsibilities.[16]

How can such debt-laden LGFVs and SOEs survive in the marketplace? The answer is government guarantee and support. In exchange for the favors that SOEs do for the government, the government will use its resources to return the favor.

First, government can persuade or sometimes order state-owned banks to make loans to SOEs in certain sectors or in certain areas. Because of the financial repression in the Chinese economy, access to credit and loans itself is already extremely valuable in enabling SOEs to survive, or even thrive. Further, because of credit rationing, the real capital in the market place is being artificially held down, which means that whoever has access to capital can easily profit from arbitraging between the regulated state banks and the free-willed credit market.

Many SOEs make handsome and easy returns by lending out the loans that they obtained from banks, because only SOEs can obtain loans directly from the banks at lower interest rates. These loans by SOEs to private enterprises and SMEs can carry a spread return of up to 10 percent per annum, a return that is higher than that of many SOEs' main lines of business.

Because the SOEs are confident that capital will flow their way no matter what their operating performance and financial status is, SOEs are willing to borrow and use such resources to help the government. Also because of the government's guarantee, banks are willing to make increasingly large loans to SOEs, part of which can be used to cover an SOE's previous loan. This symbiosis explains why SOEs can constantly behave in a way very different from what market forces predict.

The government's guarantee proves to be most valuable when SOEs get into trouble. On some occasions, the government will turn its implicit guarantee into an explicit one and use its fiscal income to guarantee the security of the loans made by local companies.[17] On other occasions, the government will provide companies with much needed government orders, which will boost the companies' short-term financial performance. On yet other occasions, the government will forego local government taxes or use fiscal subsidies to reward companies that have helped the government in the past.

In short, with the government's guarantee, the SOEs do not have to worry about the availability or the cost of their debt, and banks do not have to worry about the security of their loans. As a matter of fact, SOEs can even sometimes help banks to intermediate their loans and re-lend some to companies that would not have made the cut for borrowing directly from the banks.

By sharing the differences between SOE loan rates and the rates to private companies with the banks, the SOEs seem to be doing everyone a favor, with government support. This "too-good-to-be-true" situation just cannot seem to get any better. With the overall easy monetary policy and inflation, the real interest rate on borrowing indeed approaches zero, which allows SOEs to engage in another round of investment and asset purchases, pushing up asset prices and generating rewarding amounts of investment return. This unfortunately results eventually in overcapacity in so many industries.[18, 19]

All of the above government guarantees and soft budget approaches seem to be effective in containing Chinese corporate leverage problems. With the high savings rate among Chinese households, government sectors, and the Chinese regulated financial sector, there is still time and room for Chinese SOEs and SOE banks to work together and put off some of the most serious debt overhang problems in China's history.

The beauty, and, at the same time, the risk of the government guarantee under a soft budget is the sharing and transfer of risks between the private and public sectors. Granted, there are many successful examples of such public-private partnerships, especially during financial crisis, and the success itself can set the stage for excessive risk taking and greater crisis down the road. Despite economics and the corporate finance theory of a debt ceiling for any enterprise, China is so big, and the risks can be transferred so freely between the private and public sectors that no one can really tell where the border between SOEs and government lies (or where the debt ceiling is).

This leads to the trillion dollar question of whether the Chinese government can deal with such mounting debt problems when the time comes, which will be discussed in Chapter 9.

Other forms of guarantees

While financial guarantee is probably one of the most important and easiest to understand forms of guarantee that the Chinese government provides to SOEs, there are many other important, yet less apparent, forms of guarantee that ensure that SOEs succeed, or at the very least prevent them from failing.

Statistics from *Fortune* magazine indicate that 100 Chinese companies ranked among the top 500 companies of the entire world (ranked by revenues) in 2014, next only to the United States, which has 128 companies ranked on the list. However, among these 100 Chinese companies, 16 reported losses, whereas only four U.S. companies on the list reported losses. What is even more alarming about these 16 Chinese companies is that they are all SOEs.[20]

Another ranking of Chinese companies by the Chinese Association of Companies reveals a similar pattern. Among the 500 largest Chinese companies, 43 reported losses in fiscal year 2014, and among these, 42 were SOEs. Such comparisons make plain that the problem with Chinese SOEs is not limited to a few select examples.

Unlike SOEs in many other countries, where they are no more than simply enterprises (primarily) owned by the state, Chinese SOEs have a much closer and more intricate relationship with the Chinese government in many capacities beyond finance.

First, many SOEs derive their core competitiveness through state support. Some of China's largest SOEs operate either in the natural resources area, such as PetroChina, SinoChem; in monopolistic areas, such as State Grid, China Telecom; or in regulated areas, such as ICBC and Bank of China. Put differently, part of the SOE's competitiveness comes from the government's direct consent to let them operate in these areas. Without such state support and entry access, it is not clear whether the SOEs could have grown as big as they are now or be as profitable as they are.

Government at different levels provides other forms of implicit guarantee that support the development of SOEs. In the case of the real estate sector, it has become a common practice for a local government to move into a newly developed area of a city to jumpstart the demand in that area and boost its real estate prices.

In areas such as steel, wind turbines, and solar panels, it is common for a local government to make a direct purchase of local SOE products. If this is not enough to boost the local SOEs, especially when the SOEs are in the process of preparing for their IPOs, local governments sometimes provide aggressive tax subsidies or rollbacks, which sometimes account for 50 percent of the company's annual profit.[21]

Apart from economic and financial support and guarantees from the government, SOEs also enjoy less tangible support and guarantees. For many investment areas considered "strategically important," or of concern to state security, often times only SOEs are allowed entry.

Similarly, for many business areas related to exclusive market power (i.e. natural resources, telecommunications, transportation), market entry is granted only to SOEs and their subsidiaries, or at the very least, to joint ventures formed between the SOEs and private companies. In this way, there clearly are "glass ceilings" for private companies when it comes to the most coveted and profitable investment and business opportunities.

Of course, because local governments may, from time to time, need support and favors from SOEs, and also because of opaque corporate governance and internal controls, there are numerous related-party transactions completed between SOEs and parties with various degrees of connection to the government. The recent wave of mergers within the SOE system makes it even harder to figure out the costs and benefits of the guarantees provided to SOEs by the government.

Last, but certainly not least, most executives at SOEs belong to the Chinese Communist Party's personnel system and rotate their jobs between the government and SOEs. Consequently, the boundary or distinction between government officials and SOE leaders is blurred, especially for officials who serve within the same province. One direct result is that SOE leaders do not consider maximizing corporate profits to be their primary responsibility. Aware of their chance of working as an SOE leader in the future, government officials innately favor SOEs over private companies when working in their offices.

As a result, SOEs gain substantial advantages over private companies in many subtle yet profound ways.

What to do next?

Even with the staggering increase in Chinese SOEs' leverage, not all experts agree that the Chinese debt problem has mushroomed out of control. Official statistics from the PBoC indicate that the overall national leverage is about 183 percent,[22] far lower than the leverage ratio of developed economies such as in the United States, the United Kingdom, and Japan. Further, some experts argue that China is a major creditor to many other countries, most notably the United States, and this credit will help China navigate through its own debt problems.[23]

However, with the slowing of Chinese economic growth and less accommodative monetary and lending policies, local governments find themselves lacking the resources needed to continue helping troubled SOEs. Real estate and LGFVs, two major areas that have brought impressive profits and investment returns to SOEs in the past few years, are now coming back and haunting those SOEs with considerable exposure.[24]

In light of the softening macroeconomic situation, even the Chinese government acknowledges that SOEs have to undergo fundamental overhaul before they can improve their competitiveness and survive the next round of economic reform. How to reform SOEs has loomed as one of the key questions in the next step to Chinese economic reform, and is one area that may determine the destination of Chinese economic reform and transition.[25]

Deleverage

To curtail the ballooning debt problems, it seems apparent that SOEs need to cut their debt levels. However, many economists suggest that a quick deleveraging may not be what Chinese SOEs need at this moment. It is important to point out that the SOE debt problem has been growing over the past few years, and a sudden break in the financing binge may cut bloodlines to many corporations, especially SOEs, which are accustomed to easy and cheap financing.

With the new leadership's resolution not to repeat 2009's excessive monetary and fiscal stimulus, many SOEs would have to learn to deal with the new norm of a neutral monetary policy and moderate growth in credit expansion. With interest rate liberalization, many companies, especially SOEs, would have to learn to cope with increasing financial costs with tighter credit. Borrowing from the words of Premier LI, Keqiang, a key challenge facing many Chinese SOEs going forward will be "how to use incremental capital to solve a stock-piling inventory problem."

Interest rate liberalization

Given that available access to cheap bank credit is a critical part of the implicit guarantees the state provides SOEs, interest rate liberalization will strongly motivate SOEs to transform. Once the SOEs start facing and shouldering market-level interest rates and cost of capital, many inefficient investments and projects will have to be abandoned. This will not only make SOEs more viable and efficient, but will also help bring down the current excessive and growing leverage of Chinese SOEs.

Interest rate liberalization will also help level the field for competition between SOEs and private companies. With both types of companies gaining similar access to capital at similar costs, both can focus more on discovering their respective competitive advantages and improving their abilities to target positioning.

Deregulation

Widespread opinion holds that deregulation and permitting market entry are necessary conditions for reforming SOEs. Only by allowing private companies to be in meaningful competition with SOEs can the pros and cons of the SOE model be assessed clearly, once further reforms are realized.

Gradual deregulation will lead SOEs to rely less on monopolistic power, will limit their collateral, and will restrain their desire to borrow and invest excessively. A more market-oriented factor price (capital and land) and product price (for example, energy prices and transportation fares) will rationalize the SOEs' decision making. With the exit of implicit guarantees that government provides to SOEs through price suppression (interest rate) and price subsidies (energy prices), SOEs will gradually lose their ability and desire to borrow wantonly.[26]

Disclosures and evaluations

In conjunction with deregulation, SOEs have to provide better disclosure about their operations and financial performance and face evaluation criteria similar to that applied to private companies. The evaluation criteria of the SASAC focus more on the size of SOEs, not necessarily their efficiency and profitability. This is largely responsible for SOEs motivation to expand without restraint and also leaves loopholes by which local governments ask local SOEs to raise debt on their behalf. Better evaluation and disclosure will not only reduce local government leeway in providing implicit guarantees, but also limit SOEs incentives to receive them.[27]

Another important area for disclosure lies in the field of corporate governance. Given that many of the listed SOEs belong to larger and less transparent parent holding companies, many SOEs engage in frequent related-party transactions between the listed part and unlisted part of the parent companies. It is widely known that the parent companies sometimes use the listed companies to raise capital for the parent companies' own needs and will bail the listed companies out if necessary.[28] This practice makes it even harder to accurately assess the SOE's debt problems and the value of the implicit guarantees that SOEs enjoy. Hopefully, with improvement in disclosures and corporate governance, SOEs debt will become more transparent and hence more manageable.

Legal reform

Finally, given the unique and sensitive nature of the relationship between Chinese SOEs and Chinese sovereign and local governments, another round of deep legal reform is needed. Many questions remain to be answered. Where should the boundary between the state and SOEs be drawn? How should the whole of society be able to share SOE earnings? How should national natural resources and monopolistic resources be used and monetized? The answers to all these questions will eventually determine the efficiency and final destiny of China's SOEs.

Notes

1. China 2020, research report by the World Bank and NDRC, China, http://www.worldbank.org/content/dam/Worldbank/document/China-2030-complete.pdf
2. http://news.sohu.com/20070302/n248450942.shtml
3. Franko, 2004http://www.sciencedirect.com/science/article/pii/S0007681304000473
4. Zhu, N. 2014, On how to improve corporate valuation for Chinese companies, working paper, SAIF.
5. http://www.sciencedirect.com/science/article/pii/S0304405X05001820
6. http://www.yuqingcn.cn/www/show-27999.html
7. http://money.163.com/14/0306/08/9ML223GI00253B0H.html
8. http://finance.sina.com.cn/stock/s/20120322/022911648812.shtml
9. http://money.163.com/14/0519/00/9SINTFNU00253B0H.html
10. It is worth pointing out that this estimate is indeed on the conservative side, according to Mr. YAO, Yudong, author of another research on the same topic, Chinese non-financial corporate leverage is as high as 140 percent.
11. http://www.1000caifu.com/bencandy.php?fid-52-id-2276-page-1.htm
12. http://app.finance.china.com.cn/report/detail.php?id=2115866
13. http://finance.sina.com.cn/china/20140519/011719145466.shtml
14. http://pg.jrj.com.cn/acc/Res/CN_RES/MAC/2013/12/2/2b4632bd-215c-41f7-8d6b-2028f939b331.pdf
15. Guosen Securities, 2014, research report "The high leverage problem for Chinese non-financial companies"
16. http://www.financialnews.com.cn/sc/zq/201408/t20140823_61708.html
17. http://money.163.com/12/072%9/86RL4DMQ002529T0.html
18. http://finance.sina.com.cn/leadership/mroll/20141112/200020799925.shtml

19. http://finance.eastmoney.com/news/1345,20131206343782477.html
20. http://finance.ifeng.com/a/20140901/13034313_0.shtml?wrating Module_1_15_108
21. http://finance.people.com.cn/stock/BIG5/n/2014/0805/c67815-25402669.html
22. http://wallstreetcn.com/node/90694
23. http://wallstreetcn.com/node/90694
24. http://business.sohu.com/20140519/n399733786.shtml
25. http://finance.jrj.com.cn/people/2013/10/28003916033335.shtml
26. http://news.hexun.com/2012-05-15/141394427.html
27. http://finance.eastmoney.com/news/1344,20130513291157851.html
28. http://economy.caijing.com.cn/2014-04-23/114126308.html

9

The Mother of All Credit: The Government that Never Defaults

In the long run, we are all dead.

—John Maynard Keynes

Trust products, real estate, the stock market, state-owned enterprises—these topics discussed in previous chapters all share one thing in common: they have all survived considerable questioning and pessimism in the past and have come out stronger than ever before.

One important reason why some near-collapse products and industries surprisingly develop later into strategically important areas is government support. Chinese central and local governments, with the help of booming economic development in the past decades, have ample resources and credibility when they pledge to support a company, or even an industry.

However, things have started changing lately. Since the 2009 stimulus package, Chinese local governments have taken on huge amounts of debt to revive Chinese economic growth. The problem has become so grave that it has attracted considerable international attention. It seems that all other problems in the Chinese financial sector are just the tip of the iceberg of the implicit guarantees problem in China, which traces its roots back to the debt problems and fiscal sustainability of Chinese government itself.[1]

Partly in response to such growing concerns domestically and overseas, China's audit authorities conducted a thorough investigation of local government debt in late 2013 and made several important discoveries.

First, total Chinese government debt, including contingent debt that is guaranteed by the government, climbed to 30.3 trillion Yuan (approx. $5 trillion) as of mid-2013. This represents a debt-to-GDP ratio of close to 60 percent, the widely used international benchmark for fiscal stability.

Among the 30 trillion Yuan debt, local government debt accounts for 17.9 trillion Yuan (about $2.8 trillion), a 67 percent increase from 10.7 trillion at the end of 2010 in less than three years. Of course, there is a wide range of variation across different regions. Beijing ranks first with the highest level of debt, with the contingency debt and total debt level at 98.93 percent and 99.86 percent of local GDP. Seven other states (Chongqing, Guizhou, Yunnan, Hubei, Shanghai, and Jilin) witness total debt levels of over 80 percent.[2]

If the total amount of local government debt is not too much more than what has been expected, the speed at which local government debt has grown in the past three years is certainly alarming.[3] Based on the same rate of growth in the past three years, Chinese local government debt may well increase to over 50 trillion Yuan, the size of the Chinese GDP in 2013, by 2020.[4]

More diversified financing sources?

At the same time, the audit also provided some encouraging news that Chinese local governments have diversified their avenues of debt borrowing over the past few years. According to the national audit office's audit of local government debt in 2010, about 80 percent of local government debt came from bank loans. The ratio dropped to about 57 percent in a similar survey by the end of June 2013.

Because the bond market is underdeveloped in China, few local governments can finance debt through it, which leaves bank loans as the primary source of financing. Thus, Chinese local government debt contrasts starkly with that in developed countries, where bank loans make up less than 20 percent of local government debt in the United States, the United Kingdom, Canada, and Australia.

The risk with bank-loan dependent local government debt is that, in case of a systematic slowdown and default by Chinese local governments, the default risks may become quickly contagious within the Chinese banking sector and wreck the Chinese financial system.

Instead, China's central government has been trying to lead local governments to diversify into multiple sources of financing, other than bank loans, partly because the fast growing debt and worsening fiscal conditions at such municipalities have finally begun to worry banks.

Among alternative financing sources, bond issuance (about 1.8 trillion Yuan) has gradually become an important supplement to bank loans, thanks to the development of the Chinese bond market. In provinces where the banking sector is relatively small, such as in the Gansu, Qinghai, and Ningxia areas, bond issuance can make up as much as 20 percent of local governments' financing.

Build-Operate-Transfer (BOT) (1.5 trillion Yuan) trailed as the third most important way to finance local government, averaging 8.3 percent among all local government debt. This pattern varies considerably among different regions and areas. For provinces in the hinterland, where there is stronger need for building infrastructure and development, and a relatively weaker banking sector, BOT can make up over 30 percent of local government debt.

Trust products, which enjoyed tremendous growth during the 2010–2013 period, came in next and contributed 1.4 trillion Yuan to local government's financing needs. On average, trust products make up 8 percent of local government debt, with the ratio going as high as 26 percent for Shaanxi province.

Finally, IOUs account for about 5 percent of total local government debt. Ningxia and Inner Mongolia have the highest level of debt financed through payables, at 47.2 and 23.7 percent, respectively.

Local Government Financing Vehicles (LGFV): the financing platform

A channel through which local governments finance, the local government financing vehicles (LGFV) have attracted considerable attention both domestically and overseas.

According to the budget law, Chinese local governments lack the authority to issue local government debt unless exceptions are made by the Cabinet (as was the case for Beijing, Shanghai, Zhejiang, Guangzhou, and Shenzhen in 2009).

Instead, local governments set up LGFVs as entities to raise funds to be used primarily for costly investment infrastructure and real estate development projects. Put slightly different, LGFVs are entities backed by local government creditworthiness. Although not directly owned or operated by local governments, they are widely perceived as state-owned companies that raise funds for local governments.

According to the 2013 National Auditing Office reports, LGFVs make up about 40 percent of total debt by local governments, remaining the single most important financing platform for local governments. In many regions, such as Chongqing, Jiangsu, and Hainan, LGFVs account for more than 50 percent of local government debts. Hunan province tops the list with 63 percent of all local government debts being financed through LGFVs. It is worth noting that this has already reflected an encouraging downward shift since 2010, when LGFV made up about 47 percent of the total local government debt.

Local government agencies are the second largest platform for raising debt. Agency debts are even larger than those from LGFVs in many provinces and account for more than 50 percent of local government debt in Shaanxi, Xinjiang, and Ningxia provinces.

Local SOEs come in third as the largest debtors within local governments, accounting for an average of 30 percent of total local debt, with the highest percentage for Fujian province, which borrows 50 percent of its total debt through local SOEs.

Lastly, noncorporate direct enterprises on average make up about 15 percent of local governments' debt, with Beijing topping the list with 50 percent of its government debt coming from this source.

Direct responsibility vs. contingent liabilities

The 2013 auditing of government debt introduced a very important concept to many Chinese government officials: contingent liabilities. In addition to the liabilities that local governments take direct responsibilities for, governments are also implicitly responsible for the contingent liabilities for which the local governments are liable, in case the primary issuing entity fails to pay up its entire liability. According to the 2013 audit, debt guaranteed by government at various levels amounted to 2.93 trillion Yuan, and contingent liabilities stood at 6.65 trillion Yuan.

Contingent liability is a fairly broad definition and one that is of particular importance and relevance to China. According to the International Financial Reporting Standard (IFRS) adopted by the International Accounting Standards Board (IASB), IAS 37 generally defines contingent assets and liabilities as "assets and liabilities that arose from past events but whose existence will only be confirmed by the occurrence of future events that are not in the entity's control. It establishes that contingent assets and liabilities are not to be recognized in the financial statements, but are to be disclosed where an inflow of economic benefits is probable (assets) or the chance of outflows of resources is not insignificant (liabilities)."[5]

Like many other situations in business, reasonable estimates are difficult to make and seldom reasonable. With limited disclosure about the size and scope of the guarantees provided by various governments, it is almost impossible to understand how much government at various levels has pledged to their LGFVs, their local SOEs, or private enterprises that they have business transactions with through IOUs. Putting such liabilities and guarantees under broad daylight will not only dispel any speculations about the gravity of the problem, but also alert local governments about how far they can push the boundary of their implicit guarantees.

Transparency

Even after the round of auditing in late 2013 and the wide debate on the amount of Chinese local government debt, more questions arise regarding the accounting and transparency of Chinese local government debt capacity.

Largely because the situation is very fluid and a lot of local government debt takes place through new venues and under new covers, it becomes a lot harder to accurately pin down the total amount of local government debt. It also becomes hard to determine, among the total amount, which is local governments' direct and explicit liability, and which will become local governments' liability in case of adverse events. As a result, some remain skeptical about the accuracy of the audit estimate and feel that the number is probably the lower bound of total Chinese local Chinese government debt.[6,7]

Among all local government debts, the municipal bond is probably the most transparent. According to international practice, the local legislator would have to approve the details regarding local debt issuance. Detailed specifications such as the purpose of issuance, the total amount of issuance, the cost of financing, and the issuing underwriter would all have to be approved by the local legislators before debt can be issued.

Such local government municipal bonds account for 50 percent of total debt in Germany and about 60 percent in the United States and

Australia. In contrast, municipal bonds make up only 10 percent of total local government debt for only select local governments in China, leaving the remaining 90 percent of total government debt to other forms of less transparent financing.

Because municipal debt issuance has to make the most disclosure and is therefore the easiest to monitor, a low fraction of total local government debt financed through municipal bonds raises eyebrows in that the local legislators lack the necessary information to understand the fiscal situation and sustainability of their municipality. This would inevitably cause the local debt level to be higher than is desired. At the very least, it is important to bear in mind that Chinese local governments can take out considerable debt, without their local legislator even being aware of it.

In addition (as outlined in Chapter 10), because local government officials have incentives to boost local economic growth through borrowing, it is in the officials' best interest not to disclose their debt level so as not to dilute their personal contribution in engineering great economic growth. As a result, even though the 2003 audit provided a promising starting point to better grasp the true size and gravity of the Chinese local government debt problem, more work would have to be done and more information would have to be disclosed before the answer can become crystal clear.

Concentrated risks

According to the 2013 National Auditing Office report, even after a significant drop from 80 percent a few years ago, bank loans still made up about 60 percent of the LGFV in China. In contrast, bank loans make up less than 20 percent in the United Kingdom and Australia, and less than 10 percent of local government debt in the United States and Canada, where institutional investors (such as mutual funds and pension funds and insurance companies) and retail investors each make up about one-half of total local government debt.[8]

206 CHINA'S GUARANTEED BUBBLE

Because the Chinese bond market remains underdeveloped and the municipal bond market close to nonexistent, few Chinese local governments can finance debt through the local bond market. In addition, capital account constraints largely sever Chinese local governments' connection to international capital markets, which leaves bank loans as the primary source of financing. This was the case until trust products became immensely popular during the past few years. However, as we pointed out in earlier chapters, even many of the trust products are distributed, repackaged, and implicitly motivated or backed by Chinese commercial banks.

On one hand, such risks concentrated on banks help the local government to better manage their liabilities. Because the banks would have to worry about any potential shocks to their own stability, banks would try to avoid pressuring local governments too hard and so trigger systemic crisis. On the other hand, however, this creates another form of implicit guarantee of its own, which further encourages risk taking by local governments.

Before Chinese banks could become "too big to fail," Chinese local governments beat the banks to it and hijacked them to comply with the governments' debt problems. In case of an economic slowdown and systematic default by Chinese local government, such concentration of local government-related bank loans may spread default risks quickly within the Chinese banking sector.

In addition to the potential contagion problem of default risks, Chinese banks also worry about the mismatching term structure of local government loans. Given the long-term nature of many municipal infrastructure projects, most municipal debts in the West have a maturity of 10 years or even longer. This is also why municipal bonds typically have relatively long maturity, so as to allow the projects to generate viable cash flow to repay their debt.

In contrast, most Chinese local government debt matures in less than three years, and would have to be rolled over upon maturity. Among all local government debt, bank loans indeed have the shortest maturity average of about a year. This would require Chinese local governments to face greater liquidity risks than their international counterparts, because most of their infrastructure investment projects cannot generate the kind of cash flow to repay their bank loans in time upon maturity.

Fiscal revenues and cost of financing

Land sales generated 2.69, 3.15, and 3.91 trillion Yuan in revenue for Chinese local government in 2011, 2012, and 2013. Within each respective year, land sales contributed to 41, 27, and 35 percent of all local government revenues. If one were to include the five major tax categories directly tied to land and real estate, land sales and related taxes would contribute to 46 percent of local government revenues in 2013, highlighting local government's dependence on land sales in China.[9]

With fast appreciating land value and housing prices, Chinese local governments do not have to worry about such cash flow problems: as long as the local government can provide basic development of land and sell it off, the land can generate enough revenues to cover local governments' debt.

However, things were about to change substantially, and possibly forever. With Chinese housing prices being some of the highest in the entire world and outstripping Chinese income growth, many doubt the market's sustainability and whether land sales can remain a major financing source to local government. The real estate curb policy put in effect since 2011 has already brought a drop in real estate prices in many cities in China. This has led directly to drops in the government's land sales revenue in 2012, and more recently in 2014. According to some reports, land sales revenue in May 2014 dropped by more than 30 percent compared to a year before.[10] The uncertainties in the direction of the Chinese housing market raised the question of whether local governments can auction off more land at higher prices, a quasi-necessary condition for a Chinese local government to balance its finances.

This is partly why trust product financing has become a more popular way for local governments to make their ends meet. However, the cost of trust product financing has escalated and shot up to over 10 percent per year over the past few years. This is much higher than the returns generated by most of local governments' infrastructure investment, typically no higher than five percent. Therefore, it has become apparent that it will not take long before trust products become too expensive to support local governments' financing needs, especially now that more investors have become increasingly averse to local government debt due to concerns over default risks.[11]

Default Risks

Municipal government bonds, in general, are considered a somewhat risky investment in the West. For example, during the five years after the 2007–2008 global financial crisis, about 4.6 rated municipal bonds by U.S. local governments went into default every year. In the past four decades, about 50 different unrated municipal bonds by various U.S. local governments went into default.[12]

In contrast, not a single bond issued by any level of Chinese government has defaulted, ever. Similar to the rationale behind other aspects of this book, implicit guarantees provided, or believed to be provided, by higher level Chinese government, support the issuance, re-issuance, and credit-worthiness of many Chinese local government debts.

Because all market participants are under the belief that the central government will not allow local government debt to default, the default risks of local government debt have been largely discounted or even ignored. Related to the distorted pricing of default risk due to implicit guarantee is the underestimation of the cost of financing for local debts.

Currently, a large majority of local government debts are being financed through banks with a subsidized interest rate. Banks are willing to make such cheap loans to local governments partly because they seek their assistance and policy support in local expansion. But more importantly, the implicit guarantee can largely explain this phenomenon. Banks typically hold the belief that local governments will not default, and even if they do, higher-level local governments, or perhaps even the central government, will take responsibility for a local government's debt.

Finally, the asset quality of local government is questionable and illiquid. According to the "The Study of China's National Balance Sheet," most assets of local governments are nonfinancial assets, of which more than 80 percent comes from land value and local SOE assets.[13, 14] The value of such assets relies heavily on a region's economic conditions and industry sector performance, and therefore is highly susceptible to local economic conditions. Further, poor liquidity may discount asset value during fire sales, when local governments are under urgent pressure to repay their debts.

Hence, even though local governments may appear to have sufficient assets on their balance sheet, they may still face the risk of default if there is a considerable decline in local economic growth speed or stalling of local housing price and land values.[15]

Guarantees from central government

However, many local governments do not seem worried. Because local governments do not have their own separate balance sheets, they are not held fully accountable for their financing behavior. The central government, as a matter of fact, provides implicit credit endorsement and enhancement on behalf of the local government. This can be illustrated by a rather perverse and amusing phenomenon of local government debt issuance in 2012.

Four cities (Shanghai, Zhejiang, Guangdong, and Shenzhen) were allowed to issue local government bonds in a pilot program in 2009 and witnessed their bonds trade at lower yield than that of the Chinese Central Government Treasuries. By common logic, the lower level governments do not have as strong a financial status as the central government, and hence would entail greater credit risks and higher bond yield to compensate for such risks.

Instead, the yield on the local governments' bond is lower (which is not the international norm) than the yield on Chinese sovereign government bonds. The reason for that is that investors—who are smart enough and familiar with the implicit guarantee that the central government provides towards local government debt—bet that the central government will not allow such bonds to default. As a result, such local government debts enjoy credit support from both the local and central governments, hence are believed to be safer than even the sovereign bonds themselves.

If anything, the Chinese central government seems to be in sound fiscal health at the moment, and a reliable support should anyone need some boost in credit worthiness. The balance sheet of the Chinese government is one of the healthiest among all major economies. The total assets of SOEs was 104.1 trillion Yuan in 2013 (of which 48.6 belongs to the central government and the remaining 55.5 trillion belongs to local governments), doubling from 53.3 trillion Yuan back in 2009.[16, 17] Additionally, China boasts the largest foreign reserve in the world, valued at over $4 trillion in 2014.

Given static situations, the Chinese government's assets can easily cover its entire liabilities. Furthermore, the Chinese government's fiscal income has been growing, rapidly during the past decade, which makes most people confident that economic growth can solve any fiscal problem for the Chinese government, should there be any problems at all. Given a high savings rate and high home ownership, the private sector is reasonably well financed and can probably cope with costs associated with aging. This should allay the Chinese government concern about the social security burden and allow it to focus on dealing with its own debt problems. Finally, the fast growing domestic capital market has the potential of further enhancing central and local government's debt capacity in the years to come.[18]

The slowdown syndrome

However, with Chinese economic growth slowing down and its mode shifting, it becomes imperative to inspect fiscal sustainability for the future.

In 2012, two note worthy patterns emerged in a Chinese central government budget report. First, the growth rate of both fiscal income and expenditure was much slower in 2012 than in 2011 (24.8 percent and 21.2 percent) and most years in the past decade. Secondly, the growth in fiscal expenditure outstrips that of fiscal income by a wide margin. Fiscal income growing slower and fiscal expenditures growing faster is trending.

At the same time, it is worth stressing that the rate of governmental expenditure is very likely to increase substantially in the future. With the Chinese government's commitment to improving social welfare, such as in public education, health care, and environmental protection, the necessary government spending has to increase accordingly.

The slowdown in fiscal income growth will trigger a series of problems not confined to economics. The growth of fiscal income has outpaced that of GDP growth in past years. Put differently, more wealth has moved into the public sector as opposed to the private sector. The proportion of household income to GDP dropped from about 56 percent in 1985 to about 40 percent in 2010,[19] far lower than the range of 50–65 percent in most developed economies.[20]

As household income growth slows, the inequality in income distribution within the private sector will draw more attention and cause dissatisfaction and disappointment in the current taxation and fiscal system. According to an official report from the Ministry of Human Resources and Social Security of China, the annual income of the top 10% of households in China is 65 times higher than that of the bottom 10% of households.[21] Similar to the international trend, the income gap between corporate executives and rank and file corporate employees has been rapidly growing, causing increasing dissatisfaction in the younger generation.

Meanwhile, the government has to deal with its own share of challenges. With reduced resources, it would become much harder to create a balance between further investment and the provision of social welfare items. Although certain areas of public expenditures grew fast in 2012 (educational expenditure grew by 28.3 percent to 466.7 billion RMB, 4.08 percent of GDP, and affordable housing expenditure grew by 16.4 percent to 444.6 billion RMB), some other areas call for similarly fast growth. For example, medical expenditure only grew by 12 percent, and unemployment training and benefits only grew by 12.9 percent.[22]

With fiscal income slowing down, the government is left with only the options of decreasing expenditure growth or fiscal deficit. This is not to mention that the Chinese government requires additional resources to deal with some of the hard core reform areas, such as social security, education, and health care—areas that average Chinese households care the most about.

So far, the central government has started to take the route of expanding fiscal deficit to make up for the shortfalls due to increasing fiscal expenditure. Until now, China has maintained a modest budget deficit of 0.8 trillion Yuan in 2012, about 1.5% of China's concurrent GDP. This figure lies well within the 3 percent safety range set by the European Union and other international communities. In contrast, the fiscal deficit of the United States stood at $1.56 trillion, or 10.9% of GDP in 2011, and the fiscal deficit problem in Japan may be even worse.[23]

Despite its relatively modest size, the speed by which the Chinese fiscal deficit grew in 2013 raised some concerns. According to the China News Agency, the Chinese 2013 fiscal deficit was projected to increase to 1.2 trillion Yuan, up about 50 percent from its 2012 levels. Even with its modest size at the moment, such a growth rate in fiscal deficit leads many to worry about what will happen a few years down the road.

The Social Security

According to the 2012 national auditing report, the Chinese government faces a total of 28 trillion Yuan worth of liabilities. This should not seem too worrisome, given that the Chinese public sector's net asset is over 55 trillion Yuan, and China's foreign reserve is over $4 trillion.[24]

However, according to some recent research led by international investment banks, the total debt of the Chinese government might be as high as 100 to 120 percent of the Chinese GDP[25, 26], far greater than the estimates in the official statistics. If true, the above factors will raise substantial uncertainties on the fiscal sustainability of the Chinese government.

Even if one were to believe the official data, the underfunding of the Chinese social security system remains one of the largest pieces of uncertainty in the government's fiscal obligations, making all the above issues seem trivial. According to a report led by leading economists from international and domestic banks, even though there is no short-term cash flow pressure, the Chinese social security system faces daunting underfunding challenges. The reports estimate the underfunding gap to be 16.48 trillion Yuan in 2010 and 18.3 trillion Yuan in 2013, about one-third of China's GDP during the same period.[27, 28]

It is a major concern that the underfunding problem will not become any better over time and may deteriorate with an ageing population, resulting from increasing inflation and uncertainty in investment returns. According to the reports, the underfunding gap in China's social security system will rise to 68.2 trillion Yuan by 2033, or 39 percent of the GDP during the same period, and will exceed 50 percent of Chinese GDP by the year of 2050. The social security underfunding gap liability is so big that it may one day grow greater than the total assets of the state-owned enterprises, the biggest source of assets in the Chinese government's balance sheet.[29]

China's fast-ageing population poses an even greater challenge to the social security system than is the case in many other countries. The Chinese population over the age of 60 will increase from about 200 million in 2013 to over 500 million in 2050, and will make up about one-third of the population. The population over the age of 80 will increase from 12 million to about 120 million during the same period. At the same time, Chinese family size has decreased steadily from 3.96 people per household in 1990 to 3.02 people per household in 2012, exerting great pressure on the future household burden of taking care of the retired family members.[30, 31]

To put Chinese social security underfunding into global perspective, Norway has the most generous social security reserve, about 83 percent of GDP, in the entire world. Japan and the United States trail with 25 and 15 percent of GDP, respectively. The figure for China is about 2 percent of its GDP.

For some more market-oriented countries such as Hong Kong, Singapore, and the United States, residents prepare for their retirement by going beyond the social security system with supplemental private pension plans. For example, the total retirement savings in the United States, including social security, supplementary retirement plans, personal savings and pensions, added up to $17.9 trillion, even greater than the U.S. GDP in the same year. This is another form of luxury that Chinese households do not enjoy.[32]

Even after a decade of development and major overhaul in the Chinese pension system since 2002, when 29 out of 31 provinces could not make ends meet in their local social security systems, there are still about half (14) of the Chinese provincial-level governments facing the very same problem. Some two decades after the Chinese government vowed to set up individual retirement accounts in 1992, it still remains unclear whether the reform can be completed as planned by 2020. According to a survey conducted by the Chinese Social Academy, over 70 percent of respondents feel that the government has not made enough contributions to address the underfunding problem in the Chinese social security system.[33]

Echoing such opinions, Mr. Dai Xianglong, then commissioner of the Chinese Social Security Fund, expressed grave concerns in regards to the underfunding problem. Mr. Dai called for delaying the retirement age right away to partly address the problem. On the incremental funding to the Chinese social security system, Mr. Dai suggested that the Chinese government provide its stake in SOEs and SOE dividend payment to the Chinese social security system as soon as possible.[34]

How to reform?

Legal reform

According to Chinese Budget Law, only local legislators can authorize local governments to issue debt. In order to better monitor the purpose, size, and cost of financing of local government debt, the local legislators should be able to require local governments to constantly disclose the governments' balance sheet, income statement, and liquidity situations, and seek legislators' approval before borrowing.

At the same time, local legislators should be able to set caps on the total amount of debt that a local government can raise under different categories. Furthermore, local legislators should require local governments to propose their long-term fiscal projections and fiscal planning, in addition to their short-term cash flow pressure. Legislators should ask local governments to consider and conduct scenario analyses for fiscal risks coming from an ageing population, increasing medical-related costs and increasing demand for social welfare projects going forward.

To arm the legislative watchdog with teeth, local governments should be required to disclose their balance sheets, and such information has to be subject to constant auditing by upper-level government. Upper-level government, at the same time, should set up a monitoring system for lower-level government debt and prevent lower-level government from over-borrowing.

Fiscal stability and sustainability should be taken into consideration in the evaluation and promotion of officials. Unlike the current mentality, under which local government officials are evaluated primarily by the rate of local economic growth and hence are motivated to borrow heavily, a new paradigm needs to take effect accounting for the quality of local economic growth and local government fiscal soundness.

Fiscal and Taxation Reform

As we discussed earlier in this chapter, nearly one-half of China's local governments' fiscal revenues come from land sales and related taxations.[35]

This concentrated source of fiscal income generates strong incentives for local governments to push up local land value and therefore housing prices. Learning from the experience of Hong Kong and Singapore, most Chinese local governments believe that housing prices will keep going up, and, therefore, the land value will continue to rise. Under such a belief, local governments have expressed great enthusiasm in developing more land and artificially pushing up local housing prices and land value.

Needless to say, a direct consequence of local governments' incentive to push up land value is the prohibitively high price of housing in most Chinese cities, especially judged by the housing price-to-income and rental income ratios. As housing prices become unattainable for an increasingly large and young population coming into urban areas, the Chinese central government faces strong social pressure to stabilize housing prices, namely to prevent housing prices from rising too fast.

These real estate curb policies issued by the central government brought direct systematic risks to local governments' doorstep. Because many local governments have already sold off land in prime locations, the incremental land that local governments can afford in subsequent land offerings would fetch lower prices than in previous auctions, if location and condition were to be held constant.

Also, because newly offered land is typically located in farther away areas, it usually requires greater work and cost for local government to invest in before the land becomes available for auctioning and development. Without rising housing prices and increasing land value, many local governments find themselves stuck in "land auction blessings."

Such land sale revenues that have propelled their balance sheet expansion and economic growth in the past decade shave now come back to haunt local governments as they become harder to achieve going forward. Without a continuous and growing base for taxation, many local governments will not have the necessary resources to even support their daily operations, let alone their future development initiatives.

Consequently, there have been some very active debates about initiating property tax, or occupancy tax that would levy annually, on the basis of home ownership—a move that had been thought not feasible only a few years back, when national housing prices were already on the rise. Needless to say, existing homeowners and developers have strong resistance to the rolling out of such taxes, citing that similar taxes have already been levied at the time of apartment purchase.

However, with the worsening fiscal situations at many local governments and upcoming demographic ageing that would weaken long-term demand for real estate, it may soon prove inevitable that many Chinese local governments will have no other option but to start collecting occupancy tax in order to make their ends meet. The irony of this short-term solution, however, is that international evidence shows that property tax is a very important mechanism that would deter housing price appreciation.[36] Hence, the local governments would run the risk of shooting themselves in the foot by going too fast with the property tax, or as the Chinese expression goes, "to quench their thirst by drinking poisoned wine."

A more fundamental approach to the local government debt problem is to reform the way central and local governments split their fiscal revenues (taxation) and fiscal responsibilities (expenditure and investments). The split-tax reform in 1994 successfully solved the near-crisis in the Chinese fiscal situation some twenty years ago. The arrangement has remained largely unchanged, even though the fiscal situation in central and local governments has changed drastically over the past two decades.

According to the 2013 government budgetary report, local governments received 52 percent of total national fiscal revenues, with the remaining 48 percent going to the central government. In contrast, local governments shouldered 85 percent of total national fiscal expenditure, whereas in the central government spent the remaining 15 percent.[37]

Such an imbalance begs for reform either through enabling local governments to collect a higher proportion of the national fiscal revenues, or by reducing the local governments' fiscal expenditure proportionally. In addition to proposed property taxes, local governments should be able to collect other taxes with more stable on-going tax bases, such as special consumption tax and vehicle purchase tax.

In addition, central government needs to consider providing more fiscal support to major infrastructure and social programs at local levels. By sharing part of such local expenditures, central government will not only help local government financially, but also gain more insight into local governments' fiscal dilemma and restore the balance in local government's policy objectives.

Develop the bond market

Similar to the solution to trust products and SOE financing, developing and growing a functioning bond market holds the key to liberalizing interest rates so that they can accurately reflect the credit risks borne by different local governments.

Banks that already have considerable exposure to local government debt, can assign different risk weighting to local debt. Virtually offering different interest rates (price) to different risk tranches of local government debt, would not only help banks better manage their risks, but also form an incentive system for local governments to reduce the risk of their debt and enjoy lower financing costs.

Municipal bonds have the advantage of providing incentives and control over local governments' fiscal situation; the market interest rate can discipline local government's financing activities, diversify the systematic risks among bond holders, and diffuse the accumulating risks concentrated in the Chinese banking sector.

By allowing relatively healthy governments to issue bonds, China's central government provides incentives for such local governments to become more transparent in their fiscal management and debt management, reducing their default risks. Furthermore, with unprecedented disclosure of local governments' fiscal information, the capital market will be able to better assess different local governments' risk profiles, and discipline local governments' future financing activities.

Municipal government bonds can complement the rest of China's bond market to help the capital market better figure out the price of risks (i.e., term spread and credit spread), which will provide investors with varying degrees of risk preferences different investment vehicles.

With the pilot issuance by select local governments, many other related government agencies (such as the Ministry of Finance and its local subsidiaries) and market entities (such as rating agencies and investment banks) will gradually become familiar with the municipal bond issuing process and become more confident with providing related services.

An independent and transparent credit rating system could provide a timely and impartial evaluation of the fiscal quality of various local governments, and subject government officials to the same market criteria, benchmarks, and financial constraints as corporate executives, thereby enhancing governments' fiscal accountability.

With the bond market, various market participants will have a chance to observe how local governments' fiscal situation and financing records affect their ability to strike future financing deals and their financing costs. This practice will set a healthy and enlightening example for other local governments, motivating them to achieve better financial balance and make preparations for bond issuance some time in the future.

For infrastructure and housing projects with steady cash flow, Chinese bond markets should develop more asset-backed securities (ABS) and mortgage-backed securities (MBS), which will also provide better liquidity to local government assets. Furthermore, public-private partnerships (PPP) can attract private capital into investing in and operating local projects without incurring big up-front investment from the government side, lowering local government's leverage.[38]

Finally, to better align the term structure of local governments' assets and liabilities, future reform should aim at improving the liquidity of local government assets. The Chinese stock market should welcome more companies, including local SOEs, to go public. With their stake in SOEs becoming liquid stocks, local governments owning shares of local SOEs will find more liquid ways to raise capital, repay debt obligations, and finance new projects.

Allow default and bankruptcy

The rather amusing incident where a few local governments allowed to issue municipal bonds in 2009 witnessed their bond yield lower than that of Chinese Treasury bonds suggests that investors bet that the central government would not allow such bonds to default. Familiar with the concept of implicit guarantee that central government provides to local government debt, investors believe that such local government bonds enjoy credit support from both the local and central governments, and, hence, are safer than even Chinese Treasury bonds themselves.

More fundamentally, it highlights Chinese unfamiliarity with default and bankruptcy and the long-standing expectation that government will not let lower-level government and important companies go under. Expectations take long to form, and maybe even longer to break. There is probably no better way to shift investors' expectations, unless default and bankruptcy were allowed to happen, without much interference and support from the government.

Some isolated incidents of trust products defaulting and corporate bankruptcy have set some encouraging examples and have somewhat lead investors into a more realistic direction in assessing the risks.

However, even in these incidents, government and SOEs were reported to have played active roles in the restructuring process, and many investors still believe that lenders and investors will not have to face losses after the situations settle.[39, 40] Hence, it is conceivable that it would take even greater resolution and courage to modify investors' confidence in the securities issued by various levels of government.

Improving disclosure and transparency is therefore critical. Only with better disclosure will the market be able to identify and discern the default risks of various local governments, and trade accordingly. Even without public trading of municipal bonds, better disclosure can help investors navigate away from troublesome borrowers, or at least charge a reasonable premium for doing business with them, and therefore rein in the ever-increasing debt of local governments.

Notes

1. http://www.economist.com/news/leaders/21625785-its-debt-will-not-drag-down-world-economy-it-risks-zombifying-countrys-financial
2. The Reports on National Government Debt Audition, June, 2013, China National Audition Office, December, 2013
3. http://www.businessinsider.com/chinas-local-government-debt-3-trillion-2013-12#ixzz3FbXvWspp
4. http://finance.sina.com.cn/money/bond/20131230/163617796897.shtml
5. IAS 37 Provisions, Contingent Liabilities, and Contingent Assets, http://www.ifrs.org/IFRSs/IFRS-technical-summaries/Documents/IAS37-English.pdf
6. http://finance.qq.com/a/20140103/009550.htm
7. http://jingji.cntv.cn/2013/06/14/ARTI1371168090591807.shtml
8. The Reports on National Government Debt Audition, June, 2013, China National Audition Office, December, 2013
9. http://house.focus.cn/news/2014-07-14/5260052.html
10. http://house.focus.cn/news/2014-06-11/5134970.html
11. http://money.163.com/14/0102/00/9HHTPE9600252G50.html
12. http://en.wikipedia.org/wiki/Municipal_bond#Risk

13. http://news.hexun.com/2012-12-14/149038432.html
14. http://www.huaxia.com/tslj/lasq/2015/0¼4217940_2.html
15. http://news.xinhuanet.com/2014-03/09/c_119680243.htm
16. http://finance.sina.com.cn/china/20140729/045919844665.shtml
17. http://news.hexun.com/2013-02-20/151259255.html
18. http://blogs.wsj.com/economics/2014/04/28/imf-three-reasons-not-to-worry-about-a-crisis-in-china/
19. National Bureau of Statistics of China, 2014
20. World Bank Database
21. Institute for Labor and Wages Studies
22. 2013 National Budgetary Report, the Chinese Cabinet, 2013
23. http://news.xinhuanet.com/world/2011-03/11/c_121173817.htm
24. http://news.hexun.com/2014-12-21/171631247.html
25. http://en.wikipedia.org/wiki/Debt-to-GDP_ratio
26. http://asia.nikkei.com/Politics-Economy/Policy-Politics/Chinese-local-government-debt-hits-new-high
27. http://www.cs.com.cn/xwzx/xwzt/20120613yanglao/06/201206/t20120613_3370074.html
28. http://finance.sina.com.cn/china/20120706/181212500715.shtml
29. CAO, Yuanzheng, et al, 2012, June 13rd, Caijing Magazine.
30. http://news.xinhuanet.com/house/wh/2014-10-22/c_1112920773.htm
31. http://news.xinhuanet.com/zgjx/2014-02/25/c_133141795.htm
32. http://www.cs.com.cn/sylm/jsbd/201212/t20121217_3782475.html
33. http://finance.ifeng.com/a/20140701/12636954_0.shtml
34. http://www.cs.com.cn/sylm/jsbd/201212/t20121217_3782475.html
35. http://house.focus.cn/news/2014-07-14/5260052.html
36. http://www.sciencedirect.com/science/article/pii/0094119086900227
37. http://finance.sina.com.cn/zl/china/20140731/091719872488.shtml
38. http://blogs.wsj.com/chinarealtime/2014/01/09/a-micro-reading-of-chinas-local-government-audit/
39. http://www.cb.com.cn/finance/2014_0314/1045442.html
40. http://finance.ifeng.com/a/20140121/11515710_0.shtml

10

Voodoo Statistics

If you torture the data enough, nature will always confess.

—Ronald Coase

I N 1980, WHEN HE WAS OPPOSING RONALD REAGAN FOR THE presidential nomination, George H.W. Bush labeled Reagan's supply-side economic policies as "Voodoo Economics." Today, the term "Voodoo Statistics" could be used to describe how regions inflate the numbers used to determine China's GDP.

Early in January 2014, before three provinces had yet to report their regional GDP for 2013, the sum of GDP from the 28 provincial regions had already surpassed the official GDP of China reported by the China National Bureau of Statistics.

This is not an anomaly. As a matter of fact, since the Chinese Bureau of Statistics started reporting national and regional GDPs in 1985, the sum of the regional GDP has always been greater, sometimes as much as 10 percent greater, than the national GDP.

The discrepancy was 2.68 trillion Yuan in 2009, 3.2 trillion in 2010, 4.6 trillion in 2011, and 5.76 trillion in 2013, with a pace just catching up with the pace of GDP growth. Out of the 31 provincial level regions, all regions, with the exception of the capital city of Beijing and coastal city of Shanghai, reported economic growth speed that was faster than the national economic growth speed, a statistical stunt that is almost impossible.

Granted, some minor discrepancies exist between how central and local governments collect and define their data. There may also be the slight chance of double-counting at the regional and the national levels. However, both reasons should generally cancel out among various regions and not produce significant bias consistently.

A more plausible explanation is that local officials, motivated by their career considerations, intentionally overstate the size of the local economy and the speed of economic growth. In confirmation of widely floated conjectures, the National Bureau of Statistics has investigated and reported several incidents of intentionally falsified statistical data.

In June 2013, the National Bureau of Statistics disclosed malpractice in data collection in a city in the Guangdong province, one of the largest provincial economies in China. During the investigation, the NBS found that most of the statistics for a town in the city had been falsified in the offices of local governments. The government officials went as far as to pretend to be employees of local companies and dial into the data collection center to falsify data on the size of the local economy. In one extreme case, the local data inflated the local industries' GDP by 300 percent, from 2.1 billion to 8.4 billion Yuan.

To inflate the size of the local economy, some areas directed data collecting staff from the NBS into the relatively well established areas or sectors for data sampling, creating a sample that was biased upward for the entire region. Some areas required national or international companies with a regional presence to count their national revenues under the local areas. Some areas modified electricity usage data so that it grew at a speed consistent with inflated GDP growth. Some areas required offices and shopping malls to keep their lights, escalators, and air conditioning on during off hours so as to boost local electricity usage. There are even rumors that several areas colluded on a consensus GDP growth number that several competing areas shared so that no local government would lose face by lagging behind colleagues in other areas.

Even though the National Bureau of Statistics has vowed to ensure data quality and punish data manipulation, similar practices have been reported every year throughout the rest of the country. The GDP has become such an important criterion for government official promotion that many local officials exhaust their time and energy strategizing how to boost the GDP and neglect endeavors that residents truly care about, such as environmental protection, health care, and educational opportunities. In such cases, statistics are not only biased and unreliable, but indeed get in the way of more inclusive and sustainable economic development.[1]

Consumer price index

The Consumer Price Index, or CPI, is one of the most watched economic indicators in almost every country. The CPI reveals inflation in the economy. Because inflation strongly influences the expectations of businesses and consumers alike as to how soon money will lose its purchasing power, it has considerable impact on household consumption behavior and on corporate investment decisions, in response to expected shifts in consumer prices and consumption.

China is no exception. However, unlike many other countries that readily publish their inflation figures regularly and disclose how the statistics are compiled, China has never published how it calculates its CPI. This has intrigued and frustrated many Chinese economists, and many have tried innovative ways to unravel the mystery.

As more research has focused on this area, one thing is becoming clearer: pork prices strongly influence the Chinese CPI. Some economists have jokingly claimed that the initials of the Chinese Consumer Price Index (CPI) stand for "China Pork Index." While this is an exaggeration, almost all agree that pork is the single most important influence in determining Chinese CPI. Even though pork prices only make up about 3 percent of the CPI compilation, many suspect they can sometimes contribute up to 50 percent of the movement in CPI readings.

The role of pork prices is based not just on their importance, but also their volatility, which reflects a basic problem of the relative relationship between supply and demand. Even though the country's demand for pork remains largely stable (despite some seasonable adjustments, such as increased demand during the Chinese New Year), farmers constantly have to decide whether or not to raise more pigs, taking into account feed prices and expected supply from other farmers. To make things more complicated, hard-to-predict weather and disease-related issues often disrupt farmers' expectations and render the guess work even more challenging.

As a result, the Chinese government and central bank have been trying to stabilize pork prices so as to stabilize the CPI, in part by attempting to accumulate a stock of pork centrally controlled by the government.

Pork may be a very important ingredient in China's everyday life, but it is very hard to understand how a single product price can have so much impact on a country's CPI and its monetary and economic policy. Why not provide more transparent and relevant statistics that can reflect more reliably the overpriced consumer price movement? Why not allow the market to better understand the CPI compilation methodology so that the market may determine for itself the true gravity of the problem?

Not disclosing such information apparently benefits the government, allowing it to reduce the CPI when needed.[2] By accumulating a national stockpile of pork, the Chinese government has the option of releasing national stock to stabilize pork prices and the CPI.

However, that leads to the question of which affects what. The CPI is meant to reflect inflation, not to determine inflation. Even if pork prices can be artificially and intentionally checked or lowered, what about other meats that are consumed as substitutes to pork? What about the farmers of the feed and the prices related to feed products? By controlling pork prices, the government may gain some undesired power in influencing or even determining the CPI of any particular statistical cycle.[3]

Another more concerning aspect of the Chinese CPI is that the components and the calculation of the CPI are kept secret, leading one to wonder if the data is reliable. Even if keeping historical consistency is a valid reason not to change how the CPI is calculated, it would be beneficial to have several different gauges to reflect inflation at the same time.

One probable reason that government officials are motivated to understate the CPI is that local officials are evaluated by the real GDP growth under their governance. Based on the definition of real GDP growth (real GDP growth = nominal GDP growth − CPI), it is safe to conclude that, to achieve higher real GDP growth, one can either boost the speed of nominal GDP growth or decrease the CPI.

Put differently, a local official can boost real GDP growth by intentionally lowering the inflation level. As shown above, if local officials have such strong incentives to overstate their GDP and GDP growth, it is not farfetched that they may also manipulate the inflation data.

A shift in the Chinese lifestyle over the past couple of decades has changed Chinese consumption and spending habits. For example, as countries progress from developing to developed stages of economy and incomes increase, health care and entertainment generally make up a higher fraction of consumption.

The problem is particularly serious and sensitive in China because of the fast pace of Chinese economic growth and the nature of its transitioning economy. For example, Chinese residents did not have to pay for their health care, housing expenses, or retirement some thirty years ago. Now, every household must fend for itself to cover these expenses. Not surprisingly, the consumer's cost of living has changed accordingly. If the methodology of compiling the CPI does not change to reflect such shifts in consumer behavior, the CPI may not be as useful in guiding the decisions of government officials.

Therefore, it is imperative that the Chinese authorities adjust their handling of the CPI data. Not only should the Bureau of Statistics provide transparent, accurate, and consistent statistics and methodologies, it should keep modifying the way statistics are compiled to ensure that Chinese statistics reflect the fast pace of development in the Chinese economy and society.

Air Pollution

A serious problem for Chinese residents in the past few years has been air pollution. Air pollution is probably the most recognized among all forms of pollution because it is the most visible. However, pollution in other areas, such as water pollution and land fill pollution, has also become serious and similarly worrisome.

The World Bank published a report in collaboration with China's national environmental agency in 2007, stating that "…outdoor air pollution was already causing 350,000 to 400,000 premature deaths a year. Indoor pollution contributed to the deaths of an additional 300,000 people, while 60,000 died from diarrhea, bladder and stomach cancer and other diseases that can be caused by water-borne pollution."[4]

World Bank officials expressed concern with the Chinese statistics when "China's environmental agency insisted that the health statistics be removed from the published version of the report, citing the possible impact on 'social stability'."[5]

Unfortunately, the pollution problem has worsened ever since. Hospitals in Harbin, a major city in the Northeast of China, reported a 30 percent increase in patients with respiratory problems after air pollution spiked in the city. Lung cancer rates in China have climbed by 465 percent over the past three decades, despite there being no significant increase in smoking rates.

Scientists say the pollution in northern cities is so severe that 500 million people's lives will be shortened by an average of 5.5 years.[6] On October 21, 2013, record smog closed the Harbin Airport along with all schools in the area.[7] According to some, polluting smog from mainland China reaches as far as California during heavily polluted periods.[8]

Why is China's pollution so bad? Of course, the red-hot economic development stimulates the use of fossil fuels. Instead of a country that mainly rode bicycles some thirty years ago, China now has a middle class that owns more than 120 million cars and another 120 million motor vehicles of other kinds. In addition to auto emissions, coal is a major contributor to air pollution, with China burning almost as much coal as the rest of the world combined. The air quality in Northern Chinese cities always reaches its worst level during winter and spring when the coal-fired collective heating systems are put to work.

However, a more fundamental problem is how pollution became so bad without people noticing. Ironically, according to Chinese national and local environment protection agency statistics, the Chinese environment has been improving consistently over the past decade. For example, in the cities of ShiJiaZhuang and Xingtai, two of the cities with the worst air pollution in the heavily polluted Hebei province,[9, 10] local authorities have reported improvement in air quality in 2009 and 2011, respectively.

So what is the catch? It goes back to how air quality is being monitored and classified. Mr. Zhong Nanshan, the ex-president of the China Medical Association, pointed out in 2012 that pollution-induced lung cancer and cardiovascular disease were increasing and could be the biggest threat to Chinese health. Zhong demanded better transparency with the air pollution data, questioning official data stating that air pollution was decreasing.

Until recently, the governmental air quality index did not include ozone and PM2.5, despite the fact that they are the most dangerous to human health.[11] This accounts for the consistent discrepancy between the official Beijing data and data recorded by the U.S. Embassy in Beijing. On January 12, 2013, the official data in Beijing showed an average figure over 300 during some of the bad days (the bigger the reading, the worse the air quality), whereas the U.S. Embassy recorded readings of up to 800,[12, 13] levels that are more than 50 times the recommended daily level set by the World Health Organization.[14,15]

Controversy intensified when the U.S. Embassy asserted that Beijing's air was "very unhealthy" on June 5, 2012, with readings of 199 micrograms of particulate matter. In contrast, readings from the Beijing Municipal Environmental Protection Bureau declared Beijing air as "good;" its data showed levels between 51 and 79 micrograms for the corresponding period.[16]

Following such strongly divergent data, Chinese authorities went as far as to ask foreign consulates in Beijing to stop publishing "inaccurate and unlawful" figures and blocked internet access to the embassy website that publishes its version of the air quality readings.[17]

Local government officials also claimed that it was "not scientific to evaluate the air quality of an area with results gathered from just only one point inside that area," and asserted that official daily average PM2.5 figures for Beijing and Shanghai were "almost the same with the results published by foreign embassies and consulates."[18]

Despite such resistance, Chinese residents' first-hand experience with poor air quality is so strong that the government decided to follow the international standard and adopt stricter air pollution monitoring of ozone and PM2.5 in 2012. The implementation of the new measure will take some time, and by the end of 2015, China will publish a new air quality index with all but the smallest cities included.

State media acknowledged the role of environmental campaigners in causing this change. On one blog, more than a million positive comments were posted in less than 24 hours following the government's pledge to improve air quality, although some wondered if the standards would be effectively enforced.[19,20]

Looking at this, a perfect opportunity arises to experience how statistics can deviate from the real life experiences of millions of people in China. If air quality, probably one of the most visible aspects of life, may be measured so differently by different methodologies and different authorities, what about other statistics for factors that cannot be directly seen and felt? If the very basic statistics cannot provide an accurate and impartial basis for decision making, how can one be confident about more complex and important decision-making based on similarly unreliable data?

Housing prices

One of the most widely used housing indexes in China is the China 100 city housing index compiled by the China Index Research Academy (CIRA).[21] According to CIRA's official website, the China 100 city housing index is based on the housing projects that are currently on sale. The weighting of each project is the sales (in transaction value) of each housing project.[22]

Such an approach based on new on-sale projects has been received with questions and skepticism by scholars such as Robert Shiller and Karl Case, who were so uncomfortable with the approach that they came up with the idea of compiling a housing index based on repeated sales of existing houses/apartments. The Case-Shiller index has become one of the most widely used housing market indexes in developed countries. Shiller and Case were among the first to point out that the U.S. housing market has gone through a period of excessive pricing appreciation with potential risks of boom and eventual bust. Further, their success in prediction lends some valuable validation to the repeat sales-based housing index approach.

The authors explain that, "the repeat sales approach can avoid the problems with an ever changing sample in the index in the housing market." Alarmingly, the sample selection problem facing the original U.S. housing index approach is nothing compared to the problems in many developing countries (such as China) which have gone through drastic urbanization in the past decades that may prove mind boggling to the West.

The city of Beijing offers an excellent example. Beijing adopted a ring-road development plan. The city developed with the expansion of the ring system; the second ring was developed in the 1980s, the third ring in the early 1990s, the fourth ring in the late 1990s, the fifth ring in the 2000s, and, today, the sixth ring. The second ring is closest to city center and is 32.7 kilometers long, the third ring is 48 kilometers long, the fourth ring is 65.3 kilometers long, the fifth ring is 99 kilometers long, and the sixth ring is 192 kilometer long. With the building of the expansive ring road system, the size of urban Beijing grew.

With the expansion of the city, many people are living far from city center. About 15 years ago, when I was still a student, the area of the Asian Game Village (YaYunCun) was still considered remote; it has now become a coveted central area within the fourth ring. Similarly, the region of WangJing has developed from a remote satellite village that few people lived in 15 years ago, to an integral part of the city that now boasts over 300,000 permanent residents and is home to the Chinese headquarters of many of the world's largest Fortune 500 companies.

Compared to about 10 years ago, when most of the new housing projects were developed within the fourth ring road, most of the new projects on sale now are concentrated in areas that are outside the fifth ring road. With the fast pace in the expansion of most Chinese cities, ensuring consistency in sample composition becomes critical to generate a reliable depiction of housing market appreciation in China in the past decade.

I will illustrate the situation with some real life data.

In 2000, the new housing projects sold for 5,000 Yuan per square meter, on average, within the third ring; 3000 Yuan per square meter, on average, between the third ring and the fifth ring; and for 1000 Yuan per square meter, on average, outside the fifth ring.

In 2012, the new housing projects sold for 50,000 Yuan per square meter, on average, within the third ring; 30,000 Yuan per square meter, on average, between third ring and fifth ring; and for 10,000 Yuan per square meter, on average, outside the fifth ring.

If the geographical dispersion of the new housing projects for sale has not changed during the past 12 years, then it seems apparent that the housing prices in Beijing have increased by 900 percent. For example, assuming that among all new projects for sale, 50 percent are still located within the third ring, 40 percent are located between third ring and fifth ring, and 10 percent are located outside the fifth ring, then the average house price in Beijing in 2000 was 3,800 Yuan per square meter (5000 × 0.5 + 3000 × 0.4 + 1000 × 0.1), and the average housing price in Beijing in 2013 was 38,000 Yuan per square meter.

But the reality is that there has been some fundamental shifts in the geographical distribution of new sale projects. By the year 2012, the city of Beijing had expanded so much and the housing prices had gone up so high that most of the new sale projects were now located outside the fifth ring. As a matter of fact, among all new projects on sale in 2012, 50 percent were located outside the fifth ring, 40 percent between the fifth ring and third ring, and only 10 percent within the second ring. That is, the geographical location of the new projects for sale was reversed from what it was in 2000.

If we were to use the CIRA index methodology to calculate the housing index, the average housing price in Beijing in 2012 would be 22,000 Yuan per square meter (50000 × 0.1 + 30000 × 0.4 + 10000 × 0.5), only about one half of what it would be if there had been no change in the geographical distribution of new projects on sale.

Looking at percentages, the difference is even more striking. The method is failing to account for the change in geographical distribution, concluding that housing prices have gone up only 340 percent, even though by the repeat sale approach, housing prices have gone up 900 percent, almost three times as much.

It is worth noting that such a problem is not limited to the new house policy. Even the index for existing homes suffers from the same flaws. Again according to the official website of the CIRA, the sample used for compiling the price index for existing homes is based on "prices from 'representative' complexes with more active transactions in major areas of the city." Bigger and more remote projects grow over time (for example, the Wang Jing and Yi Zhuang areas are now two of the largest new communities in Beijing with a population of over half a million each; they are both located along the fifth ring of the city).

With more and more new projects located in more distant areas and the urban population migrating toward the close suburbs, the index of existing homes suffers from the drastic shift in sample composition with just as much bias as the index of new homes.

Such a mishandling of statistics causes the CIRA housing index to fail to capture the drastic shift in its sample composition, and consequently severely underestimates the severity of the Chinese housing boom. Thus, the methodology and resulting conclusions cause Chinese housing prices to seem at odds with the population's dissatisfaction with the cost of housing.

The misleading housing index may also explain why the price-to-rent ratio depicts a more worrisome picture for the Chinese housing market than the price-to-income ratio does. The latter takes housing prices from the understated housing index, whereas the price-to-rent ratio (rental yield) is less dependent upon sample selection. If anything, the price-to-rent ratio is indeed much higher in the neighboring areas than in the city center because of the limited consumption needs and low occupancy in more distant areas.

Since 2011, China has implemented a series of curb policies intended to bring down the raging housing prices, which have made little difference two years later. As a matter of fact, the housing market seems to have entered another bullish year since the start of 2013. To obtain a clear understanding of the housing market problem in China and launch corresponding measures to cool off the housing market, the Chinese government may want to start with the basics and get its statistics right in the first place.

Gini Coefficient

Another controversial data gauge is the Gini coefficient, named after Italian statistician and socialist Corrado Gini for his contribution in estimating social income inequality more than 100 years ago. The coefficient takes a value between 0 and 1. The closer the reading to 0, the more equal the income distribution; the opposite is true for readings closer to 1. According to international standard, a reading of a Gini co-efficient that is more than 0.40 indicates that there is substantial dispar-ity in income distribution. If the reading is more than 0.60, it indicates that the income disparity in a country is extreme.

Among major developed economies, only the United States achieves a Gini coefficient of greater than 0.4 (the after-tax Gini coefficient is ar-gued to be below 0.4 by some U.S. economists).[23] The coefficient is gen-erally smaller than 0.3 for Scandinavian countries and other developed countries with strong social welfare and taxation policies.

Following the international norm, China has been publishing its Gini coefficient statistics since the late 1970s, after the Cultural Revolution. China reported its Gini coefficient to be 0.32 in 1978, and China's Gini coefficient reached its lowest level (0.24) after the reform and opening policy was implemented.

In 2013, the China Bureau of Statistics resumed its publication of the Gini coefficient after a 10 year hiatus. According to the Bureau of Statistics, the Gini coefficient has been hovering around 0.4, before reaching its decade high of 0.49 in 2008 and gradually decreasing to 0.47 in 2012.

These data have attracted considerable controversy because the public feels that the income inequality problem has become worse since 2009. Adding some credence to the public's feelings, the China Southwest University of Finance and Economics (SWUFE) published its own version of the Gini coefficient based on its survey of Chinese household income and wealth in 2010.

According to the SWUFE reports, China's Gini coefficient in 2010 was 0.61, much higher than the 0.48 reported by the Bureau of Statistics. Further, a reading of 0.61 ranks China highest among all countries except Columbia, making China the country of greatest in-come inequality among all countries in the entire world.

Of course, these two sets of data are based on different samples, and there are differences in each survey's methodologies, which may be responsible for a reasonable portion of the differences between these two reports. Even Mr. Ma Jiantang, the chief of the Bureau of Statistics, acknowledges that household income is such a sensitive topic in China that the official surveyor may have trouble in obtaining accurate information. This problem is particularly severe, according to him, among the high-income stratus, which would choose not to participate in the survey or would underreport their income. Consequently, Mr. Ma himself admits that the official Gini coefficient may understate the income inequality problem in China these days.

The SWUFE study, explicitly accounting for the challenge in surveying the higher-income stratus, intentionally oversampled higher-income households from higher-income regions to address the potential bias in not being able to reach enough high-income subjects.

Therefore, it is probably safe to say that there are respective limitations to each study and approach. Nevertheless, the SWUFE reports seem to reflect what many people in China have felt in the past few years: the problem of income inequality became far more serious after the 2008 global financial crises and the ensuing 4 trillion Yuan stimulus package.

An unprecedentedly large amount of stimulus and credit supply could create considerable opportunities and wealth for those who benefit from such plans, but the rest of the country has to live with the depressed interest rate and see their wealth grow slower.

No matter which eventually proves to be closer to reality, the two approaches seem to agree with each other in that the income inequality problem in China has become a serious issue and must be taken seriously. Even the official study acknowledges that there is an income inequality problem and that a large fraction of government officials obtain "grey income," which not only far exceeds their official income, but also shifts their mentality and incentives towards certain government policy making.

China's Export Data in Doubt

Another example of questionable statistics is the Chinese trade data for April 2013. For that month, Chinese exports increased by

14.7 percent, far better than the previous month, and the 9.2 percent consensus reached by foreign investment bank analysts' forecasts. On the other hand, such data came in at the same time with considerable decrease in exports to Taiwan and Korea, two of China's major trade partners. It is particularly surprising that the Chinese export figures do not seem to match the import data reported by its partners.

Another issue that has been heatedly debated by economists is the sharp increase in China's exports to Hong Kong during the same month. The trade between the Chinese mainland and Hong Kong jumped by 55 percent in the month of April 2013, whereas the trade between China and the rest of the world increased by a starkly lower 12 percent. Hong Kong is so important in April's trade data that if one takes Hong Kong out of the picture, China would have sustained a $20 billion trade deficit, instead of the currently reported surplus of $18.2 billion.

Granted that Hong Kong has always been an important trade partner to mainland China, and there is always a stable relationship between the mainland's exports to and imports from Hong Kong, the discrepancy in this month's export and import data raised further doubt about the authenticity of the country's exports to its Hong Kong SAR and further concerns about potential capital influx under the camouflage of trade surplus.

The explanation offered by Chinese customs is that given a large fraction of Chinese exports to Hong Kong are trans-shipments, with the final destination undetermined, a large fraction of the export trade is being classified as exports to Hong Kong. However, this explanation has not been very convincing to the international community, especially given that the practice of trans-shipment has been a major contributor to China mainland's exports to Hong Kong for a long time. With no particular shift in the gauge of the statistics, it should not drive the sharp increase in April 2013.

A more plausible explanation may be that, given monetary easing by leading economies and the relatively high interest rate and economic growth of mainland China, many enterprises and investment companies use the differentials in interest rates in mainland China and Hong Kong to arbitrage. Because the offshore RMB market in Hong Kong offers much lower savings and loan interest rates, many enterprises borrow from the low-interest yielding offshore market and use trade to transfer the money into mainland China and earn higher yield within China's market.

Depending on varying expectations of the pace of RMB appreciation, many companies even use more advanced techniques of (mis)matching the maturity of their payables and receivables to further enhance their arbitrage returns. Such RMB interest rate arbitrage has proven to be so lucrative lately that it has drastically pushed up China's exports to Hong Kong, in light of an otherwise lackluster month in trade data.

It is worth noting that this is not the first time that Chinese economic data has been doubted. Back in the late 1990s, under the plan to ensure an 8 percent economic growth, the Chinese government published economic growth data that did not match its energy consumption in the same period, even though the two figures typically move hand in hand.

To make things even more complex, such inconsistency in the official statistics is also questioned by China's own government officials and citizens. For example, many government officials suspect that the contribution of investments to Chinese economic growth has been historically overestimated, whereas labor's contribution to Chinese economic growth has been historically underestimated at the same time. In addition, such seemingly mechanical factors, such as the leap year and the timing of Chinese New Year, have always been used as excuses for abnormal statistical data, which should have been well addressed by now to make the data historically comparable and easy to interpret when available.

Lightning strikes twice?

So far we have seen the discrepancies in the reporting of national and local economic growth, the gap between China's exports to Hong Kong and its exports to the rest of Asia in the spring of 2014, the drastic difference between the air quality readings of the official Beijing government data and those published by the U.S. Embassy in Beijing, and the stark contrast between residents' feelings about consumer and housing prices and the official data.

All these contrasts seem to point in one direction: the statistics consistently work in favor of government officials' objectives. When economic growth needs to be faster, GDP growth will increase; when the air pollution level needs be lower, the official statistics will show it lower; when Chinese exports need a rebound, the statistics will graciously present such a rebound.

All these examples question the authenticity and reliability of Chinese statistics and how much the personal interests of government officials are involved. Workers wish to get the best possible treatment with the least possible effort. This is a very basic assumption about human decision-making. Therefore, it is quite plausible that officials might pull a few strings to make their performance look better, at least better than the reality.

Such a phenomenon, loosely termed an *agency problem* in economics, is prevalent in all aspects of economies and around the entire world. However, what sets China apart is that the mandates to grow the economy as fast as possible are issued by the central government, not local residents or constituencies.

Given the hierarchal nature of Chinese government operations, a government official does not expect to serve in the same post for more than ten years. As a matter of fact, many believe one key strategy for progressing quickly in the Chinese bureaucratic system is to switch posts as often as one can. A direct result of this job promotion mechanism is short-termism. Each government official is concerned primarily with the short-term economic performance of his county or his city. When it comes down to performance evaluation, officials will try to use the statistics to give themselves a boost, if possible.

In the end, the statistics problem traces its roots back to the objective of the government. If the central government values the speed of economic growth and uses it as the most important criterion for official evaluation and promotion, it should come as no surprise that officials in lower-level government will react to the incentive system and focus on boosting economic growth speed, as measured by official statistics.

Even some famous economists admit that "economists have become increasingly interested in problems that are not necessarily important, but technically easier to measure."[24] GDP growth and fiscal income growth are far easier to measure than more subjective benchmarks such as resident satisfaction and resident happiness.

Unfortunately, without a clear and sound objective, decisions and actions will go awry. This can, in part, explain the local government debt and local government financing vehicle problems that have all of sudden started plaguing the Chinese economy. To achieve faster economic growth, local officials are motivated to borrow and invest as much as they can in order to stimulate local economic growth. Of course, it is not in the official's interest to fully disclose the cost and risk of such borrowing, which might hurt his ability to borrow more the next year.

Exactly because nobody talks about what everybody else has been doing, the risk has been accumulating without being kept in check. In some sense, this is a bit like earnings management by corporate CEOs. Some corporate executives take on excessive borrowing or excessively risky investment projects to push up short-term stock performance and their own compensation through bonuses and stock options, at the expense of jeopardizing the company's financial health and long-term growth opportunities.

The officials' situation can also explain why environmental protection has been neglected for so long in China. On one hand, environmental protection requires governmental expenditure but cannot bring any short-term help to economic growth. If anything, protecting the environment means shutting down some unregulated coal mines, steel mills, and manufacturers, and reducing the purchase and use of automobiles, which would all lead to a setback in local economic growth.

On the other hand, environmental protection is only vaguely mentioned in the criteria by which officials are assessed and lacks any measurable benchmarks. Accordingly, few local officials take pains to protect the environment and, instead, focus their attention exclusively on economic growth.

Even though Chinese statistics law mandates that citizens have to report independent and reliable statistical data, it is conceivable that the career considerations of government officials, especially local government officials, motivate them to report biased data.

Technical difficulties certainly exist, but they are not so cumbersome that they could not be overcome by the second largest economy in the entire world. What has to be reformed is monitoring of the accuracy of statistical data and the consequences of not reporting true data.

To propel such reforms, the government has to publish and disclose more details on key steps in compiling official statistics, such as the source of data, survey methods, and sample choices. Like many other aspects of the economy, this is nothing new. As long as more details are disclosed, the public will naturally and gradually become more confident and trustful of the official statistics.

The "unknown" unknown

Statistics serve as the foundation for accurate and reliable decision-making. This is the case not only for China, but for every other country.

Some feel that an unreliable housing price index led U.S. policy-makers to draw unreliable conclusions about the U.S. housing market before the collapse that directly led to the 2007–2008 global financial crises.[25]

Another important example of poor information disclosure is the sovereign debt problem of Greece. Reports show that part of the reason why the European Union and international investor community failed to foresee the breakout of the Greek debt crisis is that, with the help of some money-hungry investment banks that were motivated to issue more bonds on behalf of the Greek government,[26] the Greek government hid many of its debts under other categories that would not be easily identified as "sovereign debt." As a result, the Greek government balance sheet ballooned and deteriorated, with the European Union not being aware of any of it. In some senses, misleading statistics can cause as many, if not even more, problems among emerging economies with slower transition in the government command chain, and less efficient execution style in public administration.

The problem becomes more serious when poor statistics are not simply a result of poor scientific training or chancy sampling, but instead are deliberately intended to skew the statistics so that certain government officials may benefit from it, either through promotion, appropriation, or any other self-serving purposes.

One could argue that part of the reason behind such unreliable statistics is the lack of experience or scientific guidance from leading academics. However, China is a country that does not lag in brain power, especially in the field of statistics. If one were to browse the list of editors at internationally leading statistical journals such as the *JASA* or *Biometrica*, the Chinese seem to dominate the field. Even if there is indeed a lack of competent statisticians domestically, the problem could be easily overcome by collaborating with international experts.

The real worry is the effect that the GDP tournament incentive system can have on all levels of government official. The Chinese central government has listed economic growth among its top priorities in the past decades.[27] Statistics is a science discipline, and also a very important tool for policy making. Since the enactment of the statistics law, China has come a long way in making more data available to the rest of the world in a more reliable way. While China celebrates such progress, it should also heed some of the new challenges that progress brings.

Statistics are merely numbers, but they are numbers of great importance. In addition to doubling its capita within a decade and gaining influence in the global community, China also has to gain the trust and confidence of its own citizens and the global community. Although they are only one facet effecting the fast changes going on in China, statistics may be pivotal in China's reform efforts.

Notes

1. http://money.163.com/13/071%1/93CQO7NN00253B0H.html
2. http://business.sohu.com/20140512/n399448351.shtml
3. http://www.forbes.com/sites/jackperkowski/2011/07/14/pork-prices-and-inflation/
4. http://www.nytimes.com/2007/08/26/world/asia/26china.html?pagewanted=all&_r=0
5. http://news.bbc.co.uk/2/hi/asia-pacific/6265098.stm
6. http://theweek.com/article/index/252440/chinas-massive-pollution-problem#axzz33iIRuwP9
7. http://www.huffingtonpost.co.uk/2013/10/23/smog-cloaks-chinese-harbin-closing-schoolsairports-pictures_n_4149331.html
8. http://www.theguardian.com/world/2013/feb/16/chinese-struggle-through-airpocalypse-smog?INTCMP=SRCH
9. http://www.xtnews.gov.cn/node3/xinwen/xtxw/userobject1ai28962.html
10. http://www.xinhuanet.com/chinanews/2011-06/04/content_22936727.htm
11. http://www.euronews.com/2013/10/21/china-record-smog-levels-shut-down-city-of-harbin/
12. http://www.huffingtonpost.com/2013/01/12/air-pollution-in-beijing-china_n_2461473.html
13. http://www.huffingtonpost.com/2013/01/12/air-pollution-in-beijing-china_n_2461473.html
14. http://www.euronews.com/2013/10/21/china-record-smog-levels-shut-down-city-of-harbin/
15. www.airnow.gov
16. http://en.wikipedia.org/wiki/Pollution_in_China#cite_note-25
17. http://en.wikipedia.org/wiki/Pollution_in_China
18. http://news.xinhuanet.com/english/china/2012-06/05/c_131633044.htm
19. http://www.theguardian.com/world/2012/mar/01/china-air-pollution-tough-rules
20. http://en.wikipedia.org/wiki/Pollution_in_China
21. http://industry.fang.com/
22. http://industry.fang.com/index/HundredCityPriceIndex.aspx
23. http://groundup.org.za/article/do-wage-increases-lead-greater-inequality_1998

24. http://www.nobelprize.org/nobel_prizes/economic-sciences/laureates/1974/hayek-lecture.html

25. Burry, Michael, I Saw the Crisis Coming, Why Didn't the Fed? New York Times, April 3, 2010.

26. http://www.nytimes.com/201%2/14/business/global/14debt.html?pagewanted=all&_r=0 Wall St. Helped to Mask Debt Fueling Europe's Crises

27. http://finance.people.com.cn/n/2013/1224/c1004-23927225.html

1 1

Guaranteed to Fail? International Lessons on Implicit Guarantees

A person often meets his destiny on the road he took to avoid it.
—Jean de la Fontaine

ESPITE IMPLICIT GUARANTEE'S TREMENDOUS CONTRIBUTIONS to the Chinese economy and financial system, it is important to point out that China is neither the inventor nor the forerunner of the practice of implicit guarantee. As a matter of fact, governments and corporations in the West have been widely using government sponsorship and guarantees to solve their own share of the problem, with varied success and mixed outcomes.

A traditional and common way that a government provides guarantees to private enterprises in the West is through Government Sponsored Enterprises (GSEs). There are three types of GSEs in the United States: GSEs related to housing, to veterans services, and to farming. The U.S. Congress created the first GSE, the Farm Credit System, in 1916, followed by the Federal Home Loan Banks (GSEs in the home finance segment of the economy) in 1932, and Sallie Mae (the GSE targeted at education) in 1972.[1]

According to Lemke, Lins and Picard (2013), "The residential mortgage borrowing segment is by far the largest of the borrowing segments in which the GSEs operate. GSEs hold or pool approximately $5 trillion worth of mortgages. ... These GSEs are financial services corporations created by U.S. Congress in order to facilitate the flow of credit into certain housing markets while reducing the cost of that same credit. ... Among them, the two most widely known examples of mortgage GSEs are Fannie Mae and Freddie Mac—along with their younger sibling Ginnie Mae. ... In addition, a separate group of 12 Federal Home Loan Banks work as a mortgage GSE to facilitate lending related to the housing market."[2]

Fannie Mae (the Federal National Mortgage Association) and Freddie Mac (the Federal Home Loan Mortgage Corporation) can date their roots back to the 1929 Great Depression. Congress established GSEs aimed at improving the efficiency of capital markets and overcoming market imperfections. By providing some form of explicit and implicit guarantees, the government provides the lenders and investors in mortgage-related securities a put option, which gives holders of mortgage-related securities in the secondary market a guarantee to limit their losses.

Presently, mortgage GSEs primarily serve as financial intermediaries to help lenders and borrowers in the housing sector. Fannie Mae and Freddie Mac, the two most prominent GSEs, purchase mortgages and package them into mortgage-backed securities (MBS), reselling them to global investors. The key ingredient in this repackaging is that the GSE securities now carry the financial backing of, and credit enhancement from, Fannie Mae or Freddie Mac, which themselves are implicitly backed by the U.S. government and treasuries. These guarantees make GSE MBSs particularly attractive to investors concerned with risks and still looking for higher returns.

In addition, the GSEs created a secondary market in loans through guarantees, bonding, and securitization, which allowed primary market debt issuers to overcome risks associated with individual loans and increase loan issuance. The GSEs also provide standardized instruments (securitized securities) for investors.

Lobbyists in favor Fannie and Freddie argue that without the GSEs, there would not be such an active secondary market for MBSs, which, they argue, is integral to the boom in the U.S. real estate market. However, some international comparisons carried out by Professor Dwight Jaffe at the University of California, Berkeley question this argument. According to Professor Jaffe, many European countries with higher home ownership rates than the United States do not really have something like the GSEs on the secondary mortgage market.[3]

Indeed, one main strand of criticism of Fannie and Freddie is that, even before their collapse during the 2007–2009 global financial crisis, they had not done a satisfactory job in making housing affordable to the particular segment of the community who could not afford homeownership otherwise. According to the Congressional Budget Office, one problem facing the GSEs is their "limited effects on affordable housing."[4]

The bigger and more fundamental problem with the GSEs is the issue of implicit guarantee. On the surface, the GSEs are intermediaries in which the government does not take a stake or provide a guarantee for. Bipartisan senators and government officials uniformly deny the existence of a guarantee. Democratic Congressman Barney Frank declared in 2003, "There is no guarantee. There's no explicit guarantee. There's no implicit guarantee. There's no wink-and-nod guarantee. Invest and you're on your own. Nobody who invests in them should come looking to me for a nickel. Nor anyone else in the federal government."[5]

Consistently, this is what Fannie and Freddie have been doing to the public. They would "adamantly lash back at anybody who argued that there was in fact a government subsidy," according to *New York Times* columnist Joe Nocera.[6] However, the GSEs would be speaking a very different language when talking to another smaller—but just as powerful—group of people: the investors in the fixed-income market.

According to Scott Simon at PIMCO, the world's largest bond manager and one of the biggest buyers of Fannie and Freddie securities, "Fannie and Freddie in meetings with investors, whether it was us or anybody else, essentially just would sort of laugh and say, 'Well, you know the government will stand behind us.'"[7]

Truer Words Were Never Secretly Spoken

With this implicit guarantee, or implicit support (as rating agencies would like to put it), these mortgage GSEs enjoy a unique competitive advantage over their competitors, mostly other financial institutions involved in the real estate sector. On one hand, the implicit guarantee provided by the government allows Fannie and Freddie to venture into areas that other companies cannot or are not brave enough to venture.

On the other hand, government-backing enables Fannie and Freddie to issue debt at interest rates far lower than their competitors. With this government-backing, Fannie and Freddie quickly became some of the most profitable companies listed in the U.S. stock market.[8]

No Actual Guarantees, and Yes, Actual Federal Subsidies

Freddie Mac states in its securities prospectus that, "Securities, including any interest, are not guaranteed by, and are not debts or obligations of, the United States or any agency or instrumentality of the United States other than Freddie Mac."[9] The Freddie Mac and Freddie Mac securities are not funded or protected by the U.S. government. Freddie Mac securities carry no government guarantee that they will be repaid. This is explicitly stated in the law that authorizes GSEs, on the securities themselves, and in public communications issued by Freddie Mac.

Indeed, Freddie Mac receives no direct federal government aid. However, the investors in corporations and the securities that Freddie Mac issues believe that the securities benefit from government subsidies and are backed by some kind of *implied* federal guarantee, especially during catastrophic market roils. The Congressional Budget Office writes, "There have been no federal appropriations for cash payments or guarantee subsidies. But in the place of federal funds, the government provides considerable unpriced benefits to the enterprises."[10]

The then-director of the Congressional Budget Office, Dan L. Crippen, testified before Congress in 2001 that the "debt and mortgage-backed securities of GSEs are more valuable to investors than similar private securities because of the perception of a government guarantee."[11] "Government-sponsored enterprises are costly to the government and taxpayers. The benefit is currently worth $6.5 billion annually."[12]

2008 Global Financial Crisis

As listed companies, Fannie and Freddie are also motivated and disciplined by their shareholders and Wall Street. During the first few years of the 2000s, Fannie Mae and Freddie Mac were surprised by the sudden rise of subprime lenders increasing market shares. The profit-maximizing side of the GSE's business model required Fannie and Freddie to respond aggressively. As a result, Fannie and Freddie furthered the boundary between their social responsibility and business mandate by expanding into the subprime mortgage market, which sealed their fate.

The implicit government guarantee behind Fannie and Freddie became truly important and a self-fulfilling prophecy when Fannie and Freddie used market participants' belief that these GSEs were "too big to fail" to actually become too big to fail, by taking far greater risks than they could handle.

With the implicit guarantee, Fannie and Freddie had grown immensely by issuing and trading real estate-related securities. When the U.S. housing market crumbled in 2007, dropping housing prices, the lack of a liquid housing market started hurting not only the balance sheet but also Fannie and Freddie's cash flow.

At the peak of the financial crisis in 2008, Fannie and Freddie had finally managed to get what they had promised, and they proved what the market believed and predicted for decades: that they lived on the bloodline of the U.S. government's implicit guarantee and would be bailed out in case of emergency and crisis.

As Hank Paulson, then Secretary of the Treasury, told Congress during hearings about the government's bailout plan, "You're angry and I'm angry that taxpayers are on the hook. But guess what: They are already on the hook for the system. We all let it happen."[13] Echoing Mr. Paulson, Professor Vernon L. Smith, the 2002 Nobel Laureate in economics, has also called Fannie Mae and Freddie Mac "implicitly tax-payer-backed agencies," with "the implicit government guarantee" of FHLMC and FNMA, and the U.S. federal government.[14]

Some observers argue that there is a similar pattern when mortgage securitization was tried several times in the past in the United States. It now seems to be a familiar recurring story that "during the credit boom, underwriting standards are violated and guarantees are inadequately funded; subsequently, defaults increase and investors in mortgage-backed securities attempt to dump their investments" when the market ends up with a credit bust.[15] If anything, the reported rank cronyism, accounting fraud, and manipulations of share prices and the financial market made the collapse of Fannie Mae and Freddie Mac particularly painful and provoked another wave of public outcry and rage.[16]

The Value of Government Guarantees

Mr. Jeffrey Lacker, Chairman of the Richmond Federal Reserve, testified at the House Judiciary Committee's hearings that "the bailout of large financial institutions by the United States and other Western governments, instead of letting such financial institutions terminate in bankruptcy, created severe distortions in risk taking and incentives in the financial system."[17]

Because executives and creditors of such large financial institutions are aware that the government will not let them fall, the practice of bailout almost certainly provides stronger incentives for financial institutions and their creditors to take more-than-appropriate risks.

To make things even worse, under the mentality of providing stability to the financial system, the government will be more likely to step in and bail out financial institutions now that financial institutions have taken even more risks than they did before the last crisis. Independent studies on the U.S. and international financial systems by the National Bureau of Economic Research (NBER) and International Monetary Fund (IMF) confirm Lacker's argument and find that more government support was associated with more risk taking by banks, especially during the financial crisis in the first decade of 2000s.[18, 19]

According to a study by the Richmond Federal Reserve, the implicit guarantee to all liabilities in the U.S. financial system added up to about $3.4 trillion in 1999 (18 percent of all liabilities in the U.S. financial system and 27.6 percent of the U.S. GDP), when it first started estimating such figures. The most up-to-date estimates using the 2011 data reveals that among the total of $44.5 trillion liabilities in the U.S. financial system, a stunning $14.83 trillion (33.4 percent) carried implicit guarantees, or about 97 percent of the U.S. GDP in that year.[20]

The size of the implicit guarantee is so big that it is even greater than the better known explicit guarantees from the Federal Deposit Insurance Corporations (FDIC) ($10.6 trillion or 28.3 percent of all liabilities) to bank deposits. Unlike the FDIC, Fannie Mae and Freddie Mac are not agencies strictly created by Congress. Also different from FDIC insurance, which charges banks premiums commensurate with their respective default risks, the implicit guarantees are largely issued for free to their beneficiary.[21]

Nobel Prize-winning economist Robert Merton showed in a couple of studies that government guarantees during the course of the 2007–2008 global financial crisis were responsible for distorting the relative risks between stocks and bonds, as manifested by a lowered default boundary, or, under the pre-crisis regime, in higher stock-implied credit spreads. These patterns are particularly striking for larger firms, bonds with higher potential default correlations, and bonds with higher ratings, all corroborating that the "too-big-to-fail" rationale leads the market to misprice default risks, especially for the select group of systematically important financial institutions.[22]

With such buffering in their credit worthiness, firms that are considered too big to fail (TBTF) benefit from their access to cheaper funding during crises. Using a sample of 74 U.S. financial institutions, Merton estimated that fixed-rate short-term funding helped transfer up to $365 billion of wealth from shareholders to bond investors due to such financial institutions' TBTF status.[23]

In addition to the TBTF status, studies have shown that the guarantee of the Federal National Mortgage Association (FNMA), another form of implicit government guarantee, also provides GSEs and some financial institutions with peace of mind that the government would bail them out of trouble, and incentivizes them to take greater risks.[24]

According to Viral Acharya, a finance professor at New York University, and his co-authors, large financial institutions enjoyed an average advantage of a lower borrowing cost of 28 basis points annually during the 1990–2010 period. Of course, this implicit guarantee proved to be most valuable around the financial crisis. The authors estimated that the cost advantage peaked in 2009 at over 120 basis points, or a subsidy of over a $100 billion wealth transfer from the state to the investors in large financial institutions' bonds and stocks.[25]

Similarly, the value of the implicit guarantee provided by European governments to their respective domestic institutions had also increased considerably until the 2008–2009 financial crisis, when the sovereign credit of many European countries deteriorated, indirectly cutting the value of the guarantees that they provided to their financial institutions.[26,27]

These studies are far from being alone in their conclusions.[28] Regardless of the precise estimate, the point seems rather clear: Whatever the government has tried in order to end its implicit guarantee to large financial institutions, and shift investors' expectations of such an implicit guarantee, is not working.[29]

According to Lacker, the size of implicit guarantees ballooned "through gradual accretion of precedents." After a crisis, each bailout has been followed by an even bigger one during the past decades. With the intensive merger activities in the United States and global banking sector, there are now fewer and bigger banks. At present, 12 mega banks—or 0.17 percent of all banks—control about 69 percent of the banking assets.[30] This means that the mega banks have become bigger than ever before and, consequently, it is more difficult to solve the TBTF problem than ever before.[31]

Indeed, as some scholars argue, now that there are fewer of them around, the mega banks may enjoy even stronger bargaining power with the government. Hypothetically, if the mega banks all decided to increase their risks at the same time (be it through coordination or not), the government would have to respond by providing even stronger guarantees to the entire banking sector to prevent systemic breakdown. Increasing government guarantees would, in turn, allow and encourage the banking sector to take even greater risks.

In summary, greater risks lead to larger guarantees, and larger guarantees create even greater risks, thereby creating a vicious cycle.[32]

Implicit Guarantee: Ban Against Short Selling

Of course, during the 2008–2009 global financial crisis, stock market regulators in the Unites States and many other countries around the world showed another way that governments can prevent a market meltdown and collapse of share prices of financial institutions—through a ban on short sales.

Short sales, the selling of securities that one does not at the moment own and the buying back of securities (hopefully) at a lower price, has a history as long as the financial market and dates back to the Dutch stock market in the 17th century. Over centuries, investors who engage in short selling are always discriminated against by regulators and the rest of the market. The resentment against short selling was particularly intense under the regime of Napoleon Bonaparte, when short sellers faced the possibility of a year in prison.[33]

Even with modern financial instruments and infrastructure, short sellers are still widely viewed as red herrings at best and troublemakers at worst during a financial crisis. Even investors who make correct and successful short selling bets (such as George Soros in the collapse of the Sterling and the 1997–1998 South East Asian Financial Crisis, Jim Chanos in the 1999–2001 internet bubble, and John Paulson in the 2007–2008 global financial crisis) do not receive as much and as positive reception as investors who take the more traditional buy-and-hold investment strategies (such as Warren Buffett and Peter Lynch).

Understandably, governments and regulators are concerned that short sellers spread negative news and can cause the market to drop substantially. Granted, there have been incidents in which short-term short sellers manage to drive down share prices so much that it hurts the companies and the stock market. However, there are just as many incidents in which the short sellers played the role of whistleblower to alert the market to negative outcomes and financial fraud, as was the case in the 1997–1998 South East Asian financial crisis, the 1999–2001 internet bubble, and the 2007–2008 global financial crisis.

In a study spanning more than a decade and covering more than 40 countries, my colleagues and I conducted systematic analyses of short selling practices and their impact on the financial markets around the world. We found no convincing evidence that a ban on short selling can make a stock market more stable or less likely to fall considerably. Instead, we did find that, by imposing a ban on short sales, regulators hurt investors' incentives to reveal information to the markets and hence cause the market to operate in a less efficient way.

Yet again, regulators' good intentions were met by a rational market force. A ban on short sales prevents negative information and opinions from being incorporated into the financial market. Hence, it provides another form of important implicit guarantee by a government and maybe, subconsciously, by all societies around the globe. However, implicit guarantees to prevent crashes and support the market are yet another example of how regulators' use of short-term goals to stabilize the financial system may, in the short run, create perverse incentives to market participants and eventually cause greater risks and instability in the long run.

For example, Alessandro Beber (Cass Business School) and Marco Pagano (Center for Studies in Economics and Finance) find that, even during the global 2007–2009 financial crisis, there is little evidence that the ban on short sales was effective in stabilizing stock prices. Instead, the study found clear evidence of worsening liquidity and price discovery in the stock market, which indeed hurt investors' investment process, and confidence in the market. This discovery is consistent with the famous saying of economist Frederick Hayek decades ago, that "the road to serfdom is paved with good intentions."

Easy Monetary Policy

Yet another common but less noticeable form of implicit guarantee comes in the form of easy monetary policies. As former Federal Reserve President Paul Volcker once put it, "The easiest thing for central banks is easy money."[34] As long as inflation stays within the target zone, many central bankers admit that ensuring and supporting economic growth remains another of their primary mandate. To boost economic growth and employment, many economists believe that easy policy may be at the top of central bankers' list.

For example, Alan Greenspan has been known for his friendly attitude towards economic growth and stock market performance through active monetary policy. He engineered one of the largest, and once thought to be the greatest, balancing acts of using easy monetary policy to boost the U.S. and global economy and the stock market. At the peak of his career, Alan Greenspan used his subtle adjustment of U.S. monetary policy to avert a sudden economic slowdown after the burst of the 1998 South East Asia Financial Crisis and 1998–2000 internet stock bubble and bust. For this achievement, he was once considered by many to be the maestro of monetary policy and the greatest central banker ever.[35]

His decision to keep interest rates at historically low levels for a prolonged period of time in the early 2000s was once considered to be fresh evidence that central banks can indeed use easy monetary policies to boost economic growth and do not have to face the consequences of inflation and asset bubbles. The market seemed to have proved his wisdom, until it peaked in the summer of 2007.

What has followed, however, served as a sudden wake up call to those who believed that financial innovation has fundamentally changed the return-to-risk tradeoff in monetary policies and financial markets. It turned out that the easy monetary policies in the early 2000s not only provided strong incentives to speculate on real estate and related securities in the United States and the rest of the world, but also shifted market participants' perception of risks and expected returns. By the time the housing market in the United States and many developed economies had reached the highest prices and least affordable levels in history, it became ever clearer that the easy policy in previous few years had culminated in one of the greatest bubbles in economic history.

Once again, the government's very good intention to shore up the economy and financial markets ended up inducing unexpected and undesired shifts in the market's mentality and boldness. These shifts, indeed, caused the market and economy greater damage than what the government had intended. As an old French saying goes, "One often comes across his destiny on his way to avoiding it."[36]

Corporate Implicit Guarantees in Structured Investment Vehicles (SIVs)

Governments are not the only agencies that provide valuable guarantees. Over the past couple of decades, many financial institutions, most notably banks, have been using securitization transactions to pool various forms of debt—such as mortgages, automobile loans, and consumer loans—together, and have been selling these asset pools to investors in the form of collateralized debt obligations (CDOs).

Prior to the financial crisis of 2007–2008, these asset securitizations were a large source of bank financing and profits. By the end of 2007, the outstanding securitization market was valued at $9.3 trillion, making it over twice the outstanding size of U.S. treasuries (Securities Industry and Financial Markets Association 2007).

These pools, often termed Structured Investment Vehicles (SIVs), were established so banks could distance themselves from the asset pools. In some ways, the relationship between the founding financial institutions and SIVs is similar to the relationship between governments and the founding financial institutions themselves: the financial institutions do have direct connections to the SIVs, but nevertheless they are widely expected to guarantee the SIVs' viabilities.

Investors favor these investment options for two reasons. First, they offer higher returns than plain-vanilla bank loan products. Second, investors feel, or sometimes get assured by the originating bank, that the SIVs are being implicitly protected by their founding institutions. That is, in case such SIVs fail to repay their investors, the banks behind such SIVs will foot the losses themselves and not allow SIV investors to suffer.

For the banks, an apparent advantage is that they can operate the SIVs off their balance sheets. Before the global financial crisis in 2007–2008, the securitizations behind the SIVs were often categorized as asset sales instead of bank loans. This approach gave banks not only the luxury of generating more business without conforming to the capital requirement, but also the advantage of shrinking their balance sheets and hence the reserve requirements.

Of course, the flip side of this approach is that the SIV investors would have to take responsibility for any investment losses stemming directly from the asset pool and not hold the issuing bank liable. On one hand, this isolation alleviates some risks in investing through SIVs by hedging SIV investors against credit problems of the issuing bank. On the other, the SIV investors have no legal ability to go after the bank assets if the SIV's asset pool falters and becomes distressed. If this happens, SIV debt investors face the prospect of not being paid.

Despite SIV's popularity and the attraction to both SIV investors and banks, there has been considerable debate among finance and accounting experts about whether banks should take any responsibility if SIVs malfunction, and related to that, how financial institutions should disclose the information. Because of their attraction to, and reliance on, these innovations, banks have been trying to "bribe" SIV investors by ensuring their investment returns and preventing their investment losses coming out of the banks' own pockets. After all, innovations that could conjure money out of thin air finally seemed to have become feasible through SIVs during the first half of the 2000–2009 decade.[37]

However, it was not until the market meltdown of 2008 that the risks of these innovative and mutually beneficial products were fully revealed. SIVs took a surprising and rather disturbing turn. With dropping housing prices in the United States and many other developed economies and a credit crunch in the short-term commercial paper financing market, SIVs found themselves flanked on both financing and investment fronts.

On the financing side, the extreme circumstances like the 2007–2008 credit crunch unsettled investors in the typically stable commercial paper market. SIVs, which rely completely on commercial paper for financing, couldn't roll over their previous borrowing, and were forced to sell their assets to pay off the debts. These fire sales of long-term assets could not have come at a worse time. With real estate related assets having already dropped in price, sales by SIVs further depressed the price of assets. Essentially, they shot themselves in the foot. As a result, several SIVs had fallen victim to the liquidity crunch and defaulted in August 2007.

It is worth it to point out that the sponsoring banks were still largely intact in the summer of 2007, and indeed stepped in and bailed out some of the SIVs. As a result, it is believed that even "failed" SIVs caused no losses to SIV investors.

However, things became dire in 2008 when the sponsoring financial institutions had to struggle for their own survival. With earnings dropping by more than 90 percent for many banks and financial institutions, the implicit guarantees that they provided to their SIVs became worthless. As a result, most of the SIVs were downgraded to the lowest credit ratings and eventually defaulted. On October 2, 2008, the *Financial Times* reported that Sigma Finance, the last surviving and oldest of the SIVs, had collapsed and entered liquidation.[38]

SIVs, which owed their phenomenal ascent and success to the implicit guarantees provided by their sponsoring institutions, ended up collapsing for the very same reason.

Guarantees through inflated rating agencies[39]

Another way to provide an implicit guarantee is through the ratings assigned by rating agencies. American author and columnist Thomas Friedman once said that "we live again in a two-superpower world. There is the United States and there is Moody's. The United States can destroy a country by leveling it with bombs; Moody's can destroy a country by downgrading its bonds."[40] By downgrading a country's credit rating, rating agencies can raise the difficulty and cost of a country raising capital, which in itself can cause trouble for a country's economic growth.

After the 2007–2009 global financial crisis, many companies blamed the credit rating agencies for blindly passing many highly risky assets without scrutiny and giving them the safest credit ratings, which misled investors into stupendous investment decisions that eventually cost investors billions of dollars.

In their defense, the credit rating agencies explained that the competitive landscape made it increasingly difficult to give fair ratings. The companies being rated now have the option of "shopping around" among various rating agencies. To generate business and make bonuses, rating agencies cannot help but "race towards the bottom" by lowering their rating standard in order to make a few more transactions. With loosening standards, the rating agencies give up their watchdog role and implicitly provide support to investors' decisions to invest in many highly risky assets, without the market fully understanding the mechanism behind the curtain. By inflating credit ratings and guaranteeing the safety of toxic assets, the ratings agencies hurt the entire global financial market and economy by providing some implicit guarantees to the investors' performance.

However, Standard and Poor's downgrade of the U.S treasury barely left a dent in the trading of U.S. treasuries in 2011.[41] A few weeks later, Moody's, another highly influential credit rating agency, lowered its rating of the Japanese government bond. Surprisingly, this downgrade did not have much negative impact on the trading and pricing of Japanese sovereign debt either.[42]

Of course, there may be a myriad of macro-economic and monetary reasons that the market downplayed these rather significant downgrades. Nevertheless, it is becoming clear that the rating agencies themselves no longer have as much impact on the market as they did before the global financial crisis. By offering inflated and safe grades to many toxic assets related to the global real estate market, the credit rating agency industry has lost its credibility and cachet among many investors.

Some of the credit rating agencies have tarnished the reputations that they have built over the past century and are trying to regain their reputation by making new, bold calls that may attract investors' attention and trust. Unfortunately, as expressed in the idiom "once bitten, twice shy," it may take them another century before they can regain investors' trust. That said, one cannot help but remember one famous quote from Warren Buffett, the investment oracle from Nebraska, "Never invest in what you do not understand." It turns out that as long as the rating agencies gave the green light, many investors would forget about the risks that they faced and go straight for investments with higher return. In this regard, the ratings from the rating agencies, at least those right before the 2007–2008 global financial crisis, also provided implicit guarantees to taking risks, with their own reputations as their most valuable asset.

Dodd-Frank Act Not Solving the Problem [43]

"If the crisis has taught a single lesson, it is that the too big to fail problem must be resolved," U.S. Federal Reserve Chairman Ben Bernanke declared as he testified before the U.S. Financial Crisis Inquiry Commission in 2010. Several years later, more people around the globe agree. However, when it comes down to the question of how to address the TBTF problem and whether the current reform through Volcker's Rule and the Dodd-Frank Act can fundamentally prevent the market from suffering from a similar crisis in the future, opinions diverge.

The gist of debate is something that is rather difficult to prove or refute: expectations. Some argue that Dodd-Frank should be able to shift investors' expectations that government will bail out large financial institutions in trouble, hence terminating the TBTF expectation.

This argument seems to be valid, at least on the surface. The government indeed bears no formal obligation to bail out troubled financial institutions, even without the Dodd-Frank Act. Nevertheless, the real question is whether, in the unlikely event of a real financial crisis, the government will stick to its ex-ante promises. Put differently, market participants are virtually betting on whether the government will issue a put warrant in the future, in case that it is necessary.

To that front, governments around the world have always held a "constructive ambiguity" approach[44] designed to encourage uncertainties in investors' expectations. To prevent investors from pricing implicit support, authorities almost never publicly announce their willingness to support institutions they consider too big to fail. Instead, they prefer to be ambiguous about the conditions, if any, under which they would use measures to help an ambiguous group of financial institutions. A perfect example of such ambiguity is the Federal Reserve's decision to let go of Lehman Brothers but bail out AIG right afterwards.

Global regulators have tried this before. The Comptroller of the Currency named eleven banks too big to fail back in 1984, and the

Financial Stability Board (FSB) released its list of systematically important financial institutions after the 2008–2009 global financial crisis. However, this practice has led global authorities to walk an ever thinner line between supporting large institutions and declaring that support was neither guaranteed nor to be expected.[45]

The real relevant and important question here is whether market participants actually expect the government to refrain from taking action in case of crisis and bank failures. Professor Viral Acharya and colleagues at New York University conducted interesting research to investigate this question.

The authors postulate that, because of the TBTF doctrine, large financial institutions and their investors expect the government to back the debts of these institutions if they encounter financial difficulty. Even though government authorities do not have any explicit ex-ante commitment to implicit guarantees during bad times, market participants may still believe that the large institutions and their issued securities are safer than they would otherwise be without these implicit guarantees.

Without such implicit guarantees, investors would demand higher yields on uninsured debt issued by banks with greater risk, as a fully market-determined mechanism would predict. However, an implicit government guarantee dulls this disciplining mechanism imposed by the market. If investors expect the government to shore up troubled banks, especially large troubled banks that may cause systemic turmoil, they would not demand additional premiums to take bonds issued by these otherwise risky banks.

Hence, this expectation of implicit guarantee would lead to an alternative market equilibrium in which investors demand lower returns because of their belief in large financial institutions. Large financial institutions, in turn, become not as risky as they seem because of a good possibility of government bailout during troubled times.

By comparing the prices that investors are willing to pay for debt from certain banks with or without government guarantees, Acharya and co-authors found that, whereas a positive relationship exists between risk and credit spreads for bonds issued by financial institutions of small and medium size, the risk-to-spread relationship is not present for the largest institutions. Put differently, bond premiums do not fully reflect the (largest) institutions' risk taking. Instead, financial market participants still widely believe that the government will bail out major financial institutions in an emergency, after the Dodd-Frank Act and despite all the efforts to end the too-big-to-fail problem.

The Jury is Still Out

There has been considerable debate regarding whether the government should have bailed out the troubled financial institutions during the 2007–2008 financial crisis and whether the bailout procedure was carried out in a fair and transparent way.

The argument for the bailout is, of course, that it prevented the global economy from collapsing and the financing market from freezing. The same applies to the bailout of the U.S. and global economies' through central banks' coordinated quantitative easing. Many supporters argue that it is apparent that quantitative easing and various stimulus packages engineered by different governments halted deterioration in the global financial market and averted a complete economic meltdown.

However, it is just as clear that the ensuing European Sovereign Debt crisis and the fiscal cliff in the United States were both partly triggered by the governments' attempt to bail out the distressed financial institutions and to boost the economy in the short run. In bailing out financial institutions and the economy, sovereign governments effectively served as the guarantor of last resort in response to the 2007–2008 banking crisis, which has created at least two arguably even bigger problems.

First, with sovereign governments eventually fulfilling their implicit guarantees of bank risk taking and resulting debts, they essentially confirmed market participants' expectation of the implicit guarantees behind banks. The bailout also confirmed the banks' own confidence about their too-big-to-fail status and perversely encouraged the banks to take even greater risks within whatever would become the new regulatory framework. In this regard, the short-term bailout would unavoidably lead to long-term risk explosion.

Furthermore, several governments' attempts to salvage their troubled banking sectors have led to the doubling of the trouble. With the government's credit worthiness being tarnished after the crisis, the bailout has put a fresh dent in sovereign credit, which had already been called into question during the crisis. For some time, it appeared that both sovereign creditworthiness, and that of the financial institutions, had both deteriorated.

The matter reached such a disastrous level that the European Union, the European Central Bank, and the International Monetary Fund had to be called in to help restructure what eventually turned into the Sovereign Debt Crisis in the Euro Zone. It seems that sovereign governments will have to secure their own fiscal soundness before attempting to provide guarantees, implicit or explicit, to private enterprises in their countries.[46]

Hence, any evaluation of the TARP program and the quantitative easing program may never be complete because the evaluation will eventually be made based on balancing between the short-term outcome and long-term consequences. Modern economics and finance theory has made some very clear points about this balancing. However, because few experts stand up arguing in the interest of the far future, the theory's implications seem to always focus more on solving the short-term problems.

Such a short-term mindset coincides with that of almost all governments around the world, which put greater emphasis on gaining voters' support in the next election and delivering the same sanguine promises they made in the previous election. As a result, government officials have very strong incentives to find short-term fixes to current problems and leave the more challenging reform jobs to their successors.

In this sense, China faces the same challenges as the West and many other countries. The modern political system and voting cycle have become so pragmatic that they are beginning to resemble the running of a modern company. However, true leaders of nations, just like true leaders at companies, must learn to weigh short-term and long-term objectives and understand what they are sacrificing in the long run when succumbing to short-term gains.[47] What comes around, goes around.

Notes

1. Lemke, Lins and Picard, *Mortgage-Backed Securities*, Chapters 1 and 2 (Thomson West, 2013 ed.).
2. http://ssrn.com/abstract=2126571
3. http://www.nytimes.com/packages/pdf/jaffe_report.pdf
4. http://www.cbo.gov/publication/21992
5. http://www.npr.org/sections/money/2011/04/21/134863767/self-fulfilling-prophecy-the-bailout-of-fannie-and-freddie
6. http://www.northcountrypublicradio.org/news/npr/134863767/self-fulfilling-prophecy-the-bailout-of-fannie-and-freddie
7. http://www.npr.org/blogs/money/2011/04/21/134863767/self-fulfilling-prophecy-the-bailout-of-fannie-and-freddie
8. http://www.vanityfair.com/news/2009/02/fannie-and-freddie200902
9. http://en.wikipedia.org/freddie_mac/
10. Assessing the public costs and benefits of Fannie Mae and Freddie Mac By United States. Congressional Budget Office
11. http://en.wikipedia.org/freddie_mac/
12. Assessing the public costs and benefits of Fannie Mae and Freddie Mac By United States. Congressional Budget Office
13. "When Fortune Frowned," *The Economist*, October 11, 2008, p. 7.
14. Vernon L. Smith, The Clinton Housing Bubble, Wall Street Journal, December 18, 2007, p. A20
15. http://www.federalreserve.gov/pubs/feds/2010/201046/201046pap.pdf
16. http://financialservices.house.gov/blog/?postid=343018
17. http://www.richmondfed.org/press_room/speeches/president_jeff_lacker/2014/lacker_speech_20140211.cfm

18. http://www.imf.org/external/pubs/cat/longres.aspx?sk=40501.0
19. http://papers.ssrn.com/sol3/papers.cfm?abstract_id=811004
20. http://financialservices.house.gov/uploadedfiles/hhrg-113-ba00-wstate-jlacker-20130626.pdf
21. https://www.richmondfed.org/publications/research/special_reports/safety_net/pdf/safety_net_methodology_sources.pdf
22. http://papers.ssrn.com/sol3/papers.cfm?abstract_id=2231317
23. http://www.tsesmeli.com/JMPaper_Tsesmelidakis_Nov2011_Letter.pdf
24. http://link.springer.com/article/10.1007/BF00207901
25. http://papers.ssrn.com/sol3/papers.cfm?abstract_id=1961656
26. http://www.oecd.org/finance/financial-markets/Implicit-Guarantees-for-bank-debt.pdf
27. http://www.oecd.org/finance/financial-markets/Value_Implicit_Guarantees_Bank_Debt.pdf
28. http://www.moodysanalytics.com/~/media/Insight/Quantitative-Research/Credit-Valuation/2011/2011-14-01-Quantifying-the-Value-of-Implicit-Government-Guarantees-for-Large-Financial-Institutions-20110114.ashx
29. http://www.federalreserve.gov/events/conferences/2011/rsr/papers/Acharya.pdf
30. There were over 18,000 federally insured banks in the 1980s and 6,891 in 2010s, based on FDIC data. Among the banks that no longer existed, 17 percent collapsed and the remaining 83 percent were merged or acquired.
31. http://www.zerohedge.com/contributed/2013-12-04/%E2%80%9Cimplicit%E2%80%9D-government-guarantees-bail-out-bank-creditors-tighten-their-grip-u
32. http://www.bundesbank.de/Redaktion/EN/Downloads/Publications/Discussion_Paper_1/1999/1999_06_01_dkp_06.pdf?__blob=publicationFile
33. Bris, Goetzmann, and Zhu, 2005
34. http://www.reuters.com/article/2013/05/30/us-usa-volcker-easing-idUSBRE94S14620130530
35. http://www.jimrogers.com/content/stories/articles/For_Whom_the_Closing_Bell_Tolls.html
36. http://en.wikiquote.org/wiki/Jean_de_La_Fontaine

37. http://www8.gsb.columbia.edu/ideas-at-work/publication/767/the-value-of-an-invisible-guarantee#.U5TktXaHScI
38. Gillian Tett (2 October 2008). "Sigma collapse marks end of an era", Financial Times.
39. http://www.oecd.org/finance/financial-markets/48963986.pdf
40. Friedman, Thomas, Don't Mess with Moody's, New York Times, Feb 22nd, 1995
41. http://www.npr.org/blogs/money/2011/08/06/139038518/why-s-ps-downgrade-of-the-u-s-may-not-be-as-bad-as-it-sounds
42. http://www.ft.com/intl/cms/s/%95efb70-29f3-11e0-997c-00144feab49a.html#axzz3RnHk3erv
43. https://www.google.co.jp/search?q=The+End+of+Market+Discipline%3F+Investor+Expectations+of+Implicit+State+Guarantees&ie=utf-8&oe=utf-8&aq=t&rls=org.mozilla:en-US:official&client=firefox-a&channel=sb&gfe_rd=cr&ei=NOiUU46TLKmg8wfgyYDABA
44. (Freixas 1999; Mishkin 1999)
45. http://www.telegraph.co.uk/finance/newsbysector/banksandfinance/7914890/BIS-its-the-implicit-taxpayer-guarantee-that-drives-banks-to-get-bigger.html
46. http://www.independent.co.uk/news/business/news/implicit-german-guarantee-helps-greece-raise-euro15bn-from-investors-1943990.html
47. http://www.oecd.org/finance/financial-markets/48963986.pdf

1 2

When the Tide Goes Out:
How to Reform

Only when the tide goes out do you discover who's been
swimming naked.

—WARREN BUFFETT

CHINA HAS UNDERGONE UNPRECEDENTED AND AMAZINGLY FAST
economic growth over the past three decades. With its remarkable economic growth speed, China has overtaken Great
Britain, France, Germany, and Japan to become the world's second
largest economy, all within the past decade.

Even at the slow pace of 7 to 8 percent of GDP growth projected
for the coming decade, China's economy will still be growing at twice
the speed of most developed economies. China's relatively smooth
navigation through the last financial crisis certainly has assured some
global investors of China's ability to manage its domestic and international matters.

Many people believe that China, despite the speed and consistency
of its growth, will surpass the United States as the world's largest economy sooner rather than later. Even based on a relatively conservative projection of a 7 percent annual growth rate, China's economy is forecast to
double and become bigger than the U.S. economy in the coming decade.

The basis of China's phenomenal economic growth is shrouded in controversy. Is it the strong government? The reform and openness policies? The transitional nature of the economy? Financial repression? Pent-up entrepreneurship and strong work ethic? High savings rates? High investment levels? The list of possibilities goes on and on. ...

Using the perspective of government guarantee, however, many of these possible forces fall into one of the following three categories.

Institutional and policy guarantee

Many people credit China's economic miracle to the Chinese government and its reform and openness policy. This commitment to return China and the Chinese economy back to the global community, and to the market-oriented economy that has persisted since the late 1970s, is believed to be the reason China pulled itself out of the decade-long Cultural Revolution.

Another major shift in Chinese policy orientation came in 1992, when Deng Xiaoping started a systematic shift from a central-planning economy to a market-oriented economy.

"It doesn't matter whether the cat is black or white, as long as it catches mice," he explained. By "mice," he is referring to economic growth, which is largely the same as GDP growth in practice. This shift in policy goal and evaluation set the precedent among the Chinese to grow their economy as fast as they can.

Deng also famously said, "Developing is of overriding importance," further solidifying a shift in society and government's mentality and putting GDP growth above everything else as the most important objective of the country and its government and officials.

In some sense, Chinese economic growth over the past two decades has to be attributed to an institutional and policy guarantee for fast growth. After all, when over a billion people and their government fully align their interests and set a clear goal, the force is unstoppable. With a booming economy and rising income, the Chinese people are happy, looking forward to a better tomorrow.

Maybe even more essential for fast economic growth than specific words and policies is the Chinese government's institutional and policy guarantee generated by this pro-growth mentality. From high rank government officials to rank-and-file corporate employees, almost everyone in China has taken to heart that "to get rich quick" is an important and honorable thing to do.

The encouragement and guarantee that were critical in changing Chinese ideology and priorities back in the 1990s laid the foundation and paved the way to the Chinese growth miracle in the following decades. Concurrently, the reform of state-owned enterprises unleashed a huge number of assets and cheap skilled labor into the Chinese workforce. The sudden unemployment shock to these workers not only fundamentally changed their long standing expectations about the centrally-planned economy, but also created a massive wave of motivated entrepreneurs and workers in every sector of the Chinese economy.

This may be part of the reason why the Chinese government does not want to give up the economic growth mentality and the related policy guarantees that have helped forge such an economic miracle. The Chinese government has been trying very hard to avoid the unavoidable, and maintain the dazzling economic growth speed that China has been enjoying over the past three decades.

During the 2007–2009 global financial crisis and its aftermath, the Chinese government chose not to accept sluggish economic growth and has engineered a series of historic stimulus packages. Whether the 2008–2009 economic slowdown in China was cyclical or structural, one thing has gradually become clear: China missed some precious opportunities to engage in fundamental reforms back then, which leaves the task far more daunting for its current leaders.

In addition to reinforcing the country's confidence in its guarantee for fast economic growth in the near future, the Chinese government has become ever more active in directly driving Chinese economic growth. Such governmental commitment created not only greater confidence and enthusiasm for borrowing and investment in the private sector, but also increasing infrastructure investment related to high

272 CHINA'S GUARANTEED BUBBLE

speed trains, highways, airports, ports, and pipelines, which have contributed an increasing share of Chinese economic growth over the past few years.[1]

Just as important, Chinese SOEs, many close to the brink of bankruptcy and subject to privatization and closure some twenty years ago, are now playing an increasingly important role in Chinese economic growth. Almost all 100 Chinese enterprises ranked among the Fortune 500 list of largest enterprises around the world are controlled by the Chinese government.

Behind this successful expansion in scale, however, is the concerning decline in SOEs' profitability. SOEs generated 46.5 trillion Yuan in revenues in 2013, more than doubling that of 21 trillion in 2008. However, SOEs' profits have been increasing at a much slower pace. For example, despite the fact that SOEs' revenues grew by about 20 percent in 2013, profits increased by only 5.9 percent in 2013 and 4.3 in 2014.[2,3] Some observe that if the Fortune 500 list were compiled by profit, instead of revenue, many Chinese SOEs would not be ranked, and many would not even be considered because they report huge losses rather than profits.[4,5]

Pressure comes from more than the bottom line. More Chinese denizens citizens have become concerned with the environment that they are living in, as evidenced by a few high-profile protests against construction of chemical or waste disposable projects within certain areas.[6,7] Safety issues related to food, traffic, and business operations have also attracted increasing attention as a price paid to gain higher profits or faster GDP growth.[8] Further, even in light of the ostensibly fast growth in wealth, the fast growing income disparity now causes more frustration and discontent than satisfaction and fulfillment.[9,10]

As a result of diminishing investment returns and increasing social tensions, it has become apparent and urgent for China to switch its economic growth model going forward. With its economic growth miracle over the past decades, it is about time that Chinese leaders pay more attention to other important objectives of economic development, such as environmental protection, wealth (re)distribution, education and innovation, health care and social security, and, eventually, a more sustainable growth model. Put differently, the Chinese government needs to consider tapering off some of the guarantees that it has provided to achieve the blazing fast growth speed that China has enjoyed over the past three decades.

Capital guarantee

In addition to institutional and policy guarantees used to instill drive and confidence and boost Chinese income and national wealth, the Chinese government has successfully provided two other guarantees as important and more tangible to economic growth: the capital (liquidity) guarantee and investment (risk) guarantee.

Studies have found that scarcity in capital formation has hindered economic growth in many developing economies. For example, Nobel Laureate Ronald McKinnon pointed out in his monograph, "Money and Capital in Economic Development," that capital formation is a critical, if not indispensable, element of successful economic development."[11] Following his idea, Gregory Chow from Princeton University shows that Chinese economic growth in the past half century has been heavily sensitive to domestic capital formation.[12]

Through a series of reform measures, such as the development of capital markets, the reform and restructuring of most SOEs—including some of the largest banks in the world—and monetization of resources and properties, China has engineered an unprecedented stage of the fastest capital formation in human economic history.

As a matter of fact, as pointed out earlier in the book, many experts believe that the Chinese economic growth miracle has benefitted largely from continuously increasing input of two important elements of economic growth: labor and capital. Unfortunately, China's labor productivity has not grown by as much, partly explaining the current challenges facing the Chinese economy. With labor costs no longer cheap by many other developing countries' standards, and with the population aging quickly, China has started losing its edge with labor input and therefore has to rely more on capital formation.

Consequently, capital formation has to step up and take on an increasing role in driving the economy. Needless to say, loose monetary policy and aggressive credit expansion created much-needed liquidity at the early stages of Chinese economic growth. However, fast capital formation, which faced less direct international competition than labor input, has its own risks and limitations.

Warren Buffett once said, "Only when the tide goes out do you discover who's been swimming naked." The liquidity and available capital within a country or a market can be thought of as the "tide" in Buffett's quote. Like the saying goes, "rising tide lifts all boats," and it can sometimes be difficult to discern whether it is the tide that is rising or the boat. Fast growing capital formation can help speed up economic growth, but can also help cover many serious problems under its currents.

Before the 2007–2009 global financial crisis, the excessive liquidity around the world had turned everyone (at least everyone with a strong enough risk appetite) into investment gurus. However, it did not take long before the "day of reckoning" came. Many once highly successful companies and investors were found to have been swimming naked all along in the global rising tide of liquidity.

Similar experiences may be taking place in China right now. China has unleashed an unprecedented amount of liquidity over the past decade. First, due to its increasing trade surplus, China has accumulated an unparalleled amount of foreign currencies denominated in the U.S. dollar. This is apparent in the staggeringly large amount of foreign reserve China has been accumulating over the past decade. China' foreign reserve shot from $200 billion in 2001, to $4.5 trillion in 2013, far larger than the size of Japan's foreign reserve ($1.23 trillion), second largest in the world.[13, 14]

Because China has strict regulations over capital flow, the Chinese central bank, the PBoC, and the State Administration of Foreign

Exchange (SAFE) require mandatory conversion of foreign currencies into CNY, resulting in a surplus in Yuan supply, a practice termed *sterilization* in international finance. As such, the central bank has had to unleash RMB Yuan in the amount of $4.5 trillion (USD) (about 25 trillion Yuan based on varying foreign exchange rates between the Yuan and foreign currencies) into the Chinese economy during the same period.

In addition, after a few cyclical slowdowns in the Chinese economy, China has launched several rounds of active monetary and fiscal stimulus packages. In particular, China implemented a tremendous 4 trillion Yuan stimulus package to counter the global slowdown after the 2008 market meltdown, which many observers estimated to have resulted in over 20 trillion Yuan of additional liquidity injected into the Chinese economy.

Banks, especially some of the largest Chinese banks that are state-owned enterprises, have been very instrumental in expanding credit supplies. Several times in recent Chinese history, even without major shifts in Chinese monetary policies, Chinese banks were instructed to create credit supply to boost economic growth, under explicit guidance from government regulators such as the PBoC and CBRC.

As a result, the money supply in China has increased from a little over 10 trillion Yuan in 2000 to over 120 trillion Yuan in 2013, with a pace of almost 30 percent annual growth per year in over a decade. If one were to use a wider gauge of total societal financing, the amount of created capital increased even more in the same period.[15]

Again, because of the capital flow control, these Yuan were confined to the Chinese domestic economy. There were no other outlets for this liquidity to go to, other than the now highly controversial real estate and stock market investment channels. Furthermore, excessive liquidity has created bubble-and-burst-like speculations in many areas of the Chinese economy, such as in art, furniture, stamps, jade stones, specialty teas and liquors, and even perishables such as garlic, ginger, green peas![16]

Similar to institutional and policy guarantees, the capital guarantee that used to be critical in jumpstarting the Chinese economy is about to reach its bottleneck and may indeed have to be reined back before bigger problems arise in asset prices and bubbles.

Investment guarantee

Behavioral sciences have long found that people tend to be heavily influenced by more recent and tangible experiences when making decisions, a phenomenon termed *representativeness bias* by Nobel Laureate Daniel Kahneman.[17] In principle, extreme market performance can have long-lasting impact on investors' expectations and beliefs.

For example, a recent study in the United States shows that investors who lived through the 1929–1933 Great Depression and other lower stock market return periods are far more risk averse than those who have not, as reflected by a lower likelihood to participate in the stock market and lower asset allocation towards stocks as opposed to bonds.[18] In addition, some surveys show that Japanese investors were extremely upbeat about the outlook of the Japanese stock market during the Japanese economic bubble between 1980 and 1990. What is puzzling is that this optimism persisted towards the late 1990s, almost a decade after the Japanese stock market bubble burst.[19]

Such human behavioral patterns may be important in explaining why bubbles form in financial markets. After all, belief in non-stoppable appreciation in asset prices is one of the major reasons why investors become feverish with unreasonably high prices with little fundamental support. Indeed, scholars from M.I.T. show through theory models that, under loose liquidity conditions and overconfidence, even a slight shift in investor expectation can go a long way in blowing up asset bubbles.[20]

By such standards, Chinese economic growth in the past three decades is not only phenomenal but also long lasting. Additionally, liquidity has been extremely loose in China during the same period. Such experiences all help solidify market participants to change their expectations and believe that this fast growth will continue in the long run. The fact that China pulled off even faster growth after the 2007–2009 global financial crisis, while almost all other major economies stumbled into chaos and recession, reaffirmed Chinese belief. They seem to forget that fluctuation and recession are both indispensable and necessary components of economic growth.

To attract international and domestic investment, Chinese policies ensure good economic performance and investment returns, or at least against losses. As outlined in the first few chapters of this book, not only do Chinese investors feel that their investment returns are being guaranteed by regulators and marketing banks, investors in areas that should involve considerable risk, such as the Chinese A-shares market and the real estate market, also feel that their investments are being guaranteed by the government and hence should not suffer from losses.

These beliefs, despite being categorically false, are very pervasive in China and probably stem from the governments' investment guarantees. To avoid social dissatisfaction and maintain social harmony, the government is not willing to let the market fall, as they probably should. As the smart investors see through this layer of investment guarantees, they gradually become fearless and increasingly risk-seeking in order to profit even more. Chinese investors believe that those high-yielding investments that should be risky are indeed de facto guaranteed by the Chinese government to make them rich.

Warren Buffett's investment philosophy, "to get scared when other people are greedy, and get greedy when other people are scared," in some sense depicts how risks accumulate within an economy and market without being noticed. Many use this criterion to distinguish experienced investors from novice investors. In that regard, it is important to point out that most Chinese investors, especially those born after the founding of the People's Republic of China, have little memory of the bubbles and subsequent recessions and are therefore relatively inexperienced with economic cycles.

As things turn out, in the next few years Chinese liquidity growth will slow down and Chinese capital will start seeking investment opportunities outside the country. When such a liquidity wave retreats, it may finally be possible to tell who has been swimming naked and whose fortune is primarily buoyed only by excessive liquidity and government support. For now, it may be a good time for many Chinese executives and households to learn from an old idiom, "Don't count your chickens before they hatch." If Chinese investors cannot properly switch the investment expectations currently backed by the Chinese government's investment guarantee, risks are bound to keep building up in the Chinese financial system.

Distorted Incentive Systems

Despite all contributions to the Chinese economic growth miracle made by the aforementioned various guarantees, serious consequences arise as well.

An apparent and direct impact of the guarantees is the distortion of incentives and market forces. A direct consequence of the distortion of the incentive system for almost everyone in an economy is the misleading trade-off between the present and future, and between risk and returns.

The institutional and policy guarantees for economic growth have galvanized government officials' attention almost solely on the speed of local economic growth. Such a shift in government officials' objectives and evaluation criteria is effectively transmitted into almost every type of decision made by government officials.

Environment, civilian satisfaction and fulfillment, community engagement and participation, education, and health care have all ended up being given up or postponed, giving way to a single objective that has proved to be foolproof: to grow the economy. As a result, China's economic growth has indeed enjoyed phenomenal success and accomplishment. However, it is important to bear in mind that this success has been made at not-so-cheap costs, which will have to be amortized over the next decades.

Government officials who know that they are evaluated primarily by the recent economic growth of their governed area try to invest as much as possible and to attract as many new businesses as possible. In order to boost short-term economic growth, government officials are often willing to pay the price of exhausting future growth opportunities and local land and capital reserves.

If financing becomes a constraint, many officials will not hesitate to take out more debt, which will not have to be repaid until later, sometimes even after the conclusion of the officials' own governing period. So, "invest now, and worry about the debt later" has become a standard mentality at various levels of Chinese local governments. These practices put the burden of securing future opportunities and repaying debt unjustifiably on the shoulders of future government officials.

Facing an increasingly large supply of capital, Chinese entrepreneurs quickly figure out the best way to become successful in an era with negative real interest rates: to borrow as much as they can and speculate as much as they can. This distorted incentive system can explain how China's overcapacity problem has evolved into its current state. With expectations of a booming economy and negative real interest rates, all companies figure out that borrowing and expanding capacity is not only a lucrative, but also a very safe investment decision.

Such experiences, coupled with decreasing investment returns in many sectors of the real economy during the past few years, lured companies' investment into real estate, the stock market, and shadow banking. Entrepreneurs and executives believe that the financial sector can bring higher returns than investment in the real economy and can also be safer, thanks to the government's guarantee. Such beliefs further lead to a self-fulfilling prophecy, which has led even more business leaders to shun their traditional businesses and profit from speculating in Chinese real estate prices and the A-shares market.

This development of asset bubbles received strong support from households and enterprises that do not have access to investment opportunities in enviable areas. They, too, would like to share a piece of the too-good-to-be-true pie from investment in sectors such as real estate, finance, telecommunication, and energy and natural resources. At the bottom of the Chinese economic food chain, these households and companies are anxious to help the entrepreneurs and try their luck at any speculative areas that promise to generate unbelievably high returns.

No matter whether it is the once red-hot property market, the rollercoaster A-shares stock market, the opaque and mysterious shadow banking products such as trust products and private lending, or the recently booming internet financing, Chinese investors tend to look only at their investment returns and treat the investment's risks as if they had never existed.

The investment guarantees provided in these areas have the Chinese government to thank—or to blame. These guarantees, primarily sponsored by the government's own credit worthiness or simply by the government's expressed determination to boost or support a specific area (such as the real estate sector in the past decade and possibly the stock market in the coming decade) provide strong enough incentives for Chinese investors to forget about the very basic principles of investment and finance.

In their defense, Chinese investors have very good reasons to have strong faith in the Chinese government. As a matter of fact, many international observers and critics have become increasingly enthralled by the Chinese government's ability to steer the Chinese economy through one crisis after another and keep China on the right development course.

That said, it is important to point out that making linear projections based on recent history is one very commonly made mistake by investors and the entire human race. Given the increasing size and complexity of the Chinese economy and its involved integration in the global economic and financial orders, many coherent arguments in the past would gradually cease to work in today's new norm.

Sustainability and quality of growth

Behind distorted risk-taking is the key question of sustainability. Starting in the new millennium, many economists predicted that the Chinese economy will one day surpass that of the United States and become the largest in the world. After over a decade, this prediction seems increasingly accurate and imminent.

Over the past decades, the Chinese government seems to have been casually entertaining these predictions by setting five-year economic plans that are aimed to double the size of the Chinese economy every decade or sooner. It is worth noting that not too many countries have set economic growth speed as the government's or country's main objective, and even fewer have managed to reach their objectives.

Japan is one of the exceptions. Despite its much smaller land mass and population, it managed to surpass the United States as the worlds' largest economy for some time. Unfortunately, due to its economic and demographic structure, Japan has been busy fixing problems not well addressed during its period of fast economic growth.

Behind all the economic growth forecasts that predict China's economic dominance lies behind one key assumption: sustainable growth. After all, economic development is more like a marathon than a 100 meter dash. With its economic growth slowing down steadily during the past few years, China should probably start thinking more about how to make its economic growth sustainable instead of merely adding another percentage or two to its GDP growth scoreboard.

However, various studies point out that Chinese economic growth has been driven largely by increasing factor inputs, such as labor and capital, which will not be sustainable going forward.

For one thing, Chinese labor costs have been increasing steadily and speedily. According to U.S. Congressional statistics, Chinese labor costs increased by 11.4 percent per year between 2000 and 2013. Put in a more tangible way, Chinese labor cost was about 30 percent that of Mexico's in 2000, and has become 20–50 percent higher than that of

Mexico's today. Compared to its neighbors, China's labor cost can be twice as high as that of Vietnam, and up to 5 times as much as that of Cambodia in 2013.[21]

If China's income per capita were to double to more than $10,000 per year by 2020, as pledged by Chinese leaders, Chinese competitiveness based on cheap labor will undoubtedly disappear over time as incomes increase.[22] This trend means that China will not be able to rely on its cheap labor and competitive wages for its "world factory" status in the future. If anything, China may see its trade eventually balance or even show a deficit as the Chinese booming middle class turns to more exotic imports.

Another major driver of the Chinese economy has been the government's infrastructure investment and housing boom. Revenues from selling off local land have become a major source of local fiscal income in the past decades, which is then used to invest in infrastructure projects to further stimulate economic growth.

The curb policy on real estate since 2011, though still far from being effective in curbing or lowering housing prices, has already shown its impact on the Chinese economy and the fiscal soundness of local governments. Altogether, the real estate and related sectors combined contribute to more than 20 percent of Chinese economic growth. With China's housing prices already higher than those of many developed economies, this real estate-driven economic growth model puts the government into a policy dilemma of balancing affordable housing and maintaining economic growth.

Such a predicament is even more acute for many local governments, which have been relying heavily on land sale revenues to boost economic growth and finance for the next round of housing boom.

So far, the Chinese government has managed to keep economic growth at an acceptable pace at the cost of housing prices resuming their upward trend. Even without further appreciation, housing prices have risen by so much that they have started exerting a chain reaction on education, employment, marriage, and even divorce. With the recent real estate registration system and the rumored rolling out of a property tax system, many experts suspect that the Chinese real estate sector may have already seen its golden days. The remaining question is whether the market will gradually deflate or suffer from a drastic drop within a short period.

The capital guarantee and investment guarantee are both responsible for the phenomenal growth of the Chinese real estate and related sectors. This makes the Chinese housing market a key point of contention when it comes to asset bubbles. The Chinese housing market is very expensive, judged by any traditional valuation methods such as price-to-income ratio and price-to-rental yield ratio. However, it remains unclear the extent to which such lofty pricing is backed up by real demand and to what extent it is because there is no better substitute for investment and speculation.

The problem of housing as an investment vehicle has become so serious and prevalent that the housing problem is no longer a housing consumption problem, but a national investment problem. Almost all successful businesses and households are involved with the real estate sector, and the returns are so attractive that many are willing to give up their once successful main line of business. This has further aggravated income distribution, giving more advantages to those who have capital or at least access to capital.

Finally, getting used to the mind-boggling appreciation of the housing market, the new generation of Chinese have found creating wealth such an easy task that they gradually forget the hardworking spirit that gave the Chinese economy its current dominant status. In this regard, diffusing the housing bubble without causing too much pain in the rest of the economy will be a critical area that future reform actions will have to handle very carefully.

How to reform

In addition to sustainability, the quality of growth is just as important. Economic growth should not simply be the numbers on government officials' evaluation cards. Instead, economic growth should be felt, rather than measured. With China's economy growing at its fast pace, it is about time for China to think more about how to make the economic growth better benefit and be appreciated by its citizens, or, to borrow President Xi's words, "to help each Chinese fulfill his or her China dream."

Unlike government officials who are under the pressure of pushing the economy to grow faster, regular Chinese people care more about the same things people care about all around the world, such as job security, income distribution, and social welfare and stability. They care about having an affordable and reliable health care and social system, so that they do not have to worry about their livelihood in the future. They are also concerned with preserving the environment so that their descendants will have as good a place or even better in which to live.

Unfortunately, these are challenging tasks all over the world, and China is no exception. Faster economic growth indeed provides greater resources to be allocated to solve these problems, but at the same time, it crowds out the attention and resources that could have otherwise been allocated to do more in these areas.

Fortunately, reform will fit perfectly with the Chinese Communist Party's commitment to "strengthen the ability of administration," which is deemed just as important as "enhancing the thought level," "strengthening the political direction," "emphasizing the organization construction," and "fighting against corruption," as is the party's major agenda in the next few years. To be more effective in strengthening its administrative ability, the Chinese Communist Party and Chinese government would need to listen more carefully to the needs and dreams of the Chinese people and try to take meaningful reforms and action to address them.

Let the market play a decisive role

To meet all of the above demands and challenges, further reforms are urgently needed. One direction reform should take should be pushing the market economy forward. According to the Third Plenum of the

Chinese Communist Party's 18th Meeting, "letting the market play a decisive role in the allocation of resources" will be the main spirit of reform in all areas of the Chinese economy in the coming decade. This means that the various forms of policy, capital, and investment guarantees that the Chinese government currently provides to the economy and market participants will have to be unwound, or at the very least become transparent and transacted in the marketplace.

Some key reforms will have to take place in the financial sector because finance deals with the allocation of two very important resources: time and risk. If all the risk that has been guaranteed by the state in the past could be revealed, disclosed, and priced into the financial market, market participants would no longer be motivated to take risks that they cannot bear, or to speculate in areas that even they themselves understand to be too risky and unsustainable.

Put differently, investors' interests in speculative areas, such as the housing market and A-shares market, will wane, and rightfully so. Instead, Chinese enterprises and households will learn to allocate their resources in more diversified ways in terms of asset class, regions, currencies, and time.

Once investors' risk appetite gets restored to its proper and unguaranteed level, Chinese corporations and households will learn to set realistic expectations about the returns on their investments. This will not only help the Chinese government and citizens put more emphasis on the present state of their lives and businesses, but also help them refrain or withdraw from irresponsible investments that lead to asset bubbles and overcapacity.

Realignment between the state and market

These changes will almost certainly call for another major reform of the Chinese economy and society, namely to realign the interests and power of the state and marketplace. Over the past three decades, China has come a long way, transforming itself from a once poor centrally-planned economy into a vibrant upper middle-income world power. To continue its success and unravel its current challenges, China will have to go even further and let the market forces play an even greater role.

The state has been driving a large portion of economic growth in the past decade. This can be partly reflected by the increasing size of the SOE sector, despite their disappointing operating efficiency and investment returns, even when compared with their international counterparts. To make matters even worse, the growth of the SOE sector has reportedly crowded out many private enterprises that will be the key drivers of the Chinese economy and employment in future decades. Therefore, conscious limiting of the reach of the state and SOEs will have to take place, along with the concrete reform steps.

Needless to say, the power of the state and government will need to be constrained or even confined during this reform process. There is no question that many vested-interest groups within the bureaucratic system and state-owned enterprises are not pleased to see such changes coming. However, in order for China to go through the series of challenges that it currently faces and achieve its economic and social reform objectives, there seems to be no other option.

The rule of law

In addition to the missing market force, another element of guarantees, especially implicit guarantees, reflects some disregard for the rule of law. Following the spirit of contract, a form of the spirit of law, both parties of a contract should clearly understand what they walk into and take responsibility when things go wrong if the guarantees are properly disclosed or priced.

However, under the circumstances of implicit guarantee, because of the implicit nature of the guarantee, both sides will not acknowledge the consequences of the contract, even when they are fully aware of them. This entails difficulty in enforcing the contract when bad things happen. This explains why seemingly clear contracts in China cannot prevent protests against regulators in the event of investment losses, and why trust cannot be established in many business operations in China.

One way to foster a rule of law mentality in China may have to do with the fundamental respect for the power and enforcement of contracts. By helping the Chinese understand risks and responsibilities that they have to take personally in various investment opportunities, the tapering off of existing guarantees may help more Chinese better appreciate the force of law and understand the rule of law.

Unwind policy and the institutional guarantee

GDP Tournament mentality

The speed of economic growth has become the single most important factor in evaluating the performance of local government officials in China. In addition to the pro-growth party mentality, there are also realistic benefits to using economic growth speed as an official evaluation criterion. First, the speed of growth is a clear and transparent benchmark, so the ground for competition is seemingly level. Further, because the objective is quite uniform across the whole country, consistent evaluation criteria allow the transfer of talents and skills across provinces and regions, which was instrumental in narrowing the gap of economic growth speed across China.

Nevertheless, with the Chinese economy growing at such phenomenal speed for so long, many people contend that the GDP tournament or GDP-dominated evaluation criteria has led directly to many serious challenges facing China right now, such as the local government debt, overinvestment, overcapacity, and the deterioration of the environment. Consequently, China Communist Party leaders have to come up with a more updated mission and evaluation criteria for its cadres in order to reflect the more developed status of the current Chinese economy and the shifting priorities in economic and social reforms. Reflecting this shift, the Shanghai municipal government has become the first Chinese provincial government to give up GDP growth as its mandate in 2015.[23]

More diverse development objectives

Albeit difficult to measure, many agree that the quality of economic growth should be incorporated as an important aspect of official evaluation. Environmental protection, social stability and harmony, income distribution, and civilian satisfaction should all be included in the matrix of official evaluation. Similar to the major overhaul that has taken place in corporate executive compensation, official evaluation should focus not only on the speed of current economic growth, but also on its sustainability.

Consistent with the 3rd Plenum's mentality of "letting the market play its maximal force in allocating resources," the Chinese government and government officials need to gradually delegate more administrative power, such as entry permission, price fixing, quota allocation, and listing requirements, to be determined by market forces.

Legal and media monitoring

In order to let the market make more informed, and hence efficient, decisions, a better legal framework and enforcement are urgently needed. Some observers claim that China's legal framework looks wonderful on paper, but lacks power in enforcement.

A classic example is the investigation of insider trading and price manipulation cases in the Chinese A-shares market. Even though the CSRC has a comprehensive list of rules and regulations against such illicit behavior, the lack of cooperation between the CSRC, legal enforcement, and party disciplinary committee sometimes makes it very hard to prosecute those responsible for scandalous cases.

Throughout the Chinese anti-corruption campaigns in 2012, the Chinese media gradually began revealing illicit behavior of some very high rank government officials. This unprecedented development could bring some good news to the marketplace as well because more active media monitoring and information disclosure will provide more information for the market to savor.

As the party and Chinese society become more tolerant of revelations of reservations and criticism, more reliable and accurate information will be disclosed and revealed. Once negative information, such as slower economic growth and increasing risks, can be properly and rightfully incorporated into the marketplace, practices such as implicit guarantees will gradually lose their camouflage and appeal, and the pricing of risks will become more transparent and precise.

Once the legal framework is upheld and the public can gain more access to truthful information, the government can probably reach a better balance in delineating its relationship with the market. If the market can indeed rise up to have more influence in allocating resources, risks, or the premium for taking risks, these will be allocated more appropriately.

Along with this process, even more information will be disclosed about the implicit guarantees that have been taken out to shore up various types of risk and asset prices. Corresponding adjustment of pricing for such risks will help further facilitate the market force to play a greater role in the Chinese economy.

Unwind the capital guarantee

Another way to taper off the implicit guarantees that abound in the Chinese economy is to moderate capital supply through monetary supply, interest rate liberalization, banking credit expansion, property market and stock market (re) valuation, and, possibly most important of all, relaxation of the capital flow curb.

Monetary policy

Chinese monetary supply (M2) shot from 10 trillion CNY in 2001 to over 120 trillion in 2014. This drastic increase in monetary supply reflects the monetization process of the Chinese economy and economic growth. For example, in the late 1990s, almost all housing was provided by employers as part of employee compensation. However, these apartments could rarely be purchased or traded and therefore did not require capital stock. In contrast, the entire real estate sector was almost completely market determined and monetized by 2014, which absorbed a large fraction of the increasing Chinese monetary supply.

Nevertheless, even taking out this structural shift in the Chinese economy, the speed of the Chinese monetary supply still outpaced that of many large economies in the world and China's own economic growth. Periodic inflation, skyrocketing housing prices, speculative bubbles in many assets and commodities, increasing risk appetite, and ignorance of risks can all somehow trace their roots back to the very loose monetary policy over the past 15 years, especially after the 2007–2009 global financial crisis. Therefore, to restore the proper expectation of asset prices and risks, the speed of monetary supply has to be scaled back to a more sustainable level.

Interest rate liberalization and banking reform

It is fair to say that the super easy monetary policy has increased the total amount of liquidity to an unprecedented level. However, it is probably the distorted interest rate, in light of the extremely generous monetary supply, that has done the real damage by misallocating capital into areas where capital is least needed, leaving many promising small- and medium-sized enterprises underfunded and crying out for funding.

Hence, China has to let the market determine various interest rates in the economy. On top of the base interest rate set by the central bank, the market should be able to decide whom to provide capital to, at what interest rate, for how long, under what conditions, etc. ...

Unlike its approach in the indirect financing of the banking sector, China's approach should be to encourage more direct financing, such as the bond market and peer-to-peer financing in the future. Direct financing should enable both sides of transactions to determine their financing arrangements directly, without the intermediation of a bank professional. This reform will not only cut out the middleman and increase efficiency, but it will also provide greater flexibility to the terms of the contract, therefore improving the likelihood of a successful deal.

Throughout interest rate reform, Chinese banking will probably bear the most impact. The regulated interest rate has contributed the lion's share of Chinese banks, profits. With interest rates becoming more determined by market forces, banks will gradually lose their competitiveness and profitability. To make things worse, interest rate liberalization will unavoidably cause rising financing costs for some companies, especially less competitive companies that used to rely on cheap bank loans. The failure of these loans may cause banks' nonperforming loans to jump and banks' asset quality to deteriorate.

Further, banks have accumulated large amounts of off-balance activities in the "catch me if you can" game that they have played with the regulators over the past decade, which partly explains the explosive development of Chinese banks and other forms of financial innovation.

Instead of focusing on preventing entry and stifling competition, China's bank regulators' mentality should shift to how to better manage banking sector risks. Given banks' systematic impact and relevance to hundreds of millions of households, the Chinese government has always been extremely sensitive to any potential risks in the banking sector and hence provides consistent explicit and implicit guarantees to banks' credibility.

The Chinese government has been moving in the right direction by proposing the roll out of a deposit insurance program in late 2014, which would insulate household personal financial security from any specific banks' asset quality, hence reducing the government's commitment to shoring up nonperforming loans and nonperforming banks. In addition, Chinese regulators will have to rein in such undisclosed activities sooner or later, possibly with gradual steps so as not to cause systematic liquidity shock and "pop the bubble" in some sectors, such as real estate.

Capital account regulation

Even after decades of reform and openness, the segregation of the Chinese economy and financial markets from the rest of the world can probably still explain many of China's current economic challenges.

Capital account regulation forbids capital to flow freely across Chinese borders. Such control artificially shores up Chinese asset prices in the context of loose monetary policy by limiting excessive liquidity from monetary and fiscal stimulus to chase domestic investment opportunities. These distortions not only spawn asset bubbles, but artificially constrain Chinese households and corporate investment portfolios, limiting their returns.

Historically, the continuous appreciation of the Chinese Yuan (CNY) has helped cover up these disadvantageous asset allocations and foregone benefits of international diversification. With the CNY gradually reaching its equilibrium exchange rate and even facing the risk of depreciation, the motivation for Chinese people and Chinese companies to diversify internationally has become ever more relevant and imminent.

Discrepancies in valuation and quality of life have already attracted many Chinese to invest heavily in overseas property markets and emigrate to developed economies such as the United States, Canada, and Australia. This puts greater pressure on the Chinese government to open up its capital account, where there may be a big jump in Chinese demand for investing overseas and a diversion away from Chinese stock and real estate markets. This capital flight may undermine the performance of the Chinese stock market and real estate market in the future.

Despite opposition based on the point above, many have argued that constraining capital account flow any further in China may cause a time bomb, which could trigger greater risks of asset bubbles, underground exchange markets, and even greater negative shock when the Chinese capital account eventually has to be opened up. Therefore, the Chinese government should make up its mind and steadily, gradually, and in an orderly fashion open up its capital account.

Incremental Reform

The target of unwinding the capital guarantee is clear; so too are the pace and intensity necessary for reform. Given the large quantity of monetary supply and liquidity floating through the Chinese economy, a sudden move in moderating monetary supply and credit expansion could trigger systematic shocks and crisis.

The credit crunch in June and December 2013, and the drop in total Chinese savings in December 2014, reflected how sensitive the Chinese financial system has become in reaction to support from new capital. As the system becomes increasingly sensitive and unstable, reform in Chinese monetary policy, interest rate liberalization, bank regulatory framework, and capital account liberalization all have to take place through incremental reform.

As reflected in the financial crisis that took place in Russia and some Latin American countries in the 1980s and 1990s, "shock therapy" would probably bring too many unanticipated and uncontrollable risks and could backfire.

Unwind investment guarantees

Real Estate

Even some of the most bullish real estate developers in China are crying wolf in 2014.[24] It has become increasingly clear that the golden days of the Chinese housing sector are over. The housing sector's—and other related sectors'—leading contributions to the Chinese economy, the tremendous wealth effect that has been generated in the Chinese housing market boom, and the resulting exuberant expectations and consumer confidence, may also shift accordingly.

Although the real estate sector has singlehandedly helped the Chinese government achieve its goal of fast economic growth during the past decade, things have to change substantially in light of the oversupply of housing and one of the least affordable housing markets in the world. Once the Chinese government can make peace with itself over lower economic growth, it should, and probably will, take a softer stance with housing prices and housing markets. As long as Chinese households and investors notice some subtle shifts in the government's attitudes toward the housing market, the speculative frenzy may have to come to an end eventually.

In practice, if investors who lose money from investing in properties can no longer obtain guarantees and support from local governments and government-pressured developers, they will probably think twice about buying property. With supply already outpacing real demand (sans speculation), the shift in policy and tapering off of the government's guarantees can hopefully lead the Chinese housing market to a soft landing.

Here, similar to the reform and exit of implicit guarantees in many other areas, the pace of the tapering off is very critical. If the government acts too slowly, the housing bubble will grow beyond control. On the other hand, if the curb measure is too strict, the housing sector and national economy may run the risk of stalling and haunting the Chinese banking sector.

To reduce the real estate sector's impact on the rest of the economy and contain financial risks, it is crucial that China develop a market for mortgage-backed and asset-backed securities. The development of the MBS and ABS markets has proved highly instrumental in diversifying away the risks concentrated within the Chinese banking sector. In addition, securitization will help improve banks' liability turnover and diffuse nonperforming loans and illiquid capital losses in other sectors or other regions of the world.

Stock market

Distinct from most capital markets around the world, the Chinese A-shares market implements an approval-based listing process. All companies interested in listing their shares have to go through a lengthy, and sometimes cumbersome, approval process with the China Securities Regulatory Commission (CSRC).

In addition to its much publicized benefit of background screening and investor protection, the approval-based listing process has another clear advantage to the regulators: controlling the capital available to the market by adjusting the pace at which new companies are allowed to list their shares.

Historically, the delay of the IPO process has been widely considered bullish news and boosts market performance, whereas the start or resumption of the IPO process is considered bearish news and often crashes the market. This adjustment, seemingly effective in moving the market, also unconsciously planted the seed of implicit guarantee in investors' minds, leading them to believe that, at very least, the CSRC can still shore up the market by indefinitely prolonging the listing of new shares.

Therefore, reforms in the Chinese A-shares market have to start with the transition from an approval-based to a registration-based IPO process, which allows all qualified companies to choose the optimal timing and pricing of listing shares, without too much interference from the regulators.

Another important reform area is derivatives and short selling. Both short selling and derivatives are known for their power in helping elicit negative information and balancing the capital market. Exactly because of this effect, each has been feared by investors and regulators alike as having the power to bring down a market by itself.

Even with the introduction of a series of futures products in China, most notably the CSI 300 Index futures (2012), the Treasury bond futures (2013), and index option (2015), Chinese regulators and investors are still reluctant to let these securities and trading mechanisms play greater roles in fear of their negative impact on the market. Several years after its introduction in China, the practice of short selling remains limited among a small select group of companies.

However, only when the Chinese A-shares market can become balanced (with both positive and negative news allowed and incorporated into setting stock prices) will the information discovery function of the Chinese A-shares market operate properly. Such an informationally efficient market could instill confidence in the sustainability and long-term value of the market in investors from China and around the globe.

Last, but certainly not least, the Chinese government should set a clearer agenda for the CSRC. Currently, the CSRC shoulders the responsibility of ensuring the order of the Chinese capital market and boosting the market's development, which is interpreted by many investors to be equivalent to boosting the performance of the Chinese A-shares market. This explains why Chinese investors may target the CSRC whenever there is a big drop in the Chinese stock market, hoping to exert pressure on the CSRC so that it will launch more favorable policies for the Chinese stock market.

If this is indeed the case, it has to be made clear that these two objectives, ensuring the order of the market and boosting market development, may sometimes contradict each other. Therefore, tapering off the implicit guarantees in the Chinese A-shares market may have to start with some very fundamental adjustment of the regulator's mission and agenda.

Shadow banking (Peer-to-peer lending regulation)

Even with a clear and detailed to-do list to reform the Chinese shadow banking system, it may quickly prove to be much easier said than done. Even though local governments do not promise to take any responsibility for the financial distress of local government financing vehicles, most investors believe that they will take responsibility in case of default. Investors believe that they can turn to the central government to not let local governments fail, bailing them out when necessary.

This implicit guarantee used to apply only to debts taken out by local governments and state-owned enterprises. However, this layer of implicit guarantee has been strengthened and extended further when banks and other regulated financial institutions are involved in the origination, structuring, and marketing of these products (as in the case of the Shanxi Zhenfu product discussed at the beginning of the book).

The Chinese Banking Regulatory Committee (CBRC) has been making attempts to rein in the ballooning shadow banking problem, or at least to make the problem more transparent, in 2014. With increasing disclosure on the related financials and fiduciary responsibilities shouldered by various involved parties, investors can certainly gain increasing understanding about the viability and sustainability of many trust products and wealth management products used in shadow banking.

Now that financial innovations referred to as internet finance (such as Yu'e Bao, peer-to-peer equity financing, peer-to-peer debt financing, and various forms of private banking) all grow explosively outside formal banking regulation, it is crucial that Chinese regulators accurately estimate the size of the industry and its risk exposure.

Default and Bankruptcy (by corporations and even governments)

Most importantly, however, the central government and regulators would have to make examples out of a few specific default events. Investors learn directly from the market, not from books. Only after a few companies, financial institutions, and even local governments are allowed to default and even go bankrupt can the central government establish its reputation for letting the market forces have the most power in allocating resources.

Not until such default events take place will investors be convinced that the widely believed implicit guarantee is no longer effective in distorting risk and shoring up prices. Only through default and sustaining losses will investors learn firsthand of the risks and adjust their expectations accordingly. Only under such a proper pricing system will the government and enterprises invest and finance reasonably and responsibly.

In addition to wanting to avoid the stigma of default and bankruptcy, the Chinese are especially averse to these events because trust in the Chinese economy is largely built on personal relationships, whereas law and enforcement is vague and ineffective in disciplining debtors' behavior.[25] In addition, the Chinese government is concerned that such adverse events may trigger civilian dissatisfaction and social unrest. Furthermore, many troubled companies are owned by the state, and the conflict of interest makes the Chinese government unwilling, or at least hesitant, to let go of companies at the brink of bankruptcy.

However strong such beliefs are, one has to realize that the economy follows its own principles, and the prolonged distortion of factor productivity pricing and risks will only result in a bubble burst or prolonged recession. Consequently, restoring information disclosure and correct expectations in the financial system will prove to be critical in diffusing the increasing risks in trust company products, wealth management products, and the Chinese financial system.

Maybe Steve Jobs was right in saying that "Death is very likely the single best invention of life": failure may be the only cure to China's implicit guarantee problem and the remedy for saving and rebooting the Chinese economy and financial system.

Notes

1. http://economy.jschina.com.cn/system/2015/01/17/023375528.shtml
2. http://news.163.com/14/0123/14/9J9G1Q2O00014Q4P.html
3. http://news.xinhuanet.com/local/2015-01/24/c_127415801.htm
4. http://finance.eastmoney.com/news/1355,20140902419299684.html
5. http://news.163.com/14/0903/10/A57A5LRG00014AED.html
6. http://news.163.com/14/0512/09/9S1JTGG000014JB6.html
7. http://news.hexun.com/2014-05-06/164530212.html?from=rss
8. http://sh.wenweipo.com/?viewnews-13099
9. http://finance.sina.com.cn/china/20141022/234420613149.shtml
10. http://finance.people.com.cn/n/2014/0825/c1004-25529553.html

11. https://books.google.com/books?hl=en&lr=&id=erOVlDIY1jEC&oi=
fnd&pg=PA1&dq=%E2%80%98Money+and+Capital+in+Economic+
Development%E2%80%99&ots=LZ6hvj13Dg&sig=iSDjUSiLj8
TOTCvp_P9uX1uOckQ#v=onepage&q=%E2%80%98Money%20
and%20Capital%20in%20Economic%20Development%E2%80%99
&f=false
12. http://www.worldscientific.com/doi/pdf/10.1142/9789812812520_fmatter
13. http://news.xinhuanet.com/ziliao/2009-06/09/content_11512684.htm
14. http://gold.jrj.com.cn/2014/08/01162817725976.shtml
15. http://news.163.com/13/0411/13/8S6CKBD200014JB5.html
16. http://newpaper.dahe.cn/dhb/html/2013-10/16/content_969607.htm?
div=-1
17. http://www.sciencemag.org/content/185/4157/1124.short
18. http://www.nber.org/papers/w14813
19. http://www.jstor.org/stable/2109855
20. Acemoglu, Daron, Victor Chernozhukov, and Muhamet Yildiz (2009),
Fragility of asymptotic agreement under Bayesian learning, Working
paper, MIT.
21. http://finance.sina.com.cn/world/20130405/181315056109.shtml
22. http://business.sohu.com/20140423/n398703530.shtml
23. http://news.xinhuanet.com/cankao/2015-01/28/c_133953423.htm
24. http://house.ifeng.com/detail/2014_06_13/46808230_0.shtml
25. Fan, Huang, and Zhu, 2014. Institutional Background and Distress Resolution, Journal of Corporate Finance.

Index

ABC (Agricultural Bank of China), 35
ABN Amro, 121
ABS (asset-backed securities), 219–220, 294
Acharya, Viral, 252, 262–263
agency problem, 239
agreement savings, 112, 114
Agricultural Bank of China (ABC), 35
AIG, 261
air pollution statistics, 228–231
Alibaba, 91–92, 109–113, 138
Amsterdam Stock Exchange, 86
anti-corruption campaign, 82, 142–143, 288
apparel industry, corporate leverage ratio in, 185
Apple, 138
asset bubbles, 151–152, 280, 283, 290
asset-backed securities (ABS), 219–220, 294
assets:
   expectation of price appreciation for, 165
   financial, of Chinese households, 12
   local government asset quality, 209
   non-standardized, 33
Australia:
   bank loans as local government financing in, 205

bank loans in local government debt in, 201
emigration to, 292
municipal bonds in, 205
automobile industry, overcapacity in, 153

Bai Zhongren, 184
Baidu, 92
bailouts, 170
   expectation of, 165–166
   during global financial crisis, 17, 263–265
   implicit guarantees provided by, 158
   by local governments, 173
   size of implicit guarantees following, 253
   (See also "Too big to fail" [TBTF])
bank loans, 74, 171
   bonds as supplement to, 201
   classic problem with, 159
   commodities financing for, 123–126
   copper financing for, 120–123
   in fast-growing economies, 36
   iron ore financing for, 123–126
   and local government default risk, 208–209
   as local government financing, 205–206

bank loans (*Cont.*)
  and mutual guarantees by companies,
    126–129
  nonbank financing of, 35
  and overcapacity problem, 154, 167
  for real estate, 74
  to SOEs, 18–19, 186, 190
Bank of China (BoC), 35, 192
banking system, 34–35 (*See also* Banks;
    Shadow banking)
bankruptcy, 13
  allowance of, 220–221
  as exit, overcapacity and, 167–170
  industry-wide impacts of, 156
  reform recommendation for,
    297–298
  as taboo concept, 167–168
  of U.S. money market funds,
    111–112
  value of, 168–169
Bankruptcy Law of 2006, 169
banks:
  assets of, 35
  concentrated risks on, 205–207
  and expanding credit supplies, 275
  in fast-growing economies, 36
  and interest rate reform, 291
  IPO filings of, 45
  managing banking sector risks, 291
  mega banks, 253
  reform recommendation for,
    290–291
  savings deposit rates of, 112–113
  savings moved away from, 110
  and SIVs, 112–113, 257, 258
  and size of mutual guarantees, 128
  state-owned, 35, 50, 163–164, 186
    (*See also individual banks*)
  "too big to fail," 261–262
  trust products from, 206

BCG (Boston Consulting Group), 40
Beber, Alessandro, 255
Beijing:
  air quality in, 229–230
  debt level of, 200
  housing prices in, 60, 231–233
  housing price-to-income ratio in,
    61
  local government debt issue for,
    202
  noncorporate direct enterprise debt
    in, 203
  rents in, 60–61
  total land value of, 62
Bernanke, Ben, 261
Block, Carson, 9, 85
BMW, 142
BNP Paribas, 121
BoC (Bank of China), 35, 192
Bonaparte, Napoleon, 86, 254
bond market, 201, 218–220,
    290–291
bonds:
  as bank loan supplement, 201
  of central government, 209
  Chaori 11 bond default, 12–13,
    154–155
  default on corporate bonds, 120
  default on municipal bonds, 208
  local government bonds, 22,
    209–210
  municipal, 204–205, 208, 218–220
Boston Consulting Group (BCG), 40
BOT (Build-Operate-Transfer)
    financing, 201
budget deficit, 24–25, 212
Buffett, Warren, 177, 254, 260, 269,
    274, 277
Build-Operate-Transfer (BOT)
    financing, 201

Bush, George H. W., 223

Cambodia, labor cost in, 134, 282
Canada:
  bank loans as local government
    financing in, 201, 205
  emigration to, 292
CAO (China Aviation Oil), 89, 181
Capacity overhang (*see* Overcapacity)
capacity utilization rate, 152, 153
capital:
  access to, 18–19, 189
  cross-border flow of, 92–94
  in fast-growing economies, 36
  transfer of, 25
capital account regulation, 206, 292
capital adequacy ratio, 37–39
capital flow:
  and capital account regulation, 292
  cross-border, 92–94
  moderating capital supply through, 289
capital formation, 274
capital (liquidity) guarantee:
  economic growth from, 273–276
  and growth of real estate and related
    sectors, 283
  unwinding, 289–293
capital market(s), 23, 92–94
  and bankruptcy, 168
  investors' beliefs about, 178
  price of risks in, 219
Case, Karl, 231
Case-Shiller index, 231
CASS (Chinese Academy of Social
  Sciences), 35, 157
CBRC (*see* China Banking Regulatory
  Committee)
CCB (China Construction Bank), 35
CDO (collateralized debt obligation)
  products, 4

CDS (credit default spread), 165
cement industry:
  ban on new investments in, 15, 152
  overcapacity in, 152
Centaline.com, 60
central government:
  budget deficit of, 212
  current fiscal situation of, 22–23
  demand for housing price growth,
    72–76, 81–82
  expenditures by, 211–212
  extent of implicit guarantee from,
    161–162
  fiscal reform and guarantees from,
    209–210
  fiscal sustainability of, 23–25, 211–213
  implicit credit endorsement for local
    governments, 22
  and implicit guarantees, 3
  and overcapacity, 163–164
  push toward high speed growth from,
    16–17, 188
  reform and openness policy of, 270
  as reliable debtor, 159
  resources and credibility of, 199
  and split-tax reform, 217–218
  and statistics problem, 239–240
ChangZhou, 145
Chanos, Jim, 254
Chaori 11 bond default, 12–13,
  154–155
Chaori Solar Technology, 13, 154–155
China Audit Authority, 3
China Aviation Oil (CAO), 89, 181
China Banking Regulatory Committee
  (CBRC), 33, 36, 41, 123, 297
China Construction Bank (CCB), 35
China Credit Trust Company, 1–3,
  31–32
China Index Institute (CII), 59

China Index Research Academy (CIRA), 231, 233, 234
China 100 city housing index, 231, 233–234
China Telecom, 192
Chinese Academy of Social Sciences (CASS), 35, 157
Chinese A-shares market, 90–95
  approval-based listing process in, 294–295
  corporate governance in, 106–107
  debt-to-asset ratio of companies in, 184
  implicit guarantee for, 88
  investigation of illicit behavior in, 288
  investment gains in, 12
  investor confidence in, 106
  investor expectations for, 3
  investor wariness of SOEs in, 186
  and IPO stocks, 98
  limited alternatives in, 103
  reforms in, 295–296
  and short selling, 10
  SOEs and subsidiaries as losers in, 181
  taper off of implicit guarantees in, 296
  volatility of, 100
Chinese Association of Companies, 192
Chinese Budget Law, 215
Chinese Communist Party:
  Anti-Corruption Campaign of, 142–143
  commitment to strengthen administrative ability, 284
  economic growth promised by, 146–147
  mission and evaluation criteria of, 287
  personnel system of, 193
Chinese economy:
  interdependence within, 25–27

overcapacity and producer prices in, 3
  (*See also* Economic growth; *individual topics*)
Chinese Overseas Freight, 184
Chinese Securities Regulatory Commission (CSRC), 01.57, 16, 44–45
  investor protection by, 11–12, 99–101
  and IPO approval process, 95, 96, 101–103
  and movement of stock market, 88
  petitioning against, 10
  setting clearer agenda for, 296
Chinese State Reserve of Copper, 89–90
Chinese Yuan (CNY):
  appreciation of, 125, 292
  conversion of foreign currencies into, 274–275
  depreciation of, 126
Chongqing:
  debt level of, 200
  LGFV debt in, 202
Chow, Gregory, 273
Churchill, Winston, 1
CICC, 155
CII (China Index Institute), 59
CIRA (*see* China Index Research Academy)
Citic Pacific, 90, 121, 181
Citic Resources, 121
CNY (*see* Chinese Yuan)
coal and charcoal industry, corporate leverage ratio in, 185
coal-chemical industry, ban on new investments in, 15, 152
Coase, Ronald, 223
collateralized debt obligation (CDO) products, 4
commodities bubbles, 290
commodities financing, 123–126

Communist Party (*see* Chinese Communist Party)

companies:
  and anti-corruption campaign, 142–143
  corporate-level forces leading to overcapacity, 164–166
  deterioration in corporate earnings, 16
  in Fortune 500, 175, 183, 191–192, 272
  mutual guarantees by, 126–129
  "too big to fail" mentality in, 165–166

concrete industry, capacity utilization rate for, 15, 152

Confucius, 151

conglomerate business groups, 104

Congressional Budget Office (U.S.), 247

construction equipment industry, corporate leverage ratio in, 185

Consumer Price Index (CPI), 225–228

consumption:
  as percent of GDP, 139–140
  recent changes in, 227

consumption-based economic growth:
  move from investment-driven model to, 143–146
  need for increased household consumption, 136–139

contingent liabilities, 203–204

contracts:
  fake, 67–68
  for housing, 56

copper financing, 120–123

corporate earnings, deterioration in, 16

corporate governance:
  and SOE reform, 196
  of state-owned enterprises, 178, 181

corporate implicit guarantees, 256–259

corporate leverage ratio, 13–14, 184–186, 191

corporate strategy:
  of state-owned enterprises, 176–179
  of Western firms, 177

corporate structure, 178–179

corporate-level forces leading to overcapacity, 164–166

corruption:
  anti-corruption campaign, 82, 142–143, 288
  and gifts of luxury products, 139
  and property ownership, 68–69

cost of capital, 186–188 (*See also* Interest rate liberalization)

cost of financing, fiscal revenues and, 207–208

CPI (Consumer Price Index), 225–228

credit, 167
  credit growth, 36
  moderating capital supply through, 289

credit crunch (2013), 34, 41, 110

credit default risk, 158

credit default spread (CDS), 165

credit ratings, 160, 219, 260 (*See also* Ratings agencies)

credit risks, 46–49, 168

CreditEase, 115–120

Crippen, Dan L., 247

cross-border capital flow, 92–94

crowding out:
  as economic term, 182
  of small and medium-sized enterprises by SOEs, 182–183

CSI 300 Index futures, 295

CSI index, 10

CSRC (*see* Chinese Securities Regulatory Commission)

DaGong credit rating agency, 161

"Dai gou," 138

Dai Xianglong, 214–215
debt, 13, 193–194
    of Chinese listed companies, 184
    nation-wide, 48
    in railway industry, 184
    restructuring of, 168
    of state-owned enterprises, 184
    total Chinese government debt, 200
    (*See also* leverage)
debt ceiling, 20
debt financing, 160, 186
DeCheng, 121
decision making:
    in peer-to-peer lending, 117
    and SOE reform, 195–196
    statistics in, 241–242
default:
    allowance of, 220–221
    banking industry-wide effects of, 157
    calmness in face of, 2
    of Chaori 11 bond, 12–13, 154–155
    on corporate bonds, 120
    implicit guarantees and distorted risk
        of, 158
    on municipal bonds, 208
    in peer-to-peer lending, 117
    reform recommendation for, 297–298
    by Shanxi Zhenfu Energy Group, 1–2,
        31–32
default risks, 46–49, 168–169, 208–209
deleveraging, for SOE reform, 194–195
delinquency management, in peer-to-
        peer lending, 117–120
delistings (stocks), 101–103
demographic changes:
    and health care system, 141–142
    and housing market, 78–79
    and social security system, 141,
        213–214
Deng Xiaoping, 146–147, 270

deregulation, for SOE reform, 195–196
derivatives, 89–91
development objectives, diversifying,
        288
direct financing, 290–291
disclosure:
    to diffuse risks, 298
    improving, 221
    by local governments, 215
    by state-owned enterprises, 196
distorted incentive systems,
        consequences of, 278–280
diversification:
    by CreditEase, 116
    of financing sources, 200–202
    international, 292
    investors' preferences for, 177, 178
    into real estate and shadow banking,
        103–104
dividends, 103–107
divorces, fake, 68
Dodd-Frank Act, 261–263
domestic consumption, need for growth
        in, 136–139

easy monetary policy, 255–256
economic growth, 131–149, 269
    and anti-corruption campaign,
        142–143
    from capital guarantee, 273–276
    controversy over, 270
    cost of, 278–279
    and disappearing export advantage,
        133–135
    drivers of, 179–181
    following global financial crisis, 277
    governmental commitment to,
        271–272
    and growth of domestic consumption,
        136–139

and health care system, 141–142
impact of, 131–132
and income/income distribution,
    139–140
from institutional and policy
    guarantee, 270–273
from investment guarantee, 276–278
move from investment-driven to
    consumption-based model for,
    143–146
quality of, 132–133, 148–149, 283–284,
    288
rate/speed of, 26, 131, 132, 146–149,
    269, 287
from real estate, 73
and social security system
    development, 141–142
and stalling labor productivity,
    135–136
state-owned enterprises as future
    drivers of, 179–181
sustainability of, 149, 281–283
economic interdependence, 25–27
economics and corporate finance, theory
    of, 20
Einhorn, David, 87
electrolytic aluminum industry:
    ban on new investments in, 15, 152
    capacity utilization rate for, 15,
        152–154
emigration of Chinese, 151, 292
entrusted loans, 41–43
entry barriers, 170–171
    for non-SOEs or subsidiaries, 193
    and overcapacity problem, 167
    and SOE reform, 195
environmental protection, 240–241, 272
environmental quality statistics, 229–230
Europe:
    corporate strategy of firms in, 177

housing price gains in, 59
lack of GSEs on secondary mortgage
    market in, 247
Sovereign Debt crisis in, 263, 264
value of implicit guarantee in, 252
European Central Bank, 264
European Union, 212, 264
exit of implicit guarantees, 199–221
    allowing default and bankruptcy,
        220–221
    and amount of local government debt,
        199–200
    bond market development, 218–220
    central government guarantees,
        209–210
    concentrated risks on banks, 205–207
    and contingent liabilities, 203–204
    default risks, 208–209
    diversified financing sources, 200–202
    fiscal and taxation reform, 216–218
    fiscal revenues and cost of financing,
        207–208
    impact on housing, 81
    legal reform, 215
    local government financing vehicles,
        202–203
    and size of company's balance sheet, 167
    and slowdown syndrome, 211–212
    and social security system, 212–215
    transparency, 204–205
    (See also Reform recommendations)
expectations:
    about return on investment, 285
    for asset price appreciation, 165
    danger of, 171–172
    for economic stimulus and expansion,
        164–165
    of investors, 277
    of not allowing default/bankruptcy,
        220

expectations (*Cont.*)
  in real estate market, 7, 62–65, 80–81
  for "too big to fail" and bailout,
    165–166, 261–263
  unrealistic, of investors, 96–97
explicit government guarantees, 19
export statistics, 236–238
exports, decrease in, 133–135

fake contracts, for housing, 67–68
fake divorces, 68
false ownership information, in housing,
  68–69
family size (China), 78–79
Fang Guangyun, 69
Fannie Mae (Federal National
  Mortgage Association), 71, 245–250
Farm Credit System (U.S.), 245
Federal Deposit Insurance Corporation
  (FDIC), 251
Federal Home Loan Banks (U.S.), 246
Federal National Mortgage Association
  (FNMA), 252
financial assets, of Chinese households, 12
financial innovations, 109–115 (*See also*
  Financing channels)
financial market bubbles, 276
financial market reform, 171, 285
financial market-level forces leading to
  overcapacity, 167
Financial Stability Board (FSB), 262
financing channels, 115–129
  commodities financing, 123–126
  copper financing, 120–123
  diversification of, 200–202
  iron ore financing, 123–126
  for local government debt, 4
  mutual guarantees by companies,
    126–129
  and overcapacity problem, 167
  peer-to-peer lending, 115–120

fire sale problem, 156
fiscal deficit, 212
fiscal income:
  central government, 211, 212
  local governments, 216
five-year economic plans, 281
flat-panel glass industry:
  ban on new investments in, 15, 152
  capacity utilization rate for, 15, 152
FNMA (Federal National Mortgage
  Association), 252
Focus Media, 9
food industry, corporate leverage ratio
  in, 185
foreign reserve, 22, 210, 274
Fortune 500 companies, 175, 183,
  191–192, 272
France, living space in, 64
Frank, Barney, 247
Freddie Mac (Federal Home Loan
  Mortgage Corporation), 71,
  245–250
Friedman, Milton, 175
Friedman, Thomas, 160
FSB (Financial Stability Board),
  262
Fujian, local SOE debt in, 203
fund pools, 33–34
futures, 89–91, 295

Gansu, bond issuance in, 201
GDP growth tournament, 172–173,
  187–188
  borrowing and building motivated by,
    144–145
  negative effect of, 242
  and officials' promotion chances,
    147–148
  and tie between SOE debt and
    government, 16–17
  unwinding mentality of, 287

GDP statistics, discrepancies in, 223–225

generational attitudes toward work, 134

Germany:
corporate leverage ratio in, 184
municipal bonds in, 204
nonfinancial corporate leverage ratio in, 13
renter protection in, 69–70

"Ghost city" phenomenon, 145

Gini, Corrado, 234

Gini coefficient, 140, 234–236

Ginnie Mae, 245, 246

global commodities market, 132

global financial crisis (2007-2008), 10, 100
bailouts during, 17, 263–265
China's economy during and after, 132–133
Chinese exports during, 134
economic growth following, 277
end of SIVs during, 113
governmental leverage resulting from, 188
money market funds during, 111–112
and mortgage GSEs, 249–250
municipal bond defaults following, 208
and short selling, 86–87, 254, 255
and stimulus package, 151

Gong Aiai, 69

government debt, 20–25
and implicit guarantees, 20
state-owned enterprise debt, 184
total Chinese government debt, 200
(See also Local governments)

Government Sponsored Enterprises (GSEs):
implicit guarantees through, 245–250

mortgage GSEs, 246–250
types of, in United States, 245

government-level forces leading to overcapacity, 163–164

Great Britain, privatization of SOEs in, 181

Greece, sovereign debt of, 241–242

Green Light Capital, 87

Greenspan, Alan, 99–100, 255–256

Greenspan Put, 99–100

Gross, Bill, 131

GSEs (see Government Sponsored Enterprises)

Guangdong, local government bonds issues by, 22, 209–210

Guangzhou:
housing prices in, 60
local government debt issue for, 202
rents in, 60–61

guarantees:
capital, 273–276, 289–293
financial, for state-owned enterprises, 188–191
implicit (see Implicit guarantee)
institutional and policy, 270–273, 287–289
investment, 276–278, 293–298
mutual guarantees by companies, 126–129
non-financial, for state-owned enterprises, 191–193
from real estate developers, 71
reforming, 269–278
and regard for rule of law, 286–287
(See also Soft budget problem)

Gui Yang, 145

Guizhou, debt level of, 200

Guo Shuqing, 104, 105

Hainan:
  LGFV debt in, 202
  real estate bubble in, 173
Harbin, 228
Hayek, Frederick, 255
health, pollution and, 228–230
health care system, 141–142
home buyers, demonstrations by, 55–56
home ownership, 66–67
Hong Kong:
  exports to, 237–238
  housing prices in, 72
  renter protection in, 70
  retirement saving in, 214
  Shanghai Hong Kong Direct Trading
    Mechanism, 94
  total land value of, 62
"Hot money," 123
hotels, anti-corruption campaign and,
  142–143
household financial assets, 101
household income, 23–24, 211
housing development:
  and bond market development,
    219–220
  as driver of economic growth,
    282–283
  investment in, 144–145
housing index, 59
housing market, 4–9, 25–26, 55–82,
  293–294
  assessing housing prices, 58–62
  and asset bubbles, 283
  demand from households, 62–63
  and demographic changes, 78–79
  expectations of and speculations
    about, 62–65
  fake contracts, 67–68
  fake divorces, 68
  false ownership information, 68–69

  fast price appreciation, 58–60
  and government demand for growth,
    72–76
  government policies needed to
    change, 81–82
  guarantees for housing, 70–72
  housing price-to-income ratio, 61
  implicit guarantee in, 55–58
  prices lowered by developers, 4–6
  and property ownership, 66–67, 140
  protests and concessions in, 4–7
  rental yield, 60–61
  renter protection act, 69–70
  risks for developers, 77–78
  and shifting expectations, 80–81
  total land value, 62
housing prices, 21, 293–294
  assessing, 58–62
  and balance of affordability and GDP
    growth, 148
  and demand for houses, 62–63, 66–67
  economic impact of, 76
  fast appreciation of, 58–60
  and "ghost city" phenomenon, 145
  government demand for growth in,
    72–76
  and land value, 216
  and loose monetary policy, 290
  stabilizing, 216
  statistics on, 231–234
housing price-to-income ratio, 61
HuaRong PuYin Fund, 119
Huarui Wind Electrics, 156–157
Hubei, debt level of, 200
Hunan, LGFV debt in, 202
hydraulic energy industry, maturing
  debt in, 155

IASB (International Accounting
  Standards Board), 203

ICBC (*see* Industry and Commerce Bank
   of China)
IDG, 115
IFRS (International Financial Reporting
   Standard), 203
IMF (International Monetary Fund),
   251, 264
implicit guarantees (in China), 3, 4
   and economic interdependence,
      25–27
   gradual exit of (*see* Exit of
      implicit guarantees; Reform
      recommendations)
   for high speed train system, 158
   for housing, 55–58, 70–72
   impact on local governments, 3–4
   in real estate market, 4–14
   and regard for rule of law, 286–287
   and shadow banking system, 51
   for state-owned enterprises, 14
   for stock market, 9–12, 94
   as tip of government debt iceberg, 20
   (*See also specific topics*)
implicit guarantees (in general), 7,
   245–265
   and bailouts, 158, 263–265
   as ban against short selling, 253–255
   corporate, 256–259
   and Dodd-Frank Act, 261–263
   easy monetary policy as, 255–256
   in Structured Investment Vehicles,
      256–259
   through Government Sponsored
      Enterprises, 245–250
   through inflated ratings agencies,
      259–260
   value of, 250–253
   (*See also specific topics*)
incentives, distortion of, 278–280
income, 23–24

and cost of labor, 282
   government (*see* Fiscal income)
   household, 23–24, 211
income inequality, 23–24
   eastern-inland gap, 135
   and Gini coefficient, 234–236
   public perception of, 235
income taxes, 140
incremental reform, 293
index futures, 90, 91, 295
India:
   economic growth in, 135
   labor productivity in, 135
   privatization of SOEs in, 181
Industry and Commerce Bank of China
   (ICBC), 1–2, 31, 32, 35, 192
inflation, 151
   and Consumer Price Index, 225
   and monetary policy, 255, 290
infrastructure projects:
   and bond market development,
      219–220
   as driver of economy, 282
   investment in, 144–145
   railway system, 158–159
Inner Mongolia, debt financing in, 202
institutional and policy guarantees:
   and economic growth, 270–273
   and government decision making, 278
   unwinding, 287–289
insurance companies, 44, 48
interbank deposits, 40
interbank market (NAFMII), 157
interdependence, economic, 25–27
interest rate liberalization, 110, 112, 114
   and bond market development, 218
   moderating capital supply through, 289
   and overcapacity, 157, 167
   reform recommendation for, 290–291
   for SOE reform, 195

International Accounting Standards
   Board (IASB), 203
International Financial Reporting
   Standard (IFRS), 203
International Monetary Fund (IMF),
   251, 264
internet bubble, 100, 254, 255
internet finance, 110–111, 297
investment (risk) guarantee:
   and distortion of incentives, 280
   economic growth from, 276–278
   and growth of real estate and related
      sectors, 283
   unwinding, 293–298
investment-driven economic growth:
   change from export-driven growth to,
      133–134
   channels for, 188
   move from consumption-based model
      to, 143–146
investors:
   beliefs of, 277
   CSRC protection of, 11–12
   demand for domestic investment
      opportunities by, 93
   dislike of short selling by, 86
   expectations of, 80–81, 96–97
   implicit guarantee assumed by, 3
   lack of dividends/share repurchases
      for, 104–107
   lack of understanding among, 6
   learning by, 100
   preference for more focused
      companies by, 178
   protection of, 99–101
   in real estate, 65–67, 75, 80–81
iPhone, 138
IPOs:
   of Alibaba, 91–92
   banks filing, 45

CSRC approval process for, 95, 96,
   101–103
delaying process of, 295
phenomenal returns at, 96–97
pricing of, 94–95
requirements for, 11, 92
and secondary market investors,
   97–98
and short-term investment,
   98–99
Western screening process for,
   102
iron ore financing, 123–126

Jaffe, Dwight, 247
Japan:
   corporate leverage ratio in, 185
   corporate strategy of firms in, 177
   fiscal deficit of, 212
   housing prices in, 72
   labor productivity in, 135
   living space in, 64
   nonfinancial corporate leverage ratio
      in, 13
   privatization of SOEs in, 181
   size of economy in, 149, 281
   social security reserve in, 214
   stock market bubble in, 276
   total value of Tokyo land, 62
Japanese government bonds, 260
Jiangsu, LGFV debt in, 202
Jiangxi Saiwei, 3, 155
Jilin, debt level of, 200
Jobs, Steve, 298

Kahneman, Daniel, 276
Keynes, John Maynard, 199
Korea, exports to, 237
Krugman, Paul, 55
Kundera, Milan, 109

labor costs, 134
  and export decrease, 136
  increase in, 281–282
labor productivity:
  as current economic challenge,
    273–274
  stagnation of, 135–136
Lacker, Jeffrey, 250
land sales, revenue from, 207, 216–217
land value, 62, 216
Latin American countries, 293
Layton, Max, 123
legal reform, 196–197, 215, 288–289
Lehman Brothers, 86, 87, 111–112, 261
leverage, 13–14
  in Chaori 11 default, 13
  of Chinese households' mortgage,
    75–76
  national, 193–194
  nonfinancial corporate leverage ratio,
    13–14
  in other countries, 13
  of real estate developers, 77–78
  in state-owned enterprises, 14,
    184–186
LGFVs (see Local government financing
    vehicles)
Li Keqiang, 195
Li Xinchuang, 126
liquidity guarantee (see Capital
    (liquidity) guarantee)
liquidity squeeze (2013), 34
listing requirement (stock market),
    91–92 (See also IPO)
loans:
  from banks (see Bank loans)
  commodities financing for, 123–126
  copper financing for, 120–123
  entrusted, 41–43
  iron ore financing for, 123–126

peer-to-peer lending, 115–120
  to real estate developers, 37
  from shadow banking, 145–146
  from SOEs to small and medium-sized
    enterprises, 18
loan-to-savings ratio, 39–40
local government financing vehicles
    (LGFVs), 17–18, 47, 144, 189,
    202–203
local governments:
  agency debts for, 202–203
  audit of debt, 20
  debt taken on by, 51, 199–203, 215
  diversified borrowing by, 21
  and economic growth, 25–26,
    147–148 (See also GDP growth
    tournament)
  economic statistics inflated by,
    224–225
  excessive local investments by,
    161–162
  fiscal disclosure by, 215
  fiscal income of, 26–27
  fiscal sustainability of, 3–4
  as investment dispute mediators,
    6–7
  land sales revenue for, 207
  leverage of, 17
  liquidity of assets, 220
  in mediating housing disputes, 57
  and overcapacity, 163–164
  real estate as revenue bloodline
    for, 74
  resources and credibility of, 199
  restricting amount of debt for,
    199–200
  and SOE debt, 16
  and split-tax reform, 217–218
  subsidies to renewable energy
    companies from, 156

Louis Vuitton, 137
luxury products:
  and anti-corruption campaign, 142
  Chinese consumers' purchasing of,
    137–138
  international vs. domestic prices for,
    137–138
  reasons for buying, 139
  tariffs/taxes and cost of, 138
Lynch, Peter, 254

Ma Jiantang, 235–236
Macau casino revenue, 143
Marathon Oil, 179
market forces:
  distortion of, 278–280
  and realignment between state and
    market, 285–286
market valuation, moderating capital
    supply through, 289
market-oriented economy, 270, 284–285
marriage, in China, 79
MBS (see Mortgage-backed securities)
McKinnon, Ronald, 273
media monitoring, 288–289
mega banks, 253
Merton, Robert, 251–252
Mexico, labor cost in, 134, 282
migrant workers, 79
Millennials, 134
Ministry of Finance, 159
Ministry of Housing and Development
    (MoHD), 59, 96
Ministry of Railway, 158–161
Minsky, Hyman, 36, 146
MoHD (Ministry of Housing and
    Development), 59, 96
monetary policy:
  easy, 255–256
  incremental reform of, 293

reform recommendations for,
    289–290
monetary supply, 165, 171, 275, 289
money market funds, 111–112
monopolistic industries, 175 (See also
    State-owned enterprises (SOEs)
Moody's, 260
Morgan Stanley, 115
Morocco, labor productivity in, 135
mortgage GSEs, 246–250
mortgage-backed securities (MBS),
    219–220, 246, 294
Muddy Waters Research, 9, 85
municipal bonds, 204–205, 208,
    218–220
Murdoch, Rupert, 177
mutual guarantees by companies,
    126–129

NAFMII (interbank market), 157
NASDAQ, short selling in, 9–10, 85
National Bureau of Economic Research
    (NBER), 251
National Bureau of Statistics (NBS), 59,
    223–225, 235
National Development and Reform
    Committee (NDRC), 163, 176
NBER (National Bureau of Economic
    Research), 251
NBS (National Bureau of Statistics), 59
NDRC (National Development and
    Reform Committee), 163, 176
new energy industry, 155–157 (See also
    individual sectors of industry)
News Corporation, 177, 179
Nike, 134–135
Ningxia:
  bond issuance in, 201
  debt financing in, 202
  local government agency debts in, 203

Nocera, Joe, 247
non-financial guarantees, for state-owned
    enterprises, 191–193
nonfinancial leverage, 185
Norway, social security reserve in, 214
NQ Mobile, 9

occupancy tax, 217
oil futures, 89
options, 89–91
Ordos, 145
overcapacity, 3, 14–17, 26, 146, 151–173
    in automobile industry, 153
    and capacity utilization rate, 152
    causes of, 162–167
    in cement industry, 152
    corporate-level forces leading to,
        164–166
    and distorted incentive system, 279
    financial market-level forces leading
        to, 167
    government-level forces leading to,
        163–164
    impact of, 153–154
    and lack of bankruptcy as exit,
        167–170
    in photo voltage and wind turbine
        industries, 153
    prevalence of, 152–153
    in railway system, 158–162
    in renewable energy industry,
        154–158
    severeness of, 126
    in steel industry, 152
    and stimulus program, 151–152,
        170–173
oversupply, of housing, 78

Pagano, Marco, 255
Paulson, Hank, 250

Paulson, John, 9, 85, 254
PBoC (see People's Bank of China)
peer-to-peer lending, 115–120, 290–291
    CreditEase, 115–120
    delinquency and risk management,
        117–120
    new model for, 116–117
    reform of, 297
People's Bank of China (PBoC), 35, 36,
    43, 45, 184–185, 274–275
PetroChina, 98, 192
petroleum industry, corporate leverage
    ratio in, 185
photo voltage industry, overcapacity
    in, 153
pollution, 228–231
polycrystalline silicon industry, ban on
    new investments in, 15, 152
pork prices, 225–227
PPPs (public-private partnerships), 20,
    220
Prada, 137, 147
Prasad, Eswar, 50
price-to-income ratio (housing), 61
primary market, separation of secondary
    market and, 97–98
Prince, Chick, 4
private enterprise, 176
production capacity, 3, 14–17, 152
    (See also Overcapacity)
productivity:
    as current economic challenge,
        273–274
    stagnation of, 135–136
profit, of state-owned enterprises, 180,
    186
property ownership, 66–68, 140
property tax, 217
Prosper.com, 117–119
public expenditures, growth in, 24, 212

public-private partnerships (PPPs),
    20, 220
purchasing power, of Chinese
    consumers, 137

Qingdao Port, 121–122
Qinghai, bond issuance in, 201
Qualified Domestic Institutional
    Investors, 101
quality of economic growth, 132–133,
    148–149, 283–284, 288

railway system:
    debt of companies, 184
    overcapacity in, 158–162
ratings agencies:
    DaGong, 161
    implicit guarantees through,
        259–260
    and transparency of credit rating
        system, 219
Reagan, Ronald, 223
real estate:
    companies' diversification into,
        103–104
    curb policies for, 8, 21, 67, 68, 70, 72,
        144, 207, 216, 234, 282
    as driver of economic growth,
        282–283
    drops and corrections in, 5, 8, 56–57
    entrusted loans in, 42
    expectations for, 7
    and "ghost city" phenomenon, 145
    investment in, as percentage of GDP,
        75
    investors' confidence in, 8
    loans to developers and rise in market,
        37
    local government guarantees for, 192
    pro-growth mentality with, 147–148

    reform recommendations for,
        293–294
    and shadow banking, 47
    and vandalization of projects, 55, 56
    (See also Housing market)
real GDP growth, 227
real interest rate of borrowing, 9
reform and openness policy, 270
reform recommendations, 269–298
    banking reform, 290–291
    capital account regulation, 292
    and consequences of distorted
        incentive systems, 278–280
    default and bankruptcy, 297–298
    deleveraging, 194–195
    deregulation, 195–196
    disclosures and evaluations of SOEs,
        196
    diverse development objectives, 288
    and guarantees driving economic
        growth, 269–278
    incremental reform, 293
    interest rate liberalization, 195,
        290–291
    legal reform, 196–197, 288–289
    market's role in resource allocation,
        284–285
    media monitoring, 288–289
    monetary policy, 289–290
    and quality of growth, 283–284
    real estate, 293–294
    realignment between state and
        market, 285–286
    regard for rule of law, 286–287
    for reporting statistics, 241
    for shadow banking, 51–52, 296–297
    speed of economic growth, 287
    for state-owned enterprises, 176,
        193–197
    stock market, 294–296

and sustainability of growth, 281–283
unwinding capital guarantee, 289–293
unwinding institutional and policy
    guarantees, 287–289
unwinding investment guarantees,
    293–298
(*See also* Exit of implicit guarantees)
regulation:
    and market force in equilibrating the
        market, 171
    and peer-to-peer lending, 115–117
regulators:
    dislike of short selling by, 86
    and implicit guarantees, 3
    and shadow banking, 49–51
    (*See also* Chinese Securities
        Regulatory Commission [CSRC])
related party transactions, 106
    of CreditEase, 116
    of state-owned enterprises, 193
renewable energy industry, overcapacity
    in, 154–158
rental yield, 60–61
renter protection act, 69–70
representativeness bias, 276
resource allocation:
    diversified, 285
    market's role in, 284–285
restaurant industry:
    and anti-corruption campaign, 142
    corporate leverage ratio in, 185
retail sales, anti-corruption campaign
    and, 143
return on invested capital (ROIC):
    decrease in, 144
    for SOEs, 187
return on investment:
    decrease in, 144
    and distortion of incentives, 279–280
    investors' demand for, 114

IPOs, 96–97
    in peer-to-peer lending, 117
    real estate, 47
    realistic expectations for, 285
    for state-owned enterprises, 186–188
    Tian Hong, 111
revenues:
    and cost of financing, 207–208
    from land sales, 207, 216–217
    of Macau casino, 143
Richmond Federal Reserve, 251
risk(s):
    accumulation of, 240, 277
    concentrated, on banks, 205–207
    credit, 46–49
    default, 46–49, 158
    and financial crises, 38
    focus on returns instead of, 280
    for housing developers, 77–78
    for investors, 25
    and loose monetary policy, 290
    in peer-to-peer lending, 117–120
    for real estate developers, 77–78
    and return on investment, 114
    for SIV investors, 257
    in speculative areas, 128
    in stock market, 12, 100–101
    (*See also* Investment [risk] guarantee)
risk sharing, in housing market, 71
ROIC (*see* Return on invested capital)
rule of law, regard for, 286–287
Russia, 293

SAFE (*see* State Administration of
    Foreign Exchange)
Saiwei, 173
Sallie Mae (U.S.), 245
SASAC (*see* State-owned Assets
    Supervision and Administration
    Committee)

Scandinavian countries, Gini coefficient for, 235
Seasoned Equity Offering (SEO), 101
secondary market, separation of primary market and, 97–98
securities companies, 44–45, 48
securitization transactions, 256–257, 294
semi-monopolistic industries, 175
    (*See also* State-owned enterprises (SOEs))
senior managers, of state-owned enterprises, 180–181
SEO (Seasoned Equity Offering), 101
Shaanxi:
    local government agency debts in, 203
    trust product financing in, 202
shadow banking, 2, 31–52
    companies' diversification into, 103–104
    cost of loans from, 145–146
    default risks and credit risks in, 46–49
    difficulties in reforming, 49–52
    enterprise financing from, 2
    entrusted loans, 41–43
    as financing for local government debt, 4
    origin of, 34–40
    products and services encompassed by, 43–46
    real estate sector in, 75
    reform recommendations for, 296–297
    regulations affecting, 44–45
    rules forbidding fund pools, 33–34
    and Shanxi Zhenfu Energy Group default, 31–32
    trust products, 40–41
    types of, 43–44
    in the West, 46

Shanghai:
    debt level of, 200
    GDP growth mandate given up by, 287
    housing prices in, 60
    local government debt issue for, 22, 202, 209–210
    rents in, 60–61
Shanghai and Shenzhen 300 Composite index, 178
Shanghai Chaori Solar Technology, 13, 154–155
Shanghai Duty Free Zone, 121–122
Shanghai Hong Kong Direct Trading Mechanism, 94
Shanghai Interbank Offered Rate (Shibor), 110
Shanxi Zhenfu Energy Group default, 1–2, 31–32
share repurchases, 103–107
ShenYin WangGuo Securities, 46
Shenzhen:
    housing prices in, 60
    local government debt issue for, 22, 202, 209–210
    rents in, 60–61
Shi Zhengrong, 155
Shibor (Shanghai Interbank Offered Rate), 110
ShiJiaZhuang, 229
Shiller, Robert, 231
ship building industry:
    ban on new investments in, 15, 152
    capacity utilization rate for, 15, 152
short selling:
    in China, 10
    defined, 253
    implicit guarantees as ban against, 253–255
    lack of, 86–89
    in NASDAQ, 9–10, 85

short-term investment horizon, 98–99
Sigma Finance, 259
Simon, Scott, 248
Singapore, retirement saving in, 214
Sino Forest, 9, 85
SinoChem, 192
SIVs (Structured Investment Vehicles),
    112–113, 256–259
slowdown syndrome, 211–212
small and medium-sized enterprises
    (SMEs):
    crowded out by SOEs, 182–183
    mutual guarantees for loans of,
        127–129
    shadow banking financing for, 2
    SOE loans to, 18
Smith, Vernon L., 250
social security system, 141–142
    and fiscal reform, 212–215
    underfunding of, 141, 213–215
SOEs (*see* State-owned enterprises)
soft budget problem:
    for railway system, 158–162
    for state-owned enterprises, 17–20,
        188–191
Sofun.com, 59
solar panel industry:
    expansion in, 16
    gross margin in, 15, 153
    local government guarantees to, 192
    maturing debt in, 155
Soros, George, 254
Southeast Asian financial crisis (1997–
    1998), 134, 236, 254, 255
Southwest University of Finance and
    Economics (SWUFE), 66, 76, 140,
    235
Soviet Union, 181
soybean pressing industry, ban on new
    investments in, 15, 152

speculation:
    and distorted incentive system, 279
    and easy monetary policy, 256
    and excessive liquidity, 275
    and Greenspan Put, 100
    in housing market, 62–65
    and mutual guarantees by companies,
        127–129
speculative bubbles, 290
spending habits, recent changes in, 227
split-tax reform, 217–218
Standard and Poor's, 260
Standard Chartered Bank, 121
State Administration of Foreign
    Exchange (SAFE), 93, 122, 274–275
State Grid, 192
State-owned Assets Supervision and
    Administration Committee
    (SASAC), 176, 184, 189
state-owned banks, 35, 50, 163–164, 186
    (*See also individual banks*)
state-owned enterprises (SOEs),
    175–197
    and anti-corruption campaign, 143
    consolidation among, 166
    corporate governance of, 178
    and corporate leverage, 184–186
    corporate strategy of, 176–179
    economic growth role of, 272
    as future drivers of economic growth,
        179–181
    growth of, 286
    implicit guarantee for, 14
    investment returns for, 144
    leverage of, 16, 17
    leverage ratio of, 14
    needed reform of, 176, 193–197
    non-financial guarantees for, 191–193
    return on investment and cost of capital
        for, 186–188

state-owned enterprises (*Cont.*)
   size of, 166
   small and medium-sized enterprises
      crowded out by, 182–183
   soft budget problem for, 17–20,
      188–191
   total asset of, 210
statistics, 223–242
   air pollution, 228–231
   capacity utilization rate, 153
   Consumer Price Index, 225–228
   in decision making, 241–242
   export data, 236–238
   Gini coefficient, 234–236
   housing prices, 231–234
   quality of, 223–225
   questionable authenticity and reliability
      of, 238–241
steel industry:
   ban on new investments in, 15, 152
   capacity utilization rate for, 15, 152
   corporate leverage ratio in, 185
   local government guarantees to, 192
   overcapacity in, 152
sterilization, 275
stimulus program, 271, 275
   consequence of, 146
   and growth of shadow banking, 36–39
   to halt slowdown during financial
      crisis, 151
   liquidity following, 127
   mini-stimulus packages, 146
   and overcapacity, 151–152, 170–173
   and rate of economic growth, 132–133
   and real estate investment returns, 47
stock market, 25, 85–107
   closed for cross-border capital flow,
      92–94
   diversification into real estate and
      shadow banking, 103–104

excessive listing requirement, 91–92
implicit guarantee in, 9–12
investors' perspective on, 94–96
IPO process and delistings, 101–103
lack of derivatives, 89–91
lack of dividends and share-repurchase,
   104–107
lack of short selling, 86–89
listed companies' perspective on,
   101–107
protection of investors, 99–101
reform recommendations for,
   294–296
separation of primary and secondary
   markets, 97–98
short sales in NASDAQ, 85
short-term investment horizon and
   volatilities, 98–99
unrealistic expectations of PE
   investors, 96–97
stock prices, short sales and, 86–88
Structured Investment Vehicles (SIVs),
   112–113, 256–259
sub-prime securities, 114
SunTech Technology, 155, 173
sustainability:
   of economic growth, 133, 149,
      281–283
   fiscal, of central government, 23–25,
      211–213
   fiscal, of local governments, 3–4
   reform recommendations for, 281–283
   (*See also* Exit of implicit guarantees)
SWUFE (*see* Southwest University of
   Finance and Economics)

Taiwan, exports to, 237
Tang Ning, 116, 118
Taobao, 138
tariffs, cost of luxury products and, 138

taxes:
    and cost of luxury products, 138
    and disposable income, 140
    on housing, 81–81
    on real estate transactions, 67, 68
    taxation reform, 216–218
TBTF (*see* "Too big to fail")
Templeton, John, 31
Tepper, David, 88
Tercent, 92
Thailand, labor productivity in, 135
"3/27," 89
Tian Hong, 109–113
Tianjin, 145
"Too big to fail" (TBTF), 165–166,
    261–263
    banks as, 38
    funding for, during crises, 252
    mortgage GSEs as, 249
    peer-to-peer companies as, 119–120
    as problem to resolve, 261
    (*See also* Bailouts)
total land value, 62
trade financing, 43
trade statistics, 236–238
transparency:
    of credit rating system, 219
    and fiscal reform, 204–205
    improving, 221
    and peer-to-peer lending, 116, 117
    and SOE reform, 196
travel industry, 143, 185
Treasury bond futures, 295
treasury futures market, 89
trust companies, 4, 32, 40–41, 48
    (*See also* Shadow banking)
trust products, 40–41
    from banks, 206
    default of, 220–221
    diffusing risks in, 298

fund pools, 33–34
infrastructure-related, 51
in local government financing,
    201–202
popularity of, 208
Shanxi Zhenfu Energy Group default,
    1–3, 31–32
Tulip Mania, 164–165
21st Century Fox, 177

UBS, 153
unemployment:
    and economic expectations, 271
    and economic growth, 147
United Kingdom:
    bank loans as local government
      financing in, 201, 205
    housing prices in, 72
    living space in, 64
United States:
    bank loans as local government
      financing in, 201, 205
    bubbles in, 88–89
    China as major creditor to, 194
    corporate leverage ratio in, 185
    corporate strategy of firms in, 177
    default on municipal bonds in, 208
    emigration to, 292
    fiscal cliff in, 263
    fiscal deficit of, 212
    Gini coefficient for, 235
    household consumption as percent of
      GDP, 139–140
    housing affordability in, 61
    housing prices in, 59, 72
    implicit real estate guarantees in, 71
    internet bubble and Greenspan Put,
      99–100
    labor productivity in, 135
    market losses in, 91

United States (*Cont.*)
  municipal bonds in, 204
  nonfinancial corporate leverage ratio
     in, 13
  retirement saving in, 214
  risk aversion in, 276
  shale energy in, 153
  and short-selling of Chinese
     NASDAQ companies, 85
  SIVs and, 113, 114
  size of economy of, 132
  social security reserve in, 214
  total land value of, 62
urbanization, 63–64, 78–79
U.S. Federal Reserve, 31
  AIG bailout by, 261
  quantitative easing by, 128, 151
U.S. treasuries, 260
USD, appreciation of CNY against,
     125–126

Vietnam:
  labor cost in, 134, 282
  Nike's production in, 135
volatility (stocks), 98–99
Volcker, Paul, 255
Volcker's Rule, 261
Volkswagen Audi, 142
"Voodoo Statistics," 223 (*See also* Statistics)

Wang Yanxiu, 117, 120
Warburg, 115
warrants market, 91, 100–101
wealth, 43
  from housing boom, 76
  movement of, 23
wealth distribution, economic growth
     and, 139–140
wealth management products (WMPs),
     32, 34, 41, 43, 46–47, 50, 298
     (*See also* Shadow banking)

Wen Jiabao, 72
Wenzhou City, 128, 166
Western countries:
  corporate strategy of firms in,
     177
  Government Sponsored Enterprises
     in, 245–250
  municipal bond risk in, 208
  urbanization in, 64
wind turbine industry:
  ban on new investments in, 15,
     152
  local government guarantees to,
     192
  maturing debt in, 155
  overcapacity in, 153
  profit in, 156–157
WMPs (*see* Wealth management
     products)
World Bank, 176, 228
WuXi SunTech, 155

Xi Jinping, 149, 284
Xingtai, 229
Xinjiang, local government agency debts
     in, 203

Yingkou, 145
Yingli, 155
Yu'e Bao, 109–115
Yunnan, debt level of, 200

Zhao Haibin, 69
Zhejiang, local government debt issue
     for, 22, 202, 209–210
Zhejiang Longsheng Group Co., Ltd.,
     42–43
Zhejiang Xingrun Real Estate Co.,
     77–78
Zhong Nanshan, 229
Zhou Xiaochuan, 13, 49, 184

About the Author

Ning Zhu is a deputy dean and professor of finance at the Shanghai Advanced Institute of Finance, a faculty fellow at the Yale University International Center for Finance, and a Special Term Professor of Finance at the University of California, Davis, and at Guanghua School of Management at Beijing University. Prior to coming back to Asia, he was a tenured professor of finance at the University of California. Professor Zhu is an expert on behavioral finance, investments, corporate finance, and the Asian financial markets. He has published numerous articles in leading journals in the finance, economics, management and legal fields. In addition to his academic research, Professor Zhu helps asset management companies in a wide range of capacities. During his leave from the University of California between 2008 and 2010, he put his research into practice and led the quantitative strategies and portfolio advisory teams at Lehman Brothers and Nomura International in Hong Kong, top ranked firms in leading institutional surveys. He commands extensive consulting experience advising government agencies, such as the PBoC, CSRC, the World Bank, and the IMF, market regulators, stock and futures exchanges, and some of the largest institutional money managers and investment banks in the world. Professor Zhu is frequently featured in leading media columns, on TV programs, and as an event keynote speaker. He is the author of the best seller *The Investor's Enemy*. Professor Zhu received his B. Econ. Degree from Beijing University, Master of Science degree from Cornell University (NY), and Ph.D. (finance) from Yale University (CT).

CPSIA information can be obtained
at www.ICGtesting.com
Printed in the USA
LVOW13*0957151217
559825LV00013B/239/P